French Perceptions

of the Early American Republic,

1783–1793

MEMOIRS OF THE

AMERICAN PHILOSOPHICAL SOCIETY
Held at Philadelphia
For Promoting Useful Knowledge
Volume 180

French Perceptions

of the

Early American Republic

1783–1793

PETER P. HILL

American Philosophical Society

INDEPENDENCE SQUARE • PHILADELPHIA

1988

Library of Congress Catalog Card No.: 87-72861
International Standard Book Number: 0-87169-180-9
ISSN: 0065-9738

This Book is Dedicated to My Mother
Ruth Proal Hill
To Whom It Was Promised

TABLE OF CONTENTS

AECPE-U	Archives des Affaires Etrangères, Correspondance Politique, Etats-Unis
ANF	Archives Nationales de France
ASP,FR	*American State Papers. Class I. Foreign Relations*
CC	Correspondance Consulaire (the B^1 classification, ANF; cited by tome to 1792, by volume after 1792)
CDMC	Commissaire du Département de la Marine et des Colonies
CDRE	Commissaire du Département des Relations Extérieures
CFM	Frederick J. Turner, ed., *Correspondence of French Ministers to the United States, 1791–1797* (Washington 1904)
CMC	Commission de la Marine et des Colonies
CRE	Commission des Relations Extérieures
CSP	Comité de Salut Public
MAE	Ministre des Affaires Etrangères
MMC	Ministre de la Marine et des Colonies
MRE	Ministre des Relations Extérieures

ACKNOWLEDGMENTS

Most of those who have encouraged me in this enterprise came to my assistance at some fairly well marked stage of the creative process. Somewhere near the beginning I came under singular obligation to Georgia Robison Beale who assured me (from her own research on a consul-designate named Louis Bosc) that the French consuls posted to this country in the 1780s did more than merely report the arrivals and departures of ships and cargoes. I needed this assurance because when I first encountered these consular dispatches, many years ago, I had dismissed them as being too much taken up with ship- and cargo-counting to be of much interest to the diplomatic historian. Thanks to Professor Beale's urging that I take another and closer look, I discovered how richly the writings of these consuls amplified a theme in Franco-American relations I had already begun to explore: that of widespread French frustration in dealing with eighteenth-century Americans.

Among those who also encouraged me during the early stages, I thank the editors of the *Journal of Modern History* for publishing an article I wrote on one aspect of that frustration: the persistent disjunctures in Franco-American commerce. It appeared in the April 1977 *Supplement* under the title: "Prologue to the Quasi-War: Stresses in Franco-American Commercial Relations, 1793–96."

While feeling my way toward a larger theme, I was struck by how often and how explicitly French officials tended to blame Americans for nearly everything that went wrong in the Franco-American relationship. Few of those officials, the evidence strongly suggested, could quite shake the feeling that France would have been better served in that relationship if Americans had not shown themselves to be a thoroughly ungrateful lot. Why the French felt they had reason to expect more and better of us became the subject of a paper I read at an international colloquium (on the American Revolution and Europe) held in Paris and Toulouse in early 1978. For this opportunity to regale a live audience with my thoughts about the French perception of American ingratitude I am indebted to Professor Claude Fohlen of the Université de Paris-I and to Professor

Jacques Godechot of the Université de Toulouse–Le Mirail, the former for inviting me, the latter for his thoughtful critique of my paper.

At this point I might have dropped my research into what I had come to think of, in general terms, as "French chagrin at American ingratitude," had not Professor Beale suggested that the French consuls had more to say on the subject. As I read through their dispatches, I realized that the consuls furnished me with enough vivid detail to depict on a scale not before attempted just how deeply, how often, and in how many different ways Americans of the 1780s had offended their erstwhile French ally.

At about midpoint in my research, conducted mostly at the Library of Congress, I went to Paris on sabbatical leave with a travel grant generously furnished by the Research Committee of the George Washington University. There, in the fall of 1982, I completed my research, reading through those copies of consular dispatches, and other documents, which the Congressional Library did not have on microfilm. The following spring I wrote the first draft of this book while a resident fellow of the Camargo Foundation in Cassis, France. For the warm support and quiet collegiality which the Foundation afforded me during this creative period I owe heart-felt thanks to its former director, Russell Young, and to its then assistant and now director, Michael Pretina.

Later, during the re-write phase, I was fortunate to be able to air the substance of Chapter IV under the guise of entertaining a group of local French historians with a paper I entitled "Smuggling as a Fine Art: Americans in the French Antilles, 1784–93." This group, numbering about twenty, meets twice a year to hear its members' papers. It is so wary of becoming institutionalized that it has no name. Its principal organizer, however, is Professor Jean T. Joughin, now emerita, of the American University, whose invitation to speak on this occasion gave me the benefit of the kind of critiquing that can come only from an audience of scholars whose research interests are tangential. Those whose comments and questions led me to recast, and undoubtedly improve, the chapter on "Americans in the Antilles," include Robert Forster of Johns Hopkins University, Jack R. Censer of George Mason University, and the late Louis M. Greenberg of the University of Maryland.

Once the work was finished, I came under particular obligation to Lawrence S. Kaplan, University Professor at Kent State, who read the manuscript, said he liked it, and made the felicitous suggestion that it might find an appropriate publisher in the American Philosophical Society. No obligation, however, exceeds that which I owe to my wife Barbara whose patience, encouragement, and intelligent criticism have sustained this enterprise from its inception. She is finally persuaded, I think, that I have cut the introduction and conclusion to their optimal lengths.

Washington, D.C.   PETER P. HILL
Winter 1986

INTRODUCTION

The essays in this volume tell of the intractable disappointments and frustrations that French government officials experienced in their dealings with Americans in the period between the peace settlement of 1783 and the outbreak of Anglo-French hostilities in 1793. They point to a significantly earlier and more serious erosion of Franco-American amity on the French side than most historians have recognized. They also suggest that well before the Jay-Grenville treaty converted that amity to outright hostility, French officials had come to expect the worst of their American allies.

While these essays depict the 1780s as an era of bad feeling, one caveat should be entered at the outset: French animus toward the young republic in this decade still stands small alongside the towering sense of grievance that developed in the later 1790s. Nor can much be inferred by way of causality, or even continuity, between the animosities of one decade and the next. Clearly, the onset of the French Revolution in 1789 created a watershed beyond which old grievances paled by comparison, and new grievances changed the shape of controversy. The Revolution so altered the circumstances of Franco-American relations that any assessments of ill-will must be weighed in different scales. In the 1780s France was at peace. In the 1790s she was fighting for her life, or at least to preserve her revolution. In the latter decade, the operation of American neutrality because it favored the British ultimately drove France to take open reprisals on American shipping. By contrast, the 1780s gave rise to problems less evocative of passion, not related to the survival of either party, and capable of being passed over with minor expressions of irritation. Yet, the difficulties arising in the earlier period, for all their appearance of being low-keyed, speak to a backdrop of accumulated ill-will that ought not to be ignored.

While these essays tell a story of gathering hostility, they also shed some long-needed light on a period of Franco-American relations generally neglected by the profession. There are still students of the era who are wont to observe dismissively that if the *ancien régime* did us no particular good, at least it did us no particular harm, and leave it at that. That the inter-war period lacked for "great events" doubtless explains why scholars have consigned it to the periphery of their research. Given its unexciting quality, they can scarcely be blamed for hastening from the uneventful '80s to the more perilous and crisis-fraught '90s. These essays, then, invite a closer look at the roots of controversy in the earlier decade.

A work that has the title *French Perceptions of the Early American Republic* must also answer the question: Did any group of Frenchmen who had experience of this country in the late eighteenth century come to conclusions unified enough as to what they perceived to make this inquiry hold together? Here the answer seems to depend on what group is singled out for its perceptions. The historian Durand Echeverria, for example, doubts that any consensus existed among the Frenchmen who came and subsequently left. What these sojourners thought of Americans, he writes, did not constitute "a true group opinion, but merely a heterogeneous collection of individual impressions" which varied according to each individual's feeling of acceptance or rejection.[1] His point is well taken. Obviously, a Marquis de Lafayette returning triumphantly to visit old comrades-in-arms carried away different impressions from those of a Talleyrand who regarded his exile here as a barbarous interlude.

Nor can one find "a true group opinion" among such differently circumstanced groups as *émigré* aristocrats, refugee planters fleeing the Antilles, or those wide-eyed gentlemen who came to learn about America so that they could publish their "voyages" when they returned to Paris. The impressions the members of these groups took away seemed to depend not only on the reception they received, but also on the kinds of material and intellectual baggage they brought with them. Those who brought capital often found opportunity to invest and flourish, while those who came penniless usually scraped out a joyless existence living off the charity of friends. Those who came with philosophe-inspired visions of finding a virtuous and noble yeomanry sometimes, like Saint-John de Crèvecoeur, saw their expectations rapturously confirmed. Others came away convinced they had encountered the world's most grasping and materialistic people, surely destined to a corruption that no philosophically inclined Frenchman could approve.

Emigrés and refugees, who may have numbered as many as 50,000, clearly failed to produce a common body of opinion. That they found Americans to be at the same time generous and miserly, honest and crafty,

---

[1]*Mirage in the West: A History of the French Image of American Society to 1815* (New York 1966) 79.

industrious and lazy, thrifty and luxury-loving, passionate and cold, etc., etc., speaks more nearly to the variety of their individual encounters than it does to the likelihood of the historian finding among them "a true group opinion." Moreover, these groups were poorly motivated to penetrate beneath the surfaces of what they saw because of their all-consuming eagerness to leave—to return as soon as possible either to France or to their island homes. What they recorded of life in America obviously counted for less than the lives they hoped to return to.

Professional travel writers, to be sure, sometimes did penetrate the surfaces. They came looking for insights which, when published, would establish them as experts on the American phenomenon. There were no Tocquevilles among them, however. Men like the Comte de Volney and the Duc de La Rochefoucauld-Liancourt, though they enjoyed a wide French readership, seldom analyzed but merely described. Moreover, their works were published in the 1790s, by which time the broad lines of perception had already been fixed.

Fortunately for the purposes of this study, one group of Frenchmen-in-America did create a written record in which they not only described but also analyzed the most important tangents of the early Franco-American relationship. These were the members of the French consular establishment, consuls, vice consuls, and consular agents, posted from Portsmouth to Savannah, for whom America in the 1780s was a career workplace. Their reports, dispatches, and memoranda constitute as nearly a "true group opinion" as one can find. Out of their shared experiences and the recurrent similarities of their day-to-day dealings with Americans emerge a congeries of perceptions often consensual to the point of unanimity that is not to be found in the contemporary writings of travelers, the recollections of refugees and émigrés, or even the major reports of the French ministers plenipotentiary to this country. Here, then, in the voluminous writings of these minor French officials there exists a research base from which a decade of French disappointments and frustrations can be freshly examined.

I
FRENCH CONSULAR OBSERVERS

In signing the treaty of Paris, Britain had seemed to write off its erstwhile colonies as a total loss. Americans had not only won their political independence; they now had George III's acknowledgment of it. Moreover, by severing most of the old commercial ties as well, Britain had appeared to make the separation complete. In this latter respect, Americans found independence a bit more daunting than they had expected. Accustomed, as colonists, to strain against the mother country's wearisome trade restrictions, they had hoped nonetheless to retain the right to trade within the British Empire after the war. This was not to be. Although London had agreed that Americans might still exchange raw materials for British manufactures in direct trade, they were henceforth to be excluded from British ports in Canada, the Caribbean and, for that matter, throughout the world. Though disappointed, Americans consoled themselves with the likelihood that independence would afford new, more profitable, avenues of commerce with other nations. Separation had cost them, but it also had freed them; its opportunities seemed boundless. They were now free to explore the wider world of commerce, free to choose the international company they would keep and, above all, free to steer a course into a future in which Britain would bid for their favors, presumably with no greater advantage than any other nation.

If any European power could hope to profit from the new dispensation, it was France—and with good reason. French arms had served the outcome, and French statesmen could hardly be faulted for supposing that Americans would gratefully continue to associate themselves with France if only to affirm that Britain no longer controlled them. Indeed, France had much to offer: great power status to shield the new republic from international rivalries, goodwill, manufactures, markets for American exports, in fact all that Americans had been wont to take from England and were now at liberty to seek elsewhere. French leaders could readily envision in the United States a people who from weakness would

1

look to Paris for guidance in world politics, and whose merchants would eagerly nourish the French economy with mutually profitable exchanges of goods. In the two related spheres that counted most, those of power politics and external commerce, Americans could reasonably be expected to see that their true interests lay with France.

Neither logic nor apparent self-interest, however, reckoned with the weight of custom, cultural affinity, and long-settled habit. To most Americans, independence brought few changes to their daily lives. It was as though the British past had cast a spell. They went on much as they had before, adapting to British-wrought institutions of law and governance, renewing former business connections in London, selling the same exports in return for the same British imports and, of course, continuing to speak the mother tongue, a cultural bond as powerful as the similarities of thought process it served as a medium. Old trade lanes, to be sure, had been dislocated, but the essential nexus of Anglo-American commerce remained intact. Old loyalties were dissolved, but new ones hardly seemed necessary. The hopeful prospect of France's replacing Britain, either as political mentor or trade partner, grew dimmer as the decade progressed.

France's principal witnesses to this darkening scene were its consuls. By tradition long honored, governments send such officials overseas to look after the nation's naval and mercantile interests. With functional logic the *ancien régime* lodged its consular service within its Ministry of Navy and Colonies. To each host country the Ministry posted a consul general, usually a figure of some prestige who resided at the seat of government and directed the activities of consuls and vice consuls. Like their counterparts elsewhere, French consuls routinely collected data on shipping, tried to recover deserters, procured naval supplies, and adjudicated minor legal disputes among nationals. They also publicized marketing opportunities, occasionally operated naval hospitals, and always represented in their persons an official French presence.

What distinguished the French consular establishment in the United States was its members' early awareness of how intimately their oversight of commercial matters related to local politics. They soon realized that for want of a strong central government, American state legislatures possessed virtually complete powers to regulate commerce. To traditional duties, therefore, French consuls in America quickly added the skills of political observers. The unusually high political content of their reports meant, in turn, that the consul general in this country often had in hand more reliable, certainly more detailed, sources of political intelligence than the Foreign Office could command through its own principal agent, the minister plenipotentiary. While a consul general's access to a ready-made intelligence network made him a minister's most valued adviser, the government in Paris was left to formulate policy from disparate sources. Having the minister report to the Foreign Office while the consul general reported to the Navy so obviously fragmented the process of intelligence gathering that in 1793 Paris finally incorporated the consular service within the Ministry of Foreign Affairs. This bureaucratic shuffle meant in practice that the consuls acquired two masters. They continued to perform their usual chores for the Navy minister to whom they still reported, but the political intelligence they gathered thereafter funneled directly to the Foreign Office.[1]

High officials in Paris, as well as consuls, soon came to appreciate the thin line Americans drew between their commercial and political dealings with other nations. Foreign Minister Montmorin told the Comte de Moustier, just before the latter left for New York in 1788, that he could expect his ministerial mission to be largely taken up with matters of commerce, "an object on which the attentions of Americans are almost exclusively fixed."[2] To this contemporary linking of commerce and politics, the historian Jacques Godechot adds a perceptive note. Writing of Franco-American relations of the 1780s, Godechot found it difficult to conclude "whether it was bad commercial relations that chilled the diplomatic rapports, or the other way around."[3]

Sometime during the year 1788 the newly arrived French minister, the Comte de Moustier, filed a lengthy report assessing the strengths and shortcomings of each member of the consular corps then serving in the United States. Three or four he singled out for praise; the others, especially some of the vice consuls, he characterized as being either failed merchants, green young men, or dubious adventurers, few of whom appeared to know what they were supposed to be doing. Some, he complained, had gone into private business ventures or had become heavily involved in local political affairs. Those who had started from modest origins, he thought, had succumbed most readily to the tempting opportunities for personal advancement offered by what he described as an "unhealthily democratic environment." As evidence of their laxity, Moustier noted how irregularly they corresponded with the consul general. Nor was he pleased with the consuls' excuse that they were making their reports

---

[1]See chapter 7 in Frédéric Masson, *Le département des affaires étrangères pendant la révolution, 1787–1804* (Paris 1877).

[2]"Correspondence of the Comte de Moustier with the Comte de Montmorin, 1787–1789," *American Historical Review* 8 (1903) 710.

[3]"Les relations économiques entre la France et les Etats-Unis de 1778 à 1789," *French Historical Studies* 1 (1958) 26.

directly to the Navy ministry. If true, he wrote, this "irregularity" defeated the purpose of having a central gathering point for information.[4]

Moustier obviously relished the prospect of shaking new life into what he thought was a moribund body of civil servants. "Never," he wrote, "has a consular establishment stood in greater need of being wound up again than that of the United States."[5] He then outlined certain procedural and staff changes. They boiled down to surprisingly few. Having aired his complaints in general terms, he went on to give mixed but largely favorable reviews to seven of the ten consuls and vice consuls then in place. Only two did he suggest ought to be removed. The others simply needed to be spurred to greater activity. Moustier's glowering assessment may simply have been that of a vigorous new arrival who finds placeholders long in office and suspects them of having grown slack on the job. More charitably, one might note that, as a group, the consuls enjoyed remarkable tenure. Six of the ten had held consular office for at least four years, and three could date their continuous service from the first consular appointments made a decade earlier.[6] Moustier must have suspected that most of them, despite their supposed torpor, would still be at their posts long after he had ended his own mission.

Moustier, meanwhile, found the consuls more alive to their duties and far better informed than he had at first imagined. To test them, he asked each to draft a detailed description of his activities, tell what problems most often recurred, and relay back to Philadelphia all regional information that might be of interest to the French government.[7] The task of coordinating this project fell to the then vice consul general, Antoine Delaforest. Within two months, that is, by late February 1789, Delaforest assured the Navy ministry that his consuls would have finished their reports by July, and the ministry would have them all in hand by the end of the year. Moustier's initiative, he noted approvingly, came at a politically fortuitous moment. The newly constituted American government was about to convene, and the kinds of information the consuls were

---

[4]"Distributions des Consulats et Vice Consulats de France dans les Etats Unis," in AECPE-U, Mem. et Doc., 9: 188vo–89vo.

[5]Ibid., f. 190.

[6]Moustier urged firing G. J. A. Ducher outright for his sniping at colleagues, and recommended posting D'Annemours to another country. Ibid., ff. 192 vo, 194vo–95. The ten consular officers, with their earliest dates of appointment, were Martin Oster (1778), Philippe-André-Joseph Létombe (1779), Chevalier D'Annemours (1779), Jean Toscan (1781), Hector Saint-John de Crèvecoeur (1783), Antoine-René-Charles-Mathurin Delaforest (1784), Jean-Baptiste Petry (1784), Louis Otto (1785), Avistay de Chateaufort (1785), and the most recent arrival, G. J. A. Ducher (1786).

[7]Moustier to MMC, New York, 25 December 1788, CC (N.Y.), 910: 82–84.

gathering would lend weight and cogency to French demands for commercial concessions from a Congress more fully empowered to grant them.[8] As it was, the consuls' reports came too late. By early summer 1789, the first federal Congress had pre-empted any opportunity for concession-seeking when it roughed out tariff and tonnage laws that showed no special favor to French ships or French cargoes. Whether the reports would have altered this outcome, had they been assembled earlier, remains conjectural. The most that can be said is that the reports themselves—some of them massive and still extant—afforded those consuls who responded an opportunity to distill the misgivings of a decade.

Well before Moustier's time, the consular establishment showed promise of producing seasoned and well-informed observers. A naval agent named Jean Holker claimed to be the first French consul here, and bore that official title at Philadelphia as early as 1778.[9] But it was Martin Oster, another naval agent, who took credit for giving what he called "legal existence" to the consular establishment, and Oster outlasted nearly everyone who might have asked him what he meant. For sheer length of service, Oster topped the list. He served six years as vice consul to Barbé-Marbois in Philadelphia, then presided as vice consul at Norfolk from 1784 to 1814, a tour of duty interrupted only once (for four years) in the late 1790s.[10] Although no other consul equaled this record, most of the persons who held consular positions when the war ended in 1783 were still in service ten years later. They included the youthful Antoine Delaforest, a hard-working minor aristocrat who enjoyed a wide acquaintance with American political leaders and understood them better than most; Louis-Guillaume Otto, an Alsatian Protestant who twice served as chargé d'affaires and later had the courage to blame his own government for having forced the United States into negotiating Jay's treaty; and Philippe Létombe, a small-town lawyer already middle-aged when he arrived in Boston in 1779, and one who strove so singlemindedly to do more than his duties required that he took it as a personal affront when the Girondins replaced him.[11]

---

[8]Delaforest to same, No. 251, New York, 18 February 1789, ibid., ff. 233–36.

[9]See "Note des avances à faire aux consuls du Roy et autres . . .," enclosed in Holker to MMC, Philadelphia, 24 July 1779, CC (Phil.), 945: 5.

[10]For personal data on Oster, see unsigned affidavit, 24 July 1783, CC (Norfolk), 927: 3–4vo; also Oster to MRE, No. 1, 4 brumaire, an 5 (25 October 1796), CC (Norfolk), Tome 2, 22–25; and same to Talleyrand, 9 germinal, an 9 (30 March 1801), ibid., ff. 96–97.

[11]See Otto's *Considérations sur la conduite du gouvernement Américain envers la France, depuis le commencement de la Révolution jusqu'en 1797* (Princeton University Press for the Institut Français de Washington 1945), original in AECPE-U, 47: 401–18vo; and Létombe's "Réponse," 2 vendémiaire, an 3 (23 September 1794), CC (Philadelphia), Tome 3, 105–107.

Of lesser calibre though long in service were men like the Chevalier Charles François Adrien le Paulnier D'Annemours who, during thirteen years in Baltimore, probably engaged in private business, certainly reduced his usefulness by living openly with a black mistress, and had to be nudged to turn in routine reports; and Saint-John de Crèvecoeur whose *Letters from an American Farmer* delighted French readers but irritated his superiors. The latter felt that he painted misleading scenes of a bucolic American paradise and wished that the consul for New York would show more than sporadic interest in gathering the commercial data of that busy port.[12]

Length of service, of course, did not guarantee high performance. As shapers of French perceptions, men like François de Barbé-Marbois. Jean-Baptiste Petry, and G.J.A. Ducher, though they served briefly, doubtless exerted more influence on the way French officials ultimately came to view the Franco-American relationship than did, say, D'Annemours or even Crèvecoeur. Where long-term exposure combined with an individual's insight and vigor, however, as it did in Delaforest, Otto, and Létombe, the result was to produce some of the most influential interpreters of that relationship.

Of the three, Antoine-René-Charles-Mathurin Delaforest may have most nearly personified the bureaucratic type, not uncommonly found in any century but often associated with the eighteenth, who was both competent and corrupt. He was either one of the greatest rascals in service to France in postwar America, or he was what most of his admiring colleagues supposed him to be: a hard-driving, conscientious consul general from whom they regularly received gentle reproofs mixed with friendly counsel. The French minister, Comte de Moustier, said of Delaforest that he "unites in himself all the desirable qualities of a good Consul, active, vigilant, industrious . . . moderating the impetuosity of several of his colleagues, covering their foibles . . . and giving them advice which can only be salutary." Similar praise came from Avistay de Chateaufort to whom Delaforest turned over the Charleston consulate in July 1785. Chateaufort wrote Paris, not once but twice, expressing appreciation for the assistance Delaforest had given him during the transition.[13] Such praise for a predecessor from a newly installed consul was as rare as it must be believable. Usually, consuls came to their posts damning their predecessors

[12]For judgments on D'Annemours and Crèvecoeur, see Moustier's "Distribution des Consulats," ff. 191vo–92, 194vo–95.

[13]Ibid., ff. 190–90vo; also Chateaufort to de Castries, Nos. 7 and 3, Philadelphia and Charleston, respectively, dated 12 May 1785, and 5 July 1785, CC (Charleston), 372: 105–105vo, and 126–27.

for having left behind a disarray of garbled accounts, lost documents, and incompetent staff. No such trail of complaint ever followed Delaforest.

Charges of corruption did pursue him, however — allegations clothed with enough detail of supposed wrongdoing to lend them an air of truth and yet, in most cases, traceable to persons who could be suspected of having personal or political reasons for wanting him brought down. Shadows first fell across his career when, following the Girondin shakeup, Delaforest returned to Philadelphia in early 1794, again to serve as consul general but also equally charged with three other "commissioners" to share responsibility for a new diplomatic mission headed by the Jacobin minister, Joseph Fauchet.[14] It was Delaforest's misfortune that Fauchet harbored to a more than modest degree the paranoia that made Jacobins among the most enemy-conscious of revolutionary factions. On arrival, Fauchet found waiting for him a long memorandum that accused Delaforest of having operated a ring of profiteers which in a two-year period, 1791–92, had sold commodities to the French government of Saint Domingue for up to three times their market value. Fauchet, who already suspected Delaforest of royalist sympathies, quietly forwarded the memorandum to Paris. The accusations came, in all likelihood, from a disgruntled consul in Baltimore named Moisonnier who, alone, from his knowledge of the Baltimore business community, could have described (or fabricated) the supposed operations of the ring in such condemning detail. According to the memorandum, Delaforest had repeatedly arranged to make overpriced shipments through the Baltimore firm of Zacharie, Coopman and Company. Party to the fraud was a Saint Domingue official named Wante, reportedly a friend of Delaforest since childhood, who made sure the cargoes were accepted and paid for on arrival. The ring also included the Philadelphia export firm of Vanuxen and Lombard. To keep the operation closed and profitable, Delaforest allegedly forced any independent sellers of provisions to present their bills to him. When these outsiders found their bills of exchange discounted at 50 percent, they raised their own prices accordingly. Thus, the ring profited both by selling overpriced commodities on their own account and by redeeming at full value bills of exchange they had bought at half price. Delaforest alone was presumed to have pocketed nearly $100,000 from these transactions.[15]

Curiously, Fauchet failed to pursue these charges, perhaps because

---

[14]The other two were Jean-Baptiste Petry, former consul at Charleston, now designated consul for the State of Pennsylvania, and a legation secretary named Le Blanc. Fauchet's suspicions of Delaforest's close association with Petry shortly led him to make separate reports to Paris. For the Commissioners' instructions, see Turner, ed., *CFM* (Washington 1904) 2: 287–94.

[15]Fauchet to CRE, Philadelphia, 11 pluviôse, an 2 (30 January 1794), série D XXV, carton 59, doss. 582, 1–9, ANF.

Moisonnier, a Girondin holdover scheduled to be replaced, would have been a politically tainted witness. Moisonnier's motives can only be guessed. Quite possibly, he hoped to retain his post in Baltimore by exploiting what he knew to be a rift between Fauchet and the consul general.[16] In any event, he soon brought new charges, this time that Zacharie, Coopman and Company, with Delaforest's knowledge and complicity, had acquired two sets of payment vouchers for the same shipment of goods to Cap Français nearly a year earlier. When confronted, Zacharie explained that he had asked Paris for a duplicate set at a time when he believed the originals had been destroyed in the great Cap fire. Delaforest had certified to their probable loss. Zacharie denied he intended to ask payment for both sets of vouchers, indeed said he had already notified Paris that the originals had been recovered. Fauchet, to his credit, concluded that Moisonnier had been over-zealous and that Zacharie, who gladly surrendered the duplicate vouchers, was as blameless in this episode as was Delaforest.[17]

More interesting to Fauchet, even than allegations of profiteering, was the likelihood verging on certainty that his consul general and fellow commissioner harbored royalist sympathies. In fact, Delaforest probably showed less ardor for the Republic than any other member of the Franco-American establishment who survived it. Some of his associates in this country were sufficiently suspect to make his political loyalty a target of innuendo whenever the Republican faithful caught sight of him in questionable company. The latter included American federalists, some of whom the consul general had known for more than a decade. How Delaforest was to deploy his influence or gather reliable intelligence without gaining the confidence of federalist leaders was a question his critics obviously felt to be less important than that he echo their own ideological hostility toward a regime they were sure had betrayed its republican principles. When it was rumored that Delaforest might be named to succeed Genet, the Philadelphia Jacobin Society roundly denounced him as "a low, intriguing aristocrat" and warned Paris that "no minister could be better calculated to respond to the views of the executive power of the United States."[18]

---

[16]Though Moisonnier knew that Fauchet wanted to oust him, he later described the minister as his defender against Delaforest's charge that his accounts were short $310,000. See his letter to MAE, 2 germinal, an 4 (22 March 1796), CC (Baltimore), Tome 1, 142–47.

[17]See Moisonnier to Committees of Public Safety and Finance, 23 prairial, an 2 (11 June 1794); and Fauchet to CRE, Philadelphia, 9 messidor, an 2 (28 June 1794), ibid., ff. 102–104, and 110–11vo, respectively.

[18]"Observations sur les circonstances actuelles, relativement aux interêts de la République Française, et celles des Etats-Unis de l'Amérique," [February 1794], D XXV, carton 59, doss. 582, ANF.

Delaforest trod even more dangerous ground if, as was rumored, he fraternized with *émigrés*, those proscribed aristocrats cast into exile by their refusal to come to terms with the Republic and whom Republicans regarded as subversives relentlessly plotting the return of the *ancien régime*. Of the many who took refuge in the United States, the Vicomte de Noailles, Omer de Talon, and the former bishop of Autun, Charles Maurice de Talleyrand, were the *émigré* luminaries most often watched. Washington innocently offended Republican Paris and was never quite forgiven when he "received" Talon and Noailles. He would have granted Talleyrand an audience, too, but for the furor.[19] With Talleyrand Delaforest almost certainly had some form of communication. The two men had known each other since the early 1780s and Talleyrand was later to appoint Delaforest to high position in the Foreign Office. Indeed, one of his first acts on becoming Minister of Exterior Relations in 1797 was to bring in Delaforest to straighten out that ministry's tangled finances.[20] That the two had no clandestine contact during Talleyrand's two years in America is unlikely.

Fauchet's suspicions peaked in early summer 1794, when he noticed letters passing through the consul general's hands addressed to "suspected men." Placing spies in Delaforest's office brought confirmation. More intercepted letters suggested that Delaforest was serving as intermediary among proscribed persons and may even have helped several of them return to France. Worse, Fauchet's spies also produced letters, similarly compromising, signed by Louis Otto, former chargé d'affaires and now sensitively employed as chief of the Foreign Ministry's *premier bureau*. In one sense, Fauchet expressed little surprise: Otto and Delaforest were two of a kind, "tender friends," he wrote. Nor should it escape the ministry's attention that Otto also had $7,000 in an account with the Bank of the United States. What truly angered Fauchet was the thought that perhaps the Foreign Office had set him up. With a brashness seldom met in diplomatic correspondence, Fauchet reflected to the Foreign Minister: "I can only believe that your purpose has been to compromise me by associating me with such men."[21]

Accused of aiding *émigrés*, Delaforest escaped Jacobin justice only by

[19]Washington numbered Talleyrand among those French *émigrés* he refused to meet in an official capacity. See Washington to Hamilton, 6 May 1794, and to the Marquis of Lansdowne, Philadelphia, 30 August 1794, in John C. Fitzpatrick, ed., *The Writings of George Washington* (Washington 1940) 33: 352–53 and 482–83, respectively.

[20]Masson, *Département des affaires étrangères*, 408.

[21]Fauchet's dispatches to MAE, of 20 prairial, an 2 (8 June 1794) and no. 14 (politique), Philadelphia, 21 prairial, an 2 (9 June 1794), in *CFM*, 389 and 390, respectively.

the good fortune of not being in Paris that summer. Otto, too, was lucky in that the authorities did not get around to jailing him until after Robespierre had fallen. As the Terror loosened its grip, Otto found it possible to explain away his American bank account (it was his wife's dowry) and to refute allegations that he had transacted private business with a British agent, a charge he ascribed to his own political "moderatism." His offense consisted in having associated with Delaforest and Jean-Baptiste Petry. The latter had been consul at Charleston in the late 1780s and subsequently one of the commissioners. Fauchet had charged both with being guilty of "misconduct and aristocracy." The charges held danger only as long as the Terror lasted. In its aftermath, Otto loyally defended both Delaforest and Petry as "agents remarkable for their probity and their talents." Several years later, he concluded that whatever the evidence against Delaforest, Fauchet had imagined it. By that time, having closed out sixteen years' service in America, Delaforest was well launched in a high level diplomatic career that would last until 1839.[22]

Louis-Guillaume Otto, defender of former colleagues, began his own career in the United States in 1779, first as secretary to La Luzerne until 1784, then returning as chargé d'affaires a year later. After the Comte de Moustier's brief mission, 1788–89, Otto again took charge of the legation until Jean de Ternant, the *ancien régime*'s last fully accredited emissary, arrived in May 1791. At his own request, he returned to Paris in the spring of 1792; thereafter until his arrest, he headed the *premier bureau* where he functioned, at least briefly, as the Foreign Ministry's in-house expert on American affairs.[23]

Otto's strong personal ties with this country, as well as his dim view of French revolutionary diplomacy, doubtless help to explain his later readiness to defend Washington's foreign policy toward France. Thrust congenially into the political life of wartime Philadelphia in the heyday of the French alliance, the 25-year-old legation secretary had no difficulty making himself at ease in its social life as well. University educated at Strasbourg, and a Protestant, he fitted comfortably into what passed for the salon circuit, enlivening it with his talents as a harpist and his attention to young women. He wooed at some length but failed to win the hand of Nancy Shippen, daughter of one of Philadelphia's most prestigious families (her father discouraged the match), but went on to marry into the politically powerful Livingston clan of New York. Although Eliza

---

[22]Otto, *Considérations*, 3, 16; Masson, *Département*, 230–31.
[23]Otto, *Considérations*, 2–3; *Almanach national de France, L'An Troisième de la République* (Paris n.d.) 207.

Livingston died within a year, this union gave him access to the ranks of public figures whose views, he wrote, "carry much weight in public deliberations."[24] Three years later, in 1790, he married the daughter of New York consul Saint-John de Crèvecoeur at a ceremony in which Thomas Jefferson, recently returned from France to become Secretary of State, acted as principal witness.[25] In sum, Otto enjoyed a political and social entrée no other Frenchmen of his generation could match.

To revolutionary colleagues, however, his social connections appeared something more than a liability. Joseph Fauchet, who instinctively distrusted anyone who had served the *ancien régime*, wrote off Otto as a social ornament, a diplomat whose public record fell somewhere between frivolity and treason. "He is a man without ability or spirit," he wrote; his talents were best suited to "taking coffee and tea." Otto had a wealth of experience, Fauchet admitted, and he "chatters well enough to give the impression of understanding things, but his principles are absolutely opposed to the revolution."[26] This judgment, so damning in its entirety but so obviously marked by ideological rancor, hardly did justice to the man. On the record, Otto proved to be both spirited and able in his conduct of official business. Those social accomplishments so scorned by Fauchet enhanced his effectiveness and made him a highly acceptable French representative. Americans were pleased to find him as tactful and discreet as La Luzerne, less prickly than Moustier, and more warmly approachable than Jean de Ternant. Whenever problems arose touching on vital French interests, Paris had no more loyal or articulate a spokesman. Moreover, the dispatches he wrote as chargé d'affaires were models of informed reflection, flawed only by a deep vein of pessimism that led him, too often and with too little reason, to predict the imminent dissolution of the Union. As interpreter, though not as prophet, he had few equals.

Later, in temporary retirement, when relations between Paris and Philadelphia had reached a dangerous impasse, Otto wrote a sweeping vindication of American conduct toward France. In a memorandum clearly intended to evoke conciliatory action from the new Directorial regime, he made a powerful case that only France could supply the correctives necessary to restore a badly deteriorated relationship. Though, for what had transpired, he exonerated Americans somewhat too glibly, Otto bore down hard on the unremitting errors and provocations he believed French

---

[24]Otto to MAE, New York, 19 May 1787, AECPE-U, 32: 262vo.

[25]See Margaret M. O'Dwyer, "Louis Guillaume Otto in America (1779–91)," (Northwestern University, unpublished doctoral dissertation 1954), 2–23, and passim.

[26][Fauchet to CRE], Philadelphia, 11 pluviose, an 2 (30 January 1794), série D XXV, carton 59, doss. 582, ff. 10–11, ANF.

governments had committed in the recent past. At every critical juncture since the Revolution began, he wrote, French diplomats, either duped, over-zealous, or plain wrong-headed, had pushed the United States into defensive reactions. The result had been to squander the genuine good-will most Americans felt toward France.[27]

Where French policymakers had erred most grievously, he continued, was in supposing the Washington administration not to have pursued policies toward France sanctioned by majority opinion. French efforts to set a presumably pro-French populace against an ostensibly pro-British government dangerously mistook a fundamental reality of the American political process. No such exploitable rift existed or could exist, he wrote, in a country where "elections are as free as they are in the United States." Had Americans at any time believed their leaders not to represent their will, they would have turned them out. "If one wants to know what the majority opinion is," he added, "one need only look at their elections and the character of those who are elected." Of a piece with this vain imagining of an exploitable rift between people and government, Otto felt that French statesmen had too long exaggerated the importance of American professions of attachment to either France or Britain. Americans, he wrote, instinctively consulted their own interests first. The preferences they expressed for one or the other of the great powers were inconsequential. Frenchmen and Britons might regard them as new pawns in an old game but, in Otto's view, based on twenty years of close observation, the new republic had already defined national purposes unlikely to be useful to either. That Louis Otto should thus discern the emergence of a self-conscious, self-serving national identity perhaps was not as surprising as that so many of his contemporaries missed it.[28]

Older than most of his consular colleagues, and maybe for that reason a trifle more self-important, Philippe-André-Joseph Létombe ran the consulate in Boston like a man who had no other ambition. For fourteen years, the watchful, methodical Létombe, despite bad health and worse finances, asked nothing more than to stay at his post, cultivating that special mastery of New England affairs in which he took great pride.

---

[27]See Otto, *Considérations*, especially 10–17.

[28]Ibid., 23, 25.

[29]To get reinstated, Létombe wrote earnestly to various government committees, succeeded in generating a favorable report from the foreign office to the Committee of Public Safety, and even circulated a published defense of his conduct. See Létombe to CSP, Paris, 8 germinal, an 2 (28 March 1794), CC (Boston), Tome 3, 86–88; his "Rapport," brumaire, an 2 (22 October–20 November 1793), ibid., ff. 60–61; and his *Recueil de diverse pièces en faveur du Citoyen Létombe* (Paris 1793).

When the Girondins shook him loose in 1793, he returned to Paris in a
state of outraged shock. Denouncing the "calumniators" who had
unseated him, Létombe defended his republican, and other, virtues so
plausibly that a post-Jacobin regime sent him back as consul general in
1795.[29] Two years later when the French minister Pierre Adet quit Philadelphia on the brink of the Quasi War, it fell to Létombe, as chargé
d'affaires, to play out the diplomatic end-game.

Born in 1738, the son of a minor official in Nord Libre, Létombe
studied law at the nearby University of Douai and was already practicing
his profession in Valenciennes when his future colleagues, Delaforest and
Otto, were still in the nursery.

Drawn to Paris in the mid-1760s, Létombe continued to practice
law and began to collect patrons. When he applied in 1769 for the post of
chief legal officer to the Superior Council of Port-au-Prince, he could
number among his sponsors such renowned literary figures as the abbés
de Raynal and de Mably and the poet-novelist Montmartel. How the
young Létombe, later the archetype of a cautious, plodding civil servant,
fitted into this coterie of lively intellectuals leaves much to conjecture, no
less his warm friendship with Mlle. Claire Clairon, the darling of Paris
theatregoers. In any event, he obtained the legal post he sought in Port-
au-Prince, only to be invalided back to Paris in 1775, suffering what he
diagnosed as a blocked liver, a complaint that recurred in later years.
During a long convalescence, he wrote technical reports for the Navy on
legal matters relating to Saint Domingue and acted as an unsalaried con-
sultant to the Controller General's office. Fit enough by 1779 to accept
the consulate in Boston, he left Paris that year to take charge of the most
bustling French outpost in America.[30]

Although all consuls had Navy-related responsibilities, Létombe's
were the more burdensome because France's Atlantic squadron made
Boston an annual port of call. French naval officers familiar with New
England waters from having used Boston as a center of wartime operations appreciated the town's northerly dispensation from the equinoctial
storms that ravaged the Caribbean. Throughout the 1780s, the late summer arrival of French men-of-war levied the heaviest kinds of demands
for a variety of consular support services. Naval commanders routinely
expected Létombe to re-victual their vessels, contract for repairs, and
provide hospital facilities for scorbutic seamen. He was also expected to
cope with the problems created by scores of French seamen on shore leave.

---

[30]"Réponse de Létombe à une libelle, trouvée dans les cartons du dépôt des Relations Extérieures," 2 vendémiaire, an 3 (3 September 1794), CC (Philadelphia), Tome 3, 105–107.

Desertions, brawls, and other breaches of discipline came at least partly under his consular jurisdiction. It was Létombe's boast that in most such instances he managed to preserve the Navy's good name.

Between fleet visits, Létombe settled agreeably into Boston's commercial community, an amiable figure well liked and respected. When he was forced to leave in 1793, no fewer than twenty prominent merchants joined the governor and council of Massachusetts in sending him off with written testimonials of appreciation; and as his ship sailed, the guns of Boston gave him a consul's traditional eleven-gun salute.[31] Even the acerbic G. J. A. Ducher, who rarely had a good word for any colleague, carped only at what he supposed was Létombe's sly effort to ennoble himself by writing (as he did, occasionally) the aristocratic "de" in front of his surname. The sharp-eyed Moustier, visiting Boston in 1788, found Létombe to be exacting and "pleasantly deferential," certainly deserving of the high "esteem and affection" in which he was obviously held.[32]

No consul, however, lacked for enemies; expatriates who thought themselves wrongfully deprived of consular assistance, litigants who chafed at adverse consular rulings, and later, most troublesome, the political dissidents who projected the grievances they felt toward one Paris regime or another on to its nearest representative. In Létombe's case, moreover, his detractors found him to be overly congenial with Boston merchants. They thought his "bonhomie" offensive. To this, the consul retorted that he always spoke to Americans with candor and told them the truth. Nor was it easy, he explained, to remain on good terms with those he suspected of violating French trade regulations. "As soon as they know I am watching," he wrote, "I am no longer able to count on . . . the goodwill of my position."[33]

In this last respect, Létombe was well placed to become a minor expert on illicit trade. Given the traditional exchange of New England fish for Caribbean sugar, and considering that the French islands were forbidden to export sugar to the United States, he could hardly be otherwise. His reports, however, though they amply documented the extent of this traffic, rarely contained proposals for quashing it. Cautious by nature and apparently reluctant to draw attention to himself by offering gratuitous suggestions, he usually settled for giving detailed descriptions of the problem. He left it to others to prod Paris to take remedial measures.

---

[31]Létombe, *Recueil*, 13–14.

[32]"Notes remises par Ducher," n.d., CC (Wilmington), Tome 1, 65vo–66; and Moustier's "Distribution des Consulats," ff. 190vo–91. See also Moustier to MMC, New York, 25 December 1788, CC (New York), 910: 83vo–84.

[33]"Mémoire des Affaires du Consulat de France à Boston pendant l'année 1788," CC (Boston), 210: 331vo.

Still, Létombe's apparent intellectual passivity bespoke not so much the indifferent placeholder as it did the prudent bureaucrat. His reports left no doubt as to how seriously he regarded certain problems of trade and commerce, but they also revealed his underlying assumption that Paris itself must devise the solutions. Meanwhile, his detailed iteration of those problems served usefully to confirm the need for solutions.

Today, whatever name-recognition attaches to François de Barbé-Marbois derives mainly from the part he played in dickering up the price of Louisiana during the purchase negotiations of 1803. In the 1780s, his fame, or notoriety, rested on two other episodes. Historians of the Revolutionary War era recall him as the author of the controversial "Marbois Letter," and students of international law find him involved in this country's first extradition case, the so-called Marbois–Longchamps Affair. Neither episode did him much credit in the eyes of American contemporaries. In the first, the letter he wrote from Philadelphia during the Paris peace negotiations, he offered a consul general's considered opinion that Congress would not insist on retaining an American right to fish in Canadian waters as part of the final settlement, and that Vergennes, by dissociating France from this American objective, might get better peace terms from Britain. Unfortunately, the British intercepted Marbois's proposal and handed it over to Congress as evidence of French betrayal.[34] The letter, curiously, had less adverse impact when Congress first learned of it in early 1784 than it did in later years when American leaders, less friendly to France, used it to prove that France had always been an unreliable ally. At the time it was disclosed, the French minister La Luzerne cheerfully reported that at least some members of Congress were willing to believe the letter had been forged. Others refused to find Marbois's suggestion for relinquishing the fisheries out of line with what Congress itself had set as minimal war aims. And in any event, the French government had not taken Marbois's advice, at least to the extent that Americans had won from Britain the "liberty" to fish inshore along the Canadian coast. Only a few congressmen, La Luzerne reported, could even remember what Marbois had proposed. By early 1784, the minister had good reason to play down any lingering resentments. He had asked Paris to recall him and was recommending the consul general to become chargé d'affaires.[35] In fact, the transition was accomplished without incident, and Marbois served little more than a year before Otto replaced him, also as chargé d'affaires, in mid-1785. Only then did it appear that the episode

---

[34]For circumstances surrounding the Barbé–Marbois letter, see Richard B. Morris, *The Peacemakers: the Great Powers and American Independence* (New York, 1965) 324–26.

[35]To Vergennes, Nos. 371 and 279, Philadelphia, of 20 March and 24 May 1784, AECPE-U, 27: 212–13 and 278–79, respectively.

had not been forgotten. Otto described whimsically the difficulty Congress had in bidding Marbois farewell. Northern members, whose regional interest in the fisheries made for long memories, objected to a valedictory resolution that said Marbois "had given Congress entire satisfaction." Nor would they accept "the greatest satisfaction" as a milder substitute. When they finally settled for "great satisfaction," Otto was moved to observe that Yankees were an unforgiving lot, and Congress wasted a good deal of time on matters of little consequence.[36]

Marbois's brush with extradition also left a bad aftertaste. Nor could its timing have been worse. That same spring of 1784, as La Luzerne tried to reassure Paris that Marbois's fisheries letter had not impaired his usefulness, a disgruntled French army officer named Charles de Longchamps physically assaulted Marbois on the streets of Philadelphia. The French government immediately demanded that Longchamps be sent home for trial and punishment. When neither Congress nor the State of Pennsylvania saw fit to surrender him, Philadelphia newspapers blew the incident into a *cause célèbre*. Nor was Paris reconciled when a Pennsylvania jury found Longchamps guilty and a Pennsylvania judge gave him a stiff jail sentence. Moreover, its continuing demand that Longchamps be extradited put Marbois, now chargé d'affaires, in the uncomfortable position of seeming to be both plaintiff and prosecutor. Worse, in conveying his government's insistence that Longchamps be sent home for punishment, Marbois appeared to suggest that French justice was somehow superior to that of Pennsylvania. American leaders, for their part, were satisfied to believe that Longchamps's three-year jail sentence met the desideratum of international law that persons committing crimes against diplomats be punished with extra severity. By the time it had run its course, the incident had touched on sensitive issues of American sovereignty, legal jurisdiction, and the United States as a place of refuge.[37]

Whether Marbois's letter and his involvement with Longchamps hastened his departure the record does not show. Mid-1785, however, found him accepting appointment as intendant, the Navy's top post in Saint Domingue. Simultaneously, Otto returned from France to fill the vacated position of chargé d'affaires, and Delaforest took over as consul general. Inexplicably, however, Paris failed to send a new minister until the Comte de Moustier arrived in early 1788.[38]

[36]To Vergennes, No. 10, Philadelphia, 28 September 1785, AECPE-U, 30: 317–17vo.
[37]See chapter 6.
[38]Correspondence effecting these personnel changes, all datelined Versailles, includes letters from Navy Minister de Castries to Vergennes, 10 June 1785; Vergennes to de Castries, 12 June and two letters from Vergennes to Barbé-Marbois, both dated 20 June 1785, AECPE-U, 30; ff. 41, 45, and 57–58, respectively.

Although Marbois served only briefly as consul general (1781–84), then a year as chargé d'affaires, he showed a flair for identifying in their early phases many of the commercial and political difficulties France would face in dealing with her American ally in the postwar period. Few problems, real or potential, escaped his notice. Whether they concerned congressional impotence, the effects of the postwar depression, American traffic in contraband, or the persistence of British influence in American trade and politics, Marbois early sensed the implications these problems were likely to have for French interests.

Nor should a roll-call of the French consular establishment omit the name of G. J. A. Ducher, a man of such obscure origins that he will forever be known only by his three initials. From equally humble consular posts, those of Portsmouth, N.H., and Wilmington, N.C., Ducher's meteoric rise to power and influence doubtless astonished colleagues who saw him return to Paris to take a major hand in shaping the most fundamental changes in French commercial policies. By the early 1790s, the former consul was drafting legislation that met the Jacobin regime's wish for a more conscious protectionism. Ducher's navigation act, passed by the National Convention in September 1793, though postponed in its operation, came into effect in the early Napoleonic period, and its principles lived on in the commercial policies of the Restoration.[39]

Both during and after his American tour of duty, Ducher showed how he drew from American sources for his thinking on commercial matters. When, for example, he wrote the Jacobin navigation act, he incorporated whole sections word for word, from the tariff and tonnage laws enacted by the first federal Congress. Earlier, while still a consul but already projecting ways to improve France's world trade position, he evinced a tough-mindedness toward the United States that was to mark his economic doctrines as a whole. France could best expand her trade here, he felt, by cracking down on Americans' illicit traffic with the French Indies. That accomplished, he believed that a combination of threat and favor would turn them more fully toward France as a "natural" trade partner and put a swift end to their ostensibly unnatural commercial ties with Britain.[40]

As an observer, Ducher selected from his American environment whatever best served his theoretical predispositions. No one compiled trade statistics more avidly or studied commercial patterns more closely. He often reached conclusions, however, that seemed more the product of

[39]For a detailed examination of Ducher's influence, see Frederick L. Nussbaum, *Commercial Policy in the French Revolution: a Study of the Career of G. J. A. Ducher* (Washington, D.C. 1923).

[40]Ibid., 116–18. Ducher justified his optimism most fully in a pamphlet entitled *Nouvelle Alliance à proposer entre les Républiques Française & Américaine* (Paris 1792).

superficial logic than of insight or understanding. He expressed great certainty, for example, that Americans would never accumulate enough specie
to pay off the French debt, that American merchants would actively seek
war with Britain because they wanted the United States to become "the
only commercial power," and that North Carolina's initial refusal to ratify
the Constitution lay in her design to make a separate commercial treaty
with London. Everywhere he looked, Ducher seemed to see nothing but
economic facts and economic motives. With few French ship arrivals to
distract him, either at Portsmouth or at Wilmington, he had plenty of
time to work statistics into theories.[41]

In his solitude, Ducher also cultivated enemies. Moustier thought
him a grubby, repulsive individual who was both ignorant and insubordi-
nate. He was "detested by all who know him," wrote the minister, and
"expends his impotent rages by denigrating the entire consular corps."[42]
Indeed, Ducher seemed to relish character assassination. His slurs on his
colleagues ranged from the libelous to the petty, and few escaped his cen-
sure. According to Ducher, Jean Petry had arranged to be grossly over-
paid, Michel Mangourit was an unpunished "thief," Martin Oster's quarrels
with his wife were a "public scandal," and the Chevalier D'Annemours's
penchant for black mistresses better fitted him to have been "a good Intendant" at Saint Domingue. Moreover, Antoine Delaforest regularly
padded his expense account; Crèvecoeur was an old tory whose "novel"
about rural life in America was "as much lying as crafty"; and Jean
Toscan, the vice consul for whom Ducher substituted briefly at Portsmouth, could not be believed when he complained of straitened finances.
Toscan, he wrote, had "two fine dapplegrey horses, a pretty carriage, and
sets a good table."[43]

How Toscan managed to draw so little fire is the more remarkable
in view of the difficulty he had with Ducher in their official dealings. In
1786 when Létombe went home on leave, Toscan came down from Portsmouth to take charge of the Boston consulate, leaving Ducher to sell off
some Navy-owned masts which the French government had stored at
Portsmouth and no longer needed. Delays, rumors, and vague reports
finally led Toscan to conclude that Ducher instead of selling the masts for
cash had exchanged them for commodities which he planned to send to
St. Pierre and Miquelon. If this were so, Toscan wrote, Ducher had acted

---

[41]See his dispatches, Nos. 9, 12, and 16, of 6 February, 5 March, and 31 May 1788, CC
(Wilmington), 1: 39–40, 41–42, and 48–49, respectively.
[42]"Distributions des Consulats," ff. 194vo–95.
[43]"Notes remises par Ducher," ff. 65–66.

without authorization, and because he knew so little of "the genius of Americans," had probably been cheated. Toscan's suspicions were apparently unfounded. At least Létombe reported on his return to Boston and following a visit to Portsmouth that Ducher had done nothing untoward, and in fact showed a firm mastery of consular function. Létombe's good report on Ducher was the only one of its kind.[44]

Posted next to Wilmington, Ducher languished irritably. During his first year and a half in this North Carolina port, he saw only five French vessels. He managed, however, to make trouble for the captains of four of them. In March 1789, he asked the Navy to bring him home before idleness and a bad climate destroyed what remained of his usefulness to government service. "Here," he wrote, "there are neither nationals, nor deputies, nor chancellor, nor French commerce."[45] A year later, he turned up inexplicably in New York, refusing to explain to Delaforest why he had left his post. Only grudgingly did Ducher finally produce a letter from Paris which gave him leave to restore his health. Delaforest remarked wryly that the vice consul's health appeared to be "very good," and warned him that if he expected to be assigned to a livelier post, he would wait in vain.[46] The following year found Ducher happily back in Paris, his ambitions soon to be gratified by the part he was to play in formulating more commercial laws of the type he had recently seen so widely violated.

As a group, French ministers to the United States in this period, though their rank carried more weight and their dispatches a greater sense of immediacy, exerted a less shaping influence on the ways Paris came to perceive this country than did the consuls. Once the war ended, the Chevalier de la Luzerne continued faithfully to report the activities of Congress, but obviously wanted to be relieved. Recalled at his own request in mid-1784, he was pleased to accept the ambassadorial post in London. His only slim tie with American affairs thereafter was through his brother who served as Minister of Navy and Colonies in the late 1780s.[47] Then followed the long ministerial hiatus which Marbois and Otto filled as chargés d'affaires until the Comte de Moustier arrived in 1788. Shrewd,

[44]Toscan to MMC, No. 10, 24 July 1786; and Létombe to same, No. 33, 14 October 1786, CC (Boston), 210: 23–24, and 36–40, respectively.

[45]Ducher to MMC, Nos. 26 and 31, of 15 December 1788, and 13 March 1789, CC (Wilmington), 1: 54–54vo, and 58–58vo, respectively.

[46]Delaforest to MMC, No. 290, New York, 28 May 1790, CC (New York), 910: 296–96vo.

[47]La Luzerne's older brother, César-Henri, became Navy Minister in October 1787. La Luzerne himself served at the London post from 1788 until his death in 1791. Louis G. Michaud, *Biographie universelle ancienne et moderne* (Reprinted: Graz, Austria 1968) 25: 539–41.

articulate, intelligent, Moustier has often been under-rated, perhaps because his obsession with diplomatic protocol made him seem superficial. In fact, he listened attentively to those who knew the American scene better than he, and ultimately produced a set of recommendations for improving Franco-American commerce which, though ill-timed, distilled much of the wisdom he took from their observations. He and most of his works were soon forgotten, however, when he chose the exile of an *émigré*.[48]

Moustier's departure in October 1789 created another ministerial lapse, again filled by Louis Otto and lasting until Jean de Ternant arrived in August 1791. Of Ternant the Philadelphia bookseller and one time revolutionary Moreau de St. Méry wrote that he "merely passed through the country." Joseph Fauchet thought he lined his pockets along the way. Ternant, he believed, conducted public affairs less ably than even his consul general, Delaforest, but was just as guilty of fleecing the Republic. Moreover, he ventured, a tribunal could easily prove it. Ternant's own dispatches, however, reveal only the hard-pressed diplomat engaged in a desperate struggle to feed and supply the revolution- and famine-struck French West Indies, a man so beset by financial demands and Foreign Office neglect that it seems unlikely he had much time either to rig his own accounts or, for that matter, qualify as an expert on American affairs.[49]

Of the revolutionary ministers who followed, only Fauchet retained a post-mission interest in counseling the Foreign Office on matters relating to the United States. Unfortunately, he also persisted in viewing Americans through the eyes of a Jacobin doctrinaire, perpetuating many of the misperceptions his contemporary, Louis Otto, tried so hard to dispel. Though Fauchet continued to give advice, the ministers who came before and after him did not. His predecessor, Edmond Genet, once disgraced and disavowed, spent the rest of his days tending a farm in New York state. The third and last of the trio, Pierre Adet, came to Philadelphia mainly to threaten French vengeance against Jay's treaty, and having done so at some length and in vain, disappeared forever from the Franco-American scene.

---

[48]France's internal problems and her greater concern for the European side of diplomacy may explain the failure to replace La Luzerne with a fully accredited minister. See Ralph L. Ketcham, "French and American Politics, 1763–1793," *Political Science Quarterly* (June 1963) 216–17.

[49]See Moreau's *Voyages aux Etats-Unis de l'Amérique, 1793–98* (New Haven, 1913) 275; [Fauchet to CRE], Philadelphia, 11 pluviôse, an 2 (30 January 1794), série D XXV, carton 59, doss. 582, f. 12, ANF; and Ternant's dispatches beginning with that of 17 November 1791, in *CFM*, 72–191, passim.

It would be misleading to discount ministerial personnel altogether as shapers of the perceptual framework within which French officialdom came to view the United States in the 1780s. Ministers' dispatches, after all, went straight to the Foreign Office, where an individual emissary's views could not help but speak with authority on what was important for Paris to know about the changing elements in Franco-American relations. Where the ministers fell short as interpreters lay in their circumstance. Without exception, they served too briefly to add much that was new to the store of received wisdom already so often repeated in consular dispatches. Those ministers served best who borrowed freely from the cumulative experience of these old "America hands," and echoed what they found in the consular reports that passed regularly under their eyes before the consul general filed them with Paris.

II
THE BRITISH FACTOR

A touch of revisionist thinking inevitably crept into the French assessments of who had lost and who had gained from the recent military decision. Ostensibly, Britain had lost a sizable chunk of empire, and Americans had won the right to govern themselves. In retrospect, however, it might be asked how much the break had cost a British government which, now spared the expense of colonial administration, still enjoyed most of the advantages of the old imperial relationship. French journalist Tanguy de la Boissière thought it axiomatic that London had "lost nothing but the sterile right of sovereignty."[1] Even that, it appeared, might not be altogether irrevocable, should Americans decide that the burdens of independence were too heavy to bear. A crushing postwar depression combined with political conditions verging on anarchy loomed darkly over the future. Nor did it escape French notice that Britain still had active partisans in this country, empire loyalists to whom the outbreak of peace had given new voice and whose eventual return to the places of political influence might prepare the way. An imperial reconciliation, though few French observers thought it likely, was at least a troubling possibility.

La Luzerne, for example, wondered whether to credit the rumor that "British influence" in Congress explained why that body, even after it achieved a quorum, dawdled over ratifying the British peace treaty. Those who spread the rumor seemed to believe that a failure to act on the treaty would prove conclusively the incapacity of Congress to govern and thus open the way to a renewal of old political ties with London. The Frenchman heard the rumor often enough to report it to Paris, although privately he saw less evidence of "British influence" than of Congress exhibiting a characteristically American indifference to "business they regard

---

[1]*Mémoire sur la situation commerciale de la France avec les Etats-Unis de l'Amérique depuis l'année 1775 jusque & y compris 1795* (Paris 1796) 19. A similar view was expressed in the French-language edition of John Baker Holroyd's neo-mercantilist tract, entitled *Observations sur le commerce des Etats américains, par le Lord Sheffield* (Rouen 1789) 115–16.

as terminated." Enough that the peace treaty had been signed—Congress, he surmised, felt it could treat ratification with "a nonchalance natural to these people." British influence might be at work, but the internal political situation, he believed, would have to become a good deal worse before Americans would seriously consider forgoing their hard-won independence.[2]

The notion of distressed Americans someday opting for a return to empire constituted the ultimate threat of "British influence." Frenchmen who considered at what cost of French blood and treasure American independence had been bought stirred uneasily at the thought that the United States might fall back under the "yoke" of their ancient enemy. A year after ratification, talk of "reunion" again surfaced. Marbois picked up a warning that Americans might seek reinstatement in the empire if France pressed too importunately for repayment of the wartime debt. The new government, he was reminded, had many creditors and few sources of revenue. Should France exert too much pressure, Britain's partisans would urge reunion as a means to wipe out the French debt at one stroke. Like La Luzerne, Marbois showed little concern. Americans loyal to France, he wrote, still outnumbered the "friends of England," although he had to admit the increasing influence of politically active groups of unreconciled Loyalists. The warning had come from "persons of goodwill," he noted, and could not be entirely discounted.[3]

French fears for the worst died hard. Fifteen years later, at the height of the Quasi-War when talk of an Anglo-American alliance was in the air, Philippe Létombe reported that "the government of the United States seems to think more than ever about reunion with Great Britain." What moved the aging chargé to speculate in this vein was, apparently, the state visit to Québec of Prince Edward, Duke of Kent.[4]

However improbable a full-scale reconciliation, the certainty that Britain would seek to influence the political life of a new nation periodically darkened the dispatches French observers filed from their American outposts. A cautious man like Louis Otto wondered how France could best counter British influence without provoking an anti-French reaction. Wisdom suggested that France not appear to be intrusive. When he was named chargé in the spring of 1785, he counseled Montmorin not to instruct him to wage open warfare against John Adams. Because Adams, then on mission to London, was known to harbor sentiments hostile to

---

[2]To Vergennes, Nos. 364 and 369, Annapolis, 15 January and 1 March 1784, AECPE-U, 27: 55–61, and 183–87, respectively.

[3]To same, No. 412, New York, 17 February 1785, AECPE-U, 29: 60–62.

[4]"Extrait d'une lettre du Citoyen Létombe," Philadelphia, 6 fructidor, an 7 (23 August 1799), série AF III, carton 64, doss. 263, ANF.

France, Otto might be expected to try to offset Adams's blighting influence. But because his countrymen knew him to be an "honest man," any
attempt to discredit Adams might have adverse repercussions. Better,
Otto thought, to allow the postwar animosity Americans felt toward
Britain continue to work its poison.[5] Two years later when the Virginia
legislature acted to favor the French textile industry by proposing a stiff
import tax on British textiles, Otto again urged moderation. A somewhat lower duty on British cottons, he told a member of that body,
"would suffice to keep French importers above competition, [and] would
have the advantage moreover of not exciting the clamors and intrigues of
the English party."[6]

Otto and others, meanwhile, saw no reason to expect a similar restraint on Britain's part. They did believe, however, that because London
continued to treat the United States like an economic dependency, its
influence in this country would remain muted. Britain could not expect
to carry much weight as long as she kept her Indies ports tightly closed
to American shipping and restricted the types of goods Americans could
export to the British Isles. Thus, during the debtor uprising in Massachusetts known as Shays's Rebellion, rumors that British agents were
working to detach one or more of the New England states could be passed
over for what they were, pure rumor. Not that the presence of British
agents was to be doubted. No important event occurred in the United
States in the 1780s that was not reported back to Lord Dorchester, the
Governor-General of Canada, but French observers could be reasonably
sure that as long as Americans felt abused, those agents would function as
little more than gatherers of information.[7]

That Britain held high cards if she chose to play them, however, was
all too apparent. Any sign of goodwill from London, any indication of
forthcoming concessions to America's powerful shipping and mercantile
interests, and Britain's prestige would turn from shadow to substance in
the time it took the good news to cross the Atlantic. French officials,
knowing how quickly American attitudes could change, realized, too,
how decisive an initiative lay with their rivals, influence to be had for the

---

[5]"Mémoire remis par le Sr. Otto pour demander des instructions avant son depart, le 17
May 1785," AECPE-U, 29: 288–89. For an analysis of this long memorandum, see Paul G. Sifton,
"Otto's *Mémoire* to Vergennes, 1785," *William and Mary Quarterly* 22 (1965) 626–45.

[6]To Vergennes, No. 84, New York, 30 March 1787, AECPE-U, 32: 230vo.

[7]Otto to same, Nos. 71 and 83, New York, of 4 December 1786, and 16 March 1787,
AECPE-U, 32: 150–52vo, and 222–23, respectively, and to Montmorin, No. 23, New York,
28 August 1788, ibid., 33: 257–59vo. See Hamilton's contemporary intrigues with British agents
in Julian P. Boyd, *Number 7: Alexander Hamilton's Secret Attempts to Control American Foreign Policy*
(Princeton, N.J. 1964).

taking, about which France could do little. French revolutionaries would later denounce the *ancien régime* for failing to take its own initiatives while British prestige was at a low ebb. The lost opportunities of the 1780s, the apparent negligence or indifference of the royalist government, were oft-iterated themes in that later era. These critics erred, however, in believing that diplomats of the *ancien régime* were blind, rather than helpless. When Montmorin instructed Moustier in late 1787, he warned of a Britain working assiduously to diminish French influence, and urged the count to "steal a march on British agents." Moustier echoed the warning four months later when he reported that the British would surely use their commercial pre-eminence to "chill" relations between France and the United States.[8] But while Montmorin and Moustier agreed on the existence of a British threat, the question remained, as always in this era, what could France do about it?

London first signaled an interest in recouping at least a modicum of influence when it designated Sir John Temple to serve as consul general. In late 1785 Temple turned up in New York where for want of a formal Anglo-American consular convention Congress merely accorded him "all privileges based on the law of nations." Otto sniffed disapprovingly, but noted that if Temple had as few powers as those permitted to French consuls, his influence would be small indeed. Temple's position, in fact, remained anomalous, made so by his government's continued refusal to exchange personnel at a ministerial level. His activities, however, real or imagined, made him an object of French official concern. Two years later, Moustier commented fretfully on the consul general's seeming popularity with the pro-British element and suspected him of inspiring newspaper pieces deprecating France.[9]

Otto, too, regarded him with suspicion. Temple during his early days in New York perplexed him with his excessive cordiality. The consul general seemed altogether too eager to associate himself in the public mind with the French chargé d'affaires. His suspicions awakened, Otto wondered whether Temple's effusive friendliness related in some way to the recently negotiated Eden treaty. Because France and Britain had just negotiated a commercial rapprochement, unprecedented for its relaxation

---

[8]Instructions to Moustier, dated 10 October 1787, are published in "Correspondence of the Comte de Moustier," 710–14; see also Moustier to Montmorin, No. 4, New York, 14 February 1788, AECPE-U, 33: 37–38.

[9]See, respectively, Otto to Vergennes, No. 25, New York, 9 December 1785, AECPE-U, 30: 448–48vo; Moustier to Montmorin, No. 4, New York, 14 February 1788, ibid., 33: 38. Temple was a Boston-born loyalist whose consul-generalship Congress approved 2 December 1785. See *Journals of the Continental Congress, 1774–1789* (Washington 1933) 29: 897–98.

of cross-channel trade restrictions, Otto thought it possible that Temple was trying to frighten Americans into believing that British trade policy —a closed policy as far as the British West Indies were concerned—might also be adopted by the French government. No good could come to French influence if Americans thought they were about to lose the French Antillean trade. Otto let Paris know that hereafter he would see as little of Sir John Temple in public as possible.[10]

Otto, like Moustier, also saw Britain's afflictive hand at work in newspaper articles damaging to France. In the same dispatch in which he described Temple's over-friendliness—although he did not identify Temple as the source—Otto reported the publication of some very convincing treaty articles purporting Spain's cession to France of both the Floridas. In return, French troops were to be placed at New Orleans to block American traffic descending the Mississippi. Otto expressed shock that even the best-informed Americans had been taken in by what was obviously a British fabrication. To contain the damage, he went to the unusual length of showing John Jay a copy of Vergennes's explicit denial that any such transaction had taken place. The rumors died instantly when Jay, somewhat to Otto's dismay, published Vergennes's assurance verbatim. Though grateful that the rumor had been quashed, the chargé felt the American Secretary of Foreign Affairs had taken liberties with a confidential dispatch, and promised the foreign office that hereafter he would communicate with Jay only by word of mouth.[11]

While Otto's handling of these two episodes showed that British machinations could be countered more or less satisfactorily on a case by case basis, France clearly stood in need of devising a more systematic means of combatting British influence. Unfortunately in this regard France could be seen to be waging not one but two battles: an all but lost struggle on the commercial front and a desperate rearguard action to retain some semblance of political authority. To have lost, apparently beyond recall, the kind of influence that a flourishing commerce might have conferred and still play a powerful role in American politics obviously called for heroic measures. The *ancien régime*, however, seemed deaf to even the mildest suggestions for improving France's position. Moustier, for example, evoked no response when he proposed that the French Caribbean squadron spread its annual visits more widely among American port cities.

---

[10]To Vergennes, No. 75, New York, 19 January 1787, AECPE-U, 32: 182–84vo.
[11]Ibid.

Although the squadron wintered regularly in Boston and Newport, Moustier thought it important for France to show the flag also in New York where British influence appeared to be pervasive. Not only would the presence of a French fleet, more widely distributed, serve to deter a British attempt to seize American ports in the event of war, but it would also have a salutary effect on American attitudes toward France. Moustier's proposal was never implemented.[12]

That the French government failed, then and later, to organize a serious counter-offensive stemmed in part from a difference of perception. From Paris American affairs ranked insignificantly alongside the more preoccupying and traditional problems posed by European power politics, whereas in America French officials, catching sight of opportunities and perils at first hand, felt more keenly the need for action. Thus a foreign minister like Montmorin could reassure Louis Otto that if the Constitutional Convention, then meeting in Philadelphia, failed to preserve the Union, "this development will do us no harm." France, he explained, had "never pretended to make America a useful ally; we have had no other purpose than to take this vast continent away from Great Britain."[13] Montmorin took a similarly dispassionate line with Moustier when the latter arrived in the midst of the ratification controversy. Doubting that Americans would actually adopt the new Constitution, he wrote that His Majesty preferred to see the United States "remain in their present condition," lest it abuse any new political strength it might acquire. While Americans were making up their minds, Moustier had strict orders not to disclose whether France favored or opposed the new organic law. He was to say only that the king wanted whatever Americans thought best for their country. From whatever motives of restraint (or indifference) such equivocations emanated, they at least facilitated France's acceptance of the outcome. In the spring of 1787, Montmorin told Moustier to congratulate the new American leadership and to assure them that France "sees the new order with the greatest pleasure."[14]

Earlier, Americans whom Moustier encountered discerned all too easily what they took to be the French government's passive hostility. The minister squirmed uncomfortably in reporting their view that France had never sought more than to detach the colonies from Britain. There-

---

[12]See his Nos. 2 and 5 to Montmorin, New York, of 10 February and 25 June 1788, "Correspondence of the Comte de Moustier," 718–21, and 731, respectively.

[13]No. 4, Versailles, 30 August 1787, AECPE-U, 32: 350–50vo.

[14]See instructions to Moustier, Paris, 10 October 1787, "Correspondence of the Comte de Moustier," 713; and Montmorin to Moustier, No. 4, Versailles, 11 May 1789, AECPE-U, 34: 89vo.

after, Americans were saying, France had shown a monumental indiffer-ence to their welfare. Some took ill Moustier's refusal to say a good word for the Constitution; and if, as seemed likely, that charter produced a strong central government, Moustier feared that the perception of France as "a jealous power" could only work to Britain's advantage. Matters were not much improved when Moustier tried to assure John Jay that whatever silence he must keep on the merits of the Constitution, there could be no doubting his majesty's high regard for the alliance. Jay promptly questioned whether the alliance still existed, having been nego-tiated to accomplish what it had now achieved, that is, American inde-pendence. Moustier countered lamely that France indeed wished prosperity for the United States, to which it had already contributed by making numerous commercial concessions. Jay seemed unimpressed.[15]

How France might have acted otherwise in this situation gave pause to French officials nearest the scene. If Otto's reports were to be credited, Montmorin did wisely to enjoin them to avoid comment. Politically minded Americans, he wrote, too often insisted that foreigners "pronounce" either for or against the Constitution, but when they did, their pronounce-ments were hailed as proof of foreign intrigue.[16]

Still, if France moved so cautiously as to seem indifferent to the con-stitutional revolution taking place in the United States, her lassitude was perhaps best explained by the long-maturing view of French observers that no central government could long endure. As early as 1785, Marbois thought he foresaw a three-way sectional split with perhaps even further fragmentation. From Boston Philippe Létombe, listening to the "thunder" of political storms, compared the infant republic to "a nut tree so battered by the wind that it would produce no fruit." Louis Otto, for his part, so often predicted the dissolution of the Union that after offering several glimmers of optimism, he felt obliged to apologize for the "contradictions in my reports." By and large, however, Otto came down on the side of pessimism. Moustier, too, pondering the uncertainty of ratification, wondered gloomily whether he would have to seek separate accreditation to each independent state government.[17] Not for a moment, however, did it escape notice that if the Union dissolved, French interests would

---

[15]Moustier to Montmorin, No. 3, New York, 12 February 1788, "Correspondence of the Comte de Moustier," 723–24.

[16]To Montmorin, No. 105, New York, 26 November 1787, AECPE-U, 32: 401–401vo.

[17]Marbois to MAE, No. 438, New York, 29 August 1785, AECPE-U, 30: 257vo; Létombe to MMC, No. 7, 1 March 1787, CC (Boston), 210: 151; Otto to MAE, New York, 19 May 1787, AECPE-U, 32: 263; and Moustier to MAE, No. 15, New York, 25 June 1788, "Cor-respondence of the Comte de Moustier," 730–31.

suffer directly. In that event, the alliance could be written off, along with American debt obligations. Worst of all was the near certainty that Britain would be better able to work her will amid the fragments of an American polity. France may have had a stake in keeping the United States weak, but had much to lose if that weakness ended in each state's going its own way.[18]

By the spring of 1788, an awareness of unique, but perhaps fleeting, opportunity began to take hold. As the ratification process went forward, Moustier foresaw mounting prospects for French advantage, and danger, as well, if France failed to move. With an eye to timing and a view to winning commercial concessions, he dismissed altogether the hope of extracting anything of consequence from the dying Confederation. If, however, the new government bore out its framers' intent to have greater authority over trade, France must be ready to press for concessions. In the event, Britain, too, he suspected, would begin to "follow a fixed plan." From his post at Wilmington, G. J. A. Ducher echoed the thought when he predicted that a new and stronger government would surely open the way to an Anglo-American commercial negotiation which France must be prepared to prevent. Less alarmist but nonetheless sensitized to an awareness of great events impending, Consul General Delaforest urged Paris to watch the American political scene carefully and be ready to negotiate with a new government for tariff duties "based on reciprocity."[19]

Still clamoring for detailed instructions, Moustier in December 1788 penned a long memorandum to Paris. With the Constitution now adopted, he underscored the gravity of France's position vis-à-vis England's. No one, he wrote, knew whether the new government would succeed, but events were now certain to push the United States toward one or the other of the great powers. If Americans chose Britain, France would forfeit all the sacrifice she had made for American independence. "*Free* Americans," he warned, "will become much more dangerous enemies for us than they ever were as American colonists." If the United States could be kept on the side of France, however, the advantages to France would be "inestimable."[20] A month later, the new federal government now a looming reality, Moustier tried again to alert Paris to the need for action.

---

[18]This certainly was Otto's conclusion in his "Mémoire" to Vergennes, 17 May 1785, AECPE-U, 29: 276–78vo.

[19]See, respectively, Moustier to MAE, No. 10, New York, 21 April 1788, "Correspondence of the Comte de Moustier," 726; same to same, No. 12, New York, 29 April 1789, AECPE-U, 34: 69vo; Ducher to MMC, No. 12, 5 March 1788, CC (Wilmington), 1: 41–41vo; and Delaforest to MMC, No. 232, New York, 9 May 1788, CC (New York), 910: 53.

[20]To MAE, No. 28, New York, 25 December 1788, AECPE-U, 33: 283–85vo.

"It seems to me," he wrote, "that everything depends on this first moment and that our influence will either be established or lost forever in the United States." He added pointedly that if France did not take an active role in "consolidating" the new government, Britain would. Six weeks later, in a prophetic mood, he ruminated that the world might someday look back to this time as the moment when "this child Colossus stood up and took strength."[21]

Though he persisted in asking for instructions, Moustier curiously did not see fit to suggest what immediate course of action France might take. He alluded occasionally to a still unfinished memorandum he was drafting on ways to strengthen his country's commercial position. But even when completed, those proposals looked to long-range rather than immediate measures.[22] In sum, despite the French minister's intimations of historic urgency, neither he nor Montmorin cared to venture, or perhaps even knew, what stopgap measures France might take to win favor and influence with the new regime.

Fortunately, French concern about "British influence" proved premature. Keyed up to see the political scene become a battleground of great power rivalry, French observers relaxed perceptibly when the first Congress, having reached a quorum in early May, plunged single-mindedly into domestic problems. With scarcely a glance at foreign affairs, Congress turned to the wholly preoccupying matter of securing revenues designed to help the new government meet long-neglected debt obligations. As one of that government's principal creditors, France stood fair to become a major beneficiary of this legislative activity.

French officials also took heart from the generally pro-French cast of the new American leadership. Washington's goodwill they took for granted. The old general's well-known reliability as a comrade in arms they counted on to steer him now into policies that would at least preserve the alliance and at best favor French interests over British should choices be forced upon him. In Paris Montmorin observed contentedly that Washington could be relied on for his "patriotism." Moustier, too, thought Washington well disposed, though he worried about the President's falling under the spell of Jay and Adams.[23]

---

[21]To MAE, No. 3, New York, 4 February 1789, ibid., 34: 22; and same to same, No. 8, New York, 29 March 1789, "Correspondence of the Comte de Moustier," *American Historical Review* 9 (1903) 96.

[22]Moustier's lengthy memorandum on commerce, dated 12 May 1789, was addressed to Jacques Necker, French Minister of Finance, and may be found in AECPE-U, 34: 91–105. See chapter 3 for discussion of its contents.

[23]See Montmorin to Moustier, No. 4, Versailles, 11 May 1789, and Moustier to Montmorin, No. 3, New York, 4 February 1789, ibid., ff. 89–90vo, 21vo, respectively.

These two men whom Paris had learned most to distrust held positions of influence. John Jay as interim secretary of state and John Adams as vice president were presumably well placed to cultivate within the administration those suspicions of France and French policy which both were known to harbor. Even these shadows were dispelled, however, when it became apparent that Adams would sink into the anonymity which the Constitution had reserved for vice presidents. Even more gratifying, Jay's appointment as chief justice opened the way for Jefferson to replace him in the State Department. No Frenchman acquainted with Thomas Jefferson could imagine that France would have anything but an ardent friend in American councils when the then minister to France returned to assume direction of his country's foreign relations.[24] Alexander Hamilton, meanwhile, remained a political imponderable. The treasury secretary who was soon to emerge as the implacable leader of the "pro-British" faction had yet to register in the French perception. Not gifted with foresight, Moustier remarked mildly on Hamilton's English origins and his reported "indisposition" toward France, but found him sincere in wanting to begin payments on the French debt.[25] Except, then, for Jay's lowering but only temporary presence in the State Department, the skies of Franco-American relations looked auspiciously cloudless.

Though satisfied that London had acquired no additional advantage from the change in government, French officials still needed to test their own influence, or even to discover if they had any. Shortly after Washington's inauguration, Moustier made a fumbling overture whose awkwardness seemed to forecast more difficulties to come. Apparently thinking to "consolidate" his country's position, the French minister asked Washington for a private audience without telling him why. Miffed when the president referred him to John Jay, Moustier later learned that Washington had thought he wanted to open direct negotiations for a new commercial treaty. Washington explained apologetically that he knew little about commercial matters and could not imagine why else Moustier had asked to see him. To this the count replied, profusely and with some agitation, that he had simply wanted to reaffirm his majesty's goodwill, and regretted having been misunderstood. With less candor than the situation called for, Moustier went on to deny categorically his government's wish for a new commercial treaty. True, the French minister had no instructions in this regard, but the need for commercial arrangements

---

[24]For example, Moustier to Montmorin, No. 19, New York, 29 June 1789, and Montmorin to Otto, No. 2, Versailles, 11 September 1790, ibid., ff. 197 and 168vo–69, respectively; and Delaforest to MMC, No. 273, New York, 5 October 1789, CC (New York), 910: 258vo.

[25]To MAE, No. 27, New York, 17 September 1789, AECPE-U, 34: 273.

better than those spelled out by the old treaty of 1778 had been a recurrent topic of foreign office consideration for the past half-decade. Even as he spoke, Moustier left a false impression of French indifference to commercial matters that was being belied by events transpiring in Congress.[26]

That Congress should seek revenues by placing duties on certain imported goods surprised no one. That it should also favor American carriers by placing higher tonnage duties on incoming foreign vessels, however, gave rise to the first serious dispute between Paris and the new federal government. The controversy began when House and Senate disagreed as to whether to carry the distinction further and tax at a lower rate the vessels of nations with whom the United States had commercial treaties (France among them), and at a higher rate the carriers of nations with whom she had no commercial treaties (principally Britain). While Moustier recognized herein Congress's long-range intent to coerce London into making a formal treaty, he was also pleased to report the lower chamber's willingness to favor French carriers. He was outraged when the House, yielding to the Senate's insistence, decided instead to put *all* foreign vessels in the same high bracket without distinction.[27] Lumping French with British carriers for tax purposes touched off a lengthy exchange. First Moustier, then Otto, with strong support from Montmorin, bitterly attacked the inequity, the lack of "reciprocity," that Congress evinced — not only in 1789, but again in 1790 when the tariff and tonnage act was renewed — in not exempting French vessels altogether from a tax of the kind from which American vessels, touching at French ports, had been exempted since 1778.[28]

As a test of French influence, the tonnage duties controversy spun out a disappointing sequel. Jefferson, though sympathetic, held firmly to the view that in refusing to exempt French vessels, Congress had not breached the treaty. In lawyerly argument more tortuous than was his wont, the secretary of state cleared the administration of any wrongful

[26]Washington to Moustier, New York, 25 May 1789, *Writings of Washington* 30: 333–35; Moustier to Washington, New York, 1 June 1789, AECPE-U, 34: 135–38vo.

[27]For House action on the tonnage bill, see *The Debates and Proceedings of the Congress of the United States* (Washington 1834) (hereinafter cited as *Annals*) 1: 302. Ibid., 53, 81–82, for the Senate's amendment and House concurrence.

[28]Moustier to MAE, No. 21, New York, 7 July 1789, AECPE-U, 34: 229–30vo; Otto to same, No. 37, New York, 12 August 1790, ibid., 25: 154–58vo; and Montmorin to Controller General Charles-Guillaume Lambert, Paris, 15 August 1790, ibid., ff. 164–64vo. See also Margaret O'Dwyer, "A French Diplomat's View of Congress, 1790," *William and Mary Quarterly* 21 (1964) 408–12.

discrimination.[29] In this instance, moreover, France lacked genuine grounds for reproach. Although she had exempted American vessels from tonnage-type levies, she had continued to exact other kinds of port duties more than their equivalent.[30]

Significantly, French officials detected no sign that Congress had acted under British influence. They found no evidence that Congress had refused lower tonnage duties to the vessels of "treaty" partners for any other reason than the need for revenues. Inasmuch as a reduction in that category would have meant reduced levies on Dutch, Prussian, and Swedish vessels, as well as French, Congress had made no exception: all foreign-flag carriers discharging cargoes in American ports were to pay 50 cents per ton, American carriers 6 cents per ton.[31]

When Congress persisted in showing no special favor, Paris responded in two ways. On the retaliatory side, she placed higher duties on American vessels bringing in cargoes of tobacco and threatened to revoke certain commercial privileges. On the side of conciliation, she stepped up pressures on the Washington administration to renegotiate the old commercial treaty.[32] Meanwhile, Louis Otto probably offered the wisest counsel. France, he felt, ought not to protest too much when it considered the fundamental purpose of the American tariff and tonnage laws. The French stake in the trans-Atlantic carrying trade was extremely small compared to Britain's. By his estimation, British tonnage arriving in American ports annually outweighed French tonnage by a ratio of more than twenty to one. To the extent that American commercial legislation might succeed in shifting those cargoes to American bottoms, France would benefit from a diminution of her rival's maritime pre-eminence.[33]

Speculation on the pressures London might bring to bear on the

---

[29]"Message from the President of the United States, relative to the extra tonnage paid by French vessels in the ports of the United States, communicated to the Senate," 19 January 1791, *ASP,FR* (Washington 1832–59) 1: 109–11.

[30]James Swan, the New York merchant whom the French government later hired as a purchasing agent, argued from first-hand knowledge that the French tariff structure was so high as to give France no grounds for complaint of discrimination. See Swan's *Causes qui se sont opposées aux progrès du Commerce entre la France et les Etats-Unis de l'Amérique, avec les moyens de l'accélérer* (Paris 1790) 68.

[31]See Section 1 (An Act imposing Duties on Tonnage), Stat. I, Ch. III, July 20, 1789, *United States, Statutes at Large* (Boston 1861) 1: 27; and for subsequent assessments, Otto to MAE, No. 39, New York, 28 September 1790, AECPE-U, 35: 172vo–74, and Ternant to same, No. 12, Philadelphia, 9 October 1791, *CFM*, 57–59.

[32]See chapter 5.

[33]To MAE, No. 52, New York, 6 January 1791, AECPE-U, 35: 262–64.

American polity during the Nootka Sound crisis occupied only a small part of French official thinking during the year 1790. Alarmed at Britain's ultimatum to Spain—over a minor episode involving the latter's seizure of British merchant ships caught trading on her exclusively claimed Pacific northwest coast—French policymakers worried more realistically over the demands their Spanish ally might make, if war followed, than over any New World complication. What some of those complications might be, however, evoked a full-scale review from the French consul general in New York.

Writing at length as the crisis unfolded, Antoine Delaforest projected the likely deployment of American public attitudes and government actions, and weighed the prospects for great power advantage. It was a document of remarkably prophetic insight, as close to the mark as any set of predictions that might have been written two and a half years later when war, in fact, did engulf Europe. The likelihood that Europe's wartime supply needs would expedite, more quickly than tonnage laws, an American takeover of the Atlantic carrying trade made the mercantile North "delirious," he wrote. Southern planters, by contrast, preferred to see the crisis end peacefully because that same shortage of carriers from which the maritime North hoped to draw profit would also raise freight rates on articles of Southern export. Although popular support for Britain or Spain would rest "more on [such mercantile] calculation than on passion," Americans by and large, he felt, would favor Britain. They deeply begrudged Spain her feeble support of American independence, her subsequent closure of the Mississippi, and her providing in the Floridas a haven for escaped slaves. France's support of Spain might "temper" that grudge, but more likely Britain, because Americans valued their commerce with her, could count on their neutrality, even their "friendly assistance."[34]

Irrespective of popular predispositions, Delaforest assured Paris that the American government preferred peace in Europe. Failing that, it had every reason to remain neutral. War could only disrupt the new regime's critical efforts to establish its credit and its revenues or, worse, could result in British encirclement if British forces seized Spanish possessions to the west and south.[35]

With what difficulties the United States might maintain its neutrality under pressures from the great powers Delaforest could only guess.

[34]To MMC, Dépêches des consuls aux Ministres de la Marine, puis des Relations Extérieures, AECPE-U, Tome 5, 1re série (1790–1813) 12–21.

[35]Ibid. Otto likewise drew a distinction between what would likely be merchants' enthusiasm and official misgivings at the prospect of war, to MAE, No. 42, New York, 1 November 1790, ibid., 35: 188–88vo.

He seemed to sense, however, that Washington and his cabinet were asking themselves the same questions. Unaware of the divided counsel that
Washington was receiving during the Nootka crisis, Delaforest nonetheless wrote with a striking degree of accuracy the scenario that unfolded
two and a half years later. If war came to Europe, he predicted, the president "will announce the strict neutrality of the American Union; will enjoin all citizens to adhere to it . . . will determine the neutral extent of
the coast . . . and finally, will regulate the procedures to be followed
with respect to prizes."[36]

As it turned out, the year 1790 drew to a close without war. Spain
yielded to British demands, French and American leaders subsided with
relief; and the French foreign office was left with Delaforest's conjectures
as to what role Britain might have played in American affairs had the outcome been different. At first glance, existing treaty articles appeared to
favor France logistically in any New World theater of maritime operations. Although both European powers could rely on profit-driven
Americans to feed and provision their respective Caribbean dependencies,
France possessed privileges in American ports which, when activated in
wartime, seemed to give her a clear edge. As Delaforest reminded Paris,
Articles 17 and 22 of the commercial treaty entitled French warships having taken prizes from the British to enter American ports, make repairs,
re-victual, and depart "whenever they please," while denying similar access
to British warships. "The location of the United States," he observed,
"would make these advantages invaluable to France, as long as they are
exclusive and England is not able to counter-balance them by acquiring
them for herself."[37]

This latter possibility once more awakened French concerns about
British influence. As the Nootka crisis wore on, both Otto and Delaforest
worried about signs of a warming in Anglo-American relations. George
Beckwith's presence in New York and Gouverneur Morris's special mission to London seemed to presage a formal exchange of ministers which,
if it took place, they felt could have no other object than a treaty negotiation. Should Britain, in the course of such negotiation, oblige the United
States by surrendering the Northwest posts and by opening her West Indies
ports, she might, in return, ask for the kinds of wartime port privileges
thus far accorded exclusively to France. Britain's crisis with Spain, moreover, raised the sinister possibility that London might go still further and
propose a formal Anglo-American alliance. Otto gave no hint of know-

---

[36]Delaforest's Nootka Sound dispatch, AECPE-U, Tome 5, 1re série, f. 19.
[37]Ibid., f. 20.

ing the substance of Major Beckwith's contemporary conversations with Alexander Hamilton in which the two men had explored that possibility. He was alarmed, however, to learn subsequently that such talk had transpired in London, or so his informants had told him. What led him to inquire was Washington's "mysterious" allusion to Britain's refusal to offer any "purely commercial arrangements," this in a presidential message sent to both houses of Congress in mid-February 1791, alluding vaguely to Morris's efforts to secure a commercial treaty. Only later did Otto feel reassured when he learned of a message Washington had sent to the Senate alone. Though bearing the same date as the report sent to both chambers, Washington's communication to the Senate spelled out more fully the problems Morris had encountered. The Pitt ministry, he noted, had told Morris that it might be willing to make commercial concessions but only as an accompaniment to a formal Anglo-American alliance. On this and other issues, however, British policy seemed so unsettled that the president had told Morris to "discontinue his communications." Otto concluded that London was not yet ready for a rapprochement, and that both Congress and the president had specifically rejected the idea of an alliance.[38]

Talk of an alliance, though insubstantial, underscored the lesser but more likely possibility that London and Philadelphia might at least reach an accord on commercial matters, an event to be heralded by an exchange of ministers. Ironically, when the British government finally made its decision to send a representative, and sent young George Hammond, it did so primarily to counter what it perceived to be the threat of "French influence." Hammond came not to negotiate a commercial treaty (as Jefferson soon discovered), but in London's hope, accurate as events proved, that the appointment itself would quell the renewed efforts of the so-called "pro-French" faction in Congress to impose discriminatory tonnage duties on British vessels. Attempted twice, in 1789 and again in 1790, this move in the House seemed likely enough to succeed to call forth the appointment in the spring of 1791 of Britain's first minister to the United States.[39]

Posted to Philadelphia only two months before Hammond arrived in October 1791, Jean de Ternant, the monarchy's last minister to this

---

[38]Otto to MAE, No. 56, Philadelphia, 10 March 1791, AECPE-U, 35: 305–305vo; and for Washington's messages of 15 February 1791, James D. Richardson, ed., *Messages and Papers of the Presidents, 1789–1897* (Washington 1896) 1: 96. A more detailed account of the Beckwith–Hamilton conversations is in Boyd's *Number 7*, chap. 4; and of the Morris mission to London, in Charles R. Ritcheson, *Aftermath of Revolution: British Policy Toward the United States, 1783–1795* (New York 1969) 95–115.

[39]Ibid., 137–44; and for Hammond's instructions, 4 July 1791, see Bernard Mayo, ed., *Instructions to the British Ministers to the United States, 1791–1812* (Washington 1941) 5–13.

country, nonetheless grasped quickly the inherent limits of British diplomacy. He could not know, of course, that the new British minister's instructions authorized him to discuss but not to treat on commercial matters. He guessed correctly, however, that London's emissary would find it difficult to swallow the conditions Americans would set for a commercial treaty. One of those conditions, he knew (from earlier conversation with Alexander Hamilton), included the opening of British West Indies ports.[40] The likelihood of a commercial, or any other kind of, rapprochement faded rapidly when Hammond, with more zeal than good judgment, set about that part of his instructions that bade him build a legal case for U.S. treaty violation in order to justify his government's non-fulfillment of the Treaty of Paris. Once enmeshed in the fine points of treaty infraction, Hammond found himself outmatched, indeed soon skewered on the still finer points that emanated from the mordant pen of Thomas Jefferson.[41] Although French officials did not know just how badly Hammond's mission was going, they could sense that British influence at the official level held no immediate threat.

On other fronts, however, the year 1792 gave little cause for complacency. Food shortages in Saint Domingue, complicated by civil unrest, put Ternant to the increasingly painful task of meeting demands for financial aid without having Paris's explicit permission to do so. When, as sometimes happened, island deputies made direct appeals to state legislatures, Ternant was hard put to maintain his authority as France's official spokesman—a status made more uncertain by an instability in France itself where no fewer than five foreign ministers ostensibly directed foreign policy in a twelve-month period.[42] As the year wore on, events in Europe picked up in tempo and violence. In April France declared war on Austria. In September the monarchy gave way to the first Republic. Soon after, the Girondin-controlled National Convention announced the Republic's crusade against its monarchist enemies, and indeed against monarchism everywhere. As if to confirm the virulence of that crusade, Louis XVI went to the guillotine on 21 January 1793. Within two weeks Britain had joined Holland, Spain, and the Holy Roman Empire in the war of the first coalition.

Once Britain and France were at war, French officials long condi-

---

[40]To MAE, Nos. 12 and 15, Philadelphia, of 9 October and 13 November 1791, *CFM*, 59, and 69, respectively.

[41]Still one of the liveliest accounts of the Jefferson–Hammond duel is in chapter 5 of Samuel F. Bemis's *Jay's Treaty: A Study in Commerce and Diplomacy* (New York 1924).

[42]See, for example, those parts of Ternant's dispatches published in *CFM*, 48, 72–75, 76, 89–93, 97–102, 119–21.

tioned to watch for signs of British influence found their worst fears borne out. So sensitized were Genet and his consuls to this apprehension that they may have imagined more evidence of it than existed. Nevertheless, there was no mistaking how inexorably the Anglo-American ties of language, law, and custom, increasingly bonded by a profitable wartime traffic in material goods, weighed in Britain's favor. Even appeals to a common republicanism, they discovered, counted for little alongside the life-giving imperatives of Anglo-American commerce. That American neutrality could have been anything but pro-British in its commercial operation (and ultimately in its political effect) was, perhaps, too much to be expected, although looking back several years later, Louis Otto felt that a persistently ill-conceived and maladroit French diplomacy had much to answer for in this regard.[43]

Long aware of Britain's potential capacity for moving and shaking the American polity, French officials nonetheless blinked in astonishment at the swiftness of its fulfillment. Little in the recent history of the 1780s prepared them for the rapidity and, some might add, the completeness with which British influence replaced their own. Those tranquil years of peace when Americans attracted scant attention from either power they might well view in retrospect as an era of modest French political ascendency. To be sure, the visible resurgence of a politically active "British faction" gave some cause for concern. But Britain herself, by her patently uncaring refusal to accommodate the United States on any of the troubling issues left unresolved by the peace of 1783, tended to reassure French policymakers that London's capacity for influencing the political life of the new nation was far less than their own.

Heartening reports from America over the years had lent substance to optimism. Franklin, for example, notified Vergennes in September 1784 that Congress, although it planned to negotiate commercial treaties with other powers, wanted the king to rest assured that it "will place no People on more advantageous ground than the subjects of his Majesty." A few months later, Marbois reported that despite the political busyness of the "friends of England here," the partisans of France greatly outnumbered them and still held the principal offices in the state governments. Louis Otto gave even more sweeping assurance. Congress, he wrote in May 1785 "has come to regard the Alliance as the safeguard of the liberty of America, to cherish our interests, to ask for our counsel, to conform to our views because gentle experience has taught them that we defer only to the safety and well-being of our allies." Five years later, Otto still felt

---

[43]*Considérations*, 12–22.

that "even the greatest detractors of France" acknowledged the French alliance as "the keystone of the independence of the United States."[44]

Though occasionally exaggerated, such sanguine depictions of French hegemony were not altogether illusory. France in the 1780s did, in fact, retain the image of a benign presence to which Americans readily accorded some modicum of deference with a view to self-interest. At a time when Britain offered nothing, France projected the benevolence of great power protection. As long as Europe remained at peace and Britain saw no reason to be solicitous, France enjoyed prestige without cost and an influence that was seldom tested.

France's loss of political leverage, once the war began, came as less of a shock, perhaps, than did the accompanying change for the worse in American attitudes. Not only did many Americans take political comfort, as well as profit, from supporting the British cause, but they also began more often to express an open hostility toward France and Frenchmen. To what extent this anti-French feeling sprang from a francophobic colonial past or from the contemporary machinations of British propagandists evoked varying opinions. Some, like the Count de Volney, whose frequent encounters with other visiting Frenchmen commended him as an expert on French sensitivities, felt that his countrymen had always found Americans to be "strongly tinctured with the old English prejudice and animosity against us." Marbois, too, blamed an ancestral "British prejudice" for the low esteem in which many Americans held France. Even Brissot de Warville, usually irrepressible in his admiration for Americans, ascribed their occasional "contempt for visiting foreigners" to a xenophobia they had inherited from a British past.[45]

Had the renewal of Anglo-French warfare not been played out against a backdrop of revolutionary turbulence in France, Britain's opportunities for discrediting her enemy would certainly have been fewer. As it was, inherited prejudices aside, French informants soon found Britain's subtle hand at work everywhere, plucking sour notes from the joyous music of liberation. They took for granted, of course, that some Americans, notably merchant Federalists, would join the anti-French chorus out of con-

[44]See, respectively, Franklin to Vergennes, Passy, 3 September 1784, AECPE-U, 28: 171; Marbois to same, No. 412, New York, 17 February 1785, ibid., 29: 64–64vo; Otto's "Mémoire remis," 17 May 1785, ibid., ff. 276–276vo; and Otto to MAE, No. 17, New York, 7 February 1790, ibid., 35: 47.

[45]See, respectively, Constantin François Chasseboeuf, Comte de Volney, *A View of the Climate and Soil of the United States of America* . . . (Philadelphia, 1804) xvii; Marbois to MAE, No. 429, New York, 15 July 1785, AECPE-U, 30: 140vo; and Jacques Pierre Brissot de Warville, *New Travels in the United States of America, 1788* (Cambridge, Mass. 1964) 195. See also D'Annemours to MMC, 21 July 1782, CC (Baltimore), 1: 6vo–7.

cern for their material ties with British commerce. Some, however, like Antoine Delaforest, worried lest other Americans be persuaded by British propaganda—or perhaps after consulting their own republican traditions—that French revolutionaries were shaping institutions not consonant with American precepts of liberty and stability. Writing as early as November 1790, he noted:

. . . some of the British Ministry's anxieties about the consequences of the French revolution seem to have slipped into the minds of the most influential members of the United States government. If on the one hand, one sees the keys of the Bastille hanging in the audience chamber of the President of the United States, it is no less true that the leading citizens show much ill-humor against the doctrine of a single legislative branch established by the French Constitution. They are far from wishing its success in this country where, today, they think that if civil equality and public liberty are not to be founded on excessively democratic principles, a measure of aristocracy is necessary to the composition of the legislative power.[46]

Otto conceded even less to British influence. Americans, he thought (writing at a safe interval after the Terror), had needed no prompting to detect flaws in French revolutionary ideology, had feared its divisive impact on American politics, and had wisely opted to retain for its stability their own less daring federal system.[47] Such indigenous explanations of American coolness toward the Great Republic came, of course, from men well versed in American political thought who, themselves, were not particularly enamored of revolutionary excess. Indeed, revolutionary ardor in the individual usually determined how much British influence he perceived. Flaming ideologues like Edmond Genet and his Girondin consuls saw it everywhere, turning people as well as government against the French cause.[48] Best typifying this paranoia was Michel Mangourit, Genet's consul at Charleston who regularly blamed most of his official problems, even those he created for himself, on British influence. He readily identified the enemy. They included "numerous Englishmen," tories, native aristocrats, and disaffected refugee "colons" from Saint Domingue. Their purveying of "false news and insolent diatribes" had intimidated the residents of Charleston, he fumed, weakened support for the French cause, and frightened Charleston shipmasters into believing that conditions in France were so disrupted as to make it risky to clear vessels for French ports. Mangourit fought back with counter-measures. He saw to it that Charleston newspapers were furnished with enthusiastic accounts of French political and commercial conditions and, like other French con-

---

[46]Delaforest's Nootka Sound dispatch, f. 19.
[47]*Considérations*, 9.
[48]*CFM*, 201–86, passim.

suls, he took a hand in organizing a pro-French political club. Pleased with what he saw to be his success in drawing together the "Friends of Liberty and Equality," he dashed off to Savannah to do further battle against British influence. "That city," he wrote Genet, "is even more asphyxiated by English coal fumes than is Charleston."[49]

Embittered as the year 1793 produced growing evidence of a Girondin failure to enlist the kind of wholehearted American support he had hoped for, Mangourit placed the blame ever more certainly on Britain's pervasive presence. England, he wrote, continues to hold American commerce "under its yoke." American debtors are the "serfs of British credit," and the erstwhile colonies still the "provinces of Great Britain." His anger undiminished in early 1794, he thought he had found an explanation for failure in the polyglot immigrant character of the people. Because the spirit of Americans "is of too many different minds to have a genius in itself. . . . it is vassal to British ways, laws, customs, and statutes."[50]

Convinced of Britain's malign influence, most French revolutionary officials either ignored, refused to recognize, or feared to report the possibility that the turbulent course of the Revolution itself had adversely affected American attitudes. A seemingly innocent monarch executed, political enemies regularly dispatched by guillotine, governments made alternately formless or lethal by factional strife and, at closer range, the neutrality-endangering activities of a Citizen Genet arming French privateers in U.S. ports while recruiting troops to invade the Spanish and British borderlands—all gave Americans ample cause for dismay. They needed no British agents whispering in their ears to tell them that such events were unseemly. And in vain did spokesmen of the Republic try to persuade them that only by such measures could Frenchmen consolidate a revolution vastly different from their own.[51] Except to those Americans invincibly persuaded that Republican France could do no wrong—and they grew fewer in number every day—pleas for understanding and support counted for less in shaping public attitudes than did the multiplying reports of sanguinary excess that flowed in from Europe with every arriving vessel.

In retrospect, the war France declared on Britain in early 1793 was

---

[49]See his Nos. 9 and 8 to MMC, of 26 November 1792, and 6 May 1793, in CC (Charleston), vol. 372, 412vo; Tome 2, 21vo, respectively.

[50]Nos. 38 and 10 to MAE, of 17 October 1793, and 21 February 1794, ibid., ff. 135, and 205, respectively.

[51]See, for example, the apologia published in Paris in 1793 by A. Didot, *Précis sur la Révolution et le caractère français, adressé aux citoyens des Etats-Unis d'Amérique*, which sought to persuade Americans that had they been subjected to tyrannies comparable to those borne by Frenchmen, they would have acted with similar violence.

waged on three fronts in America. The struggle to win a share of American markets, the commercial battle, was all but lost when the war began. For a year or two American grain ships continued importantly to provision the French Métropole, and throughout the war they fed and supplied her Antilles, but the hope of finding an American market for French manufactures comparable to Britain's had virtually disappeared. On the diplomatic front, the struggle to realize a tactical advantage from the wording of old treaties also went badly. As long as the Washington administration read its treaty obligations in the context of traditional neutral duties, no French emissary after Genet discovered anything but a pro-British bias in the operation of American neutrality. It was on the third front—in the battle to win and hold the sympathies of the American people—that French revolutionaries least expected to suffer defeat and, in a sense, came most bitterly to resent Britain's victory. They seemed not to realize that to retain those sympathies (which at first ran strongly in their favor) would require the sort of "hard sell" public relations campaign they lacked the means to sustain. Inescapably, the revolution in France conveyed scenes of increasing confusion and violence. Not surprisingly, its "bad press" in this country was less the product of ancestral prejudice or even British propaganda than it was a reaction to events which Americans either saw too clearly for their liking or were at a loss to integrate into their own political experience. This is not to suggest that all American "press coverage" put the Revolution in an unfavorable light. France, as well as Britain, had her defenders, her loyal press organs and, moreover, public figures who could be counted on to speak and write in her behalf. But the sheer volume of "news" that came from Europe by way of England, which, of course, needed no translation, militated against French efforts to depict events in ways favorable to the Revolution.[52]

Americans were long accustomed to take their opinions from newspapers. Like no other people in the world, they read newspapers daily, avidly, and usually with an eye to events across the Atlantic. Even those not directly engaged in shipping looked to Europe for news that might affect them: farmers and planters to learn the European market prices for their exportable crops; retailers and customers eager to know the latest

---

[52]For the importance of newspapers in shaping public opinion, see Donald H. Stewart, *The Opposition Press of the Federalist Period* (Albany, 1969) chap. 1; Bernard Faÿ, *The Revolutionary Spirit in France and America* (New York, 1966) 33–34; Allen J. Barthold, "French Journalists in the United States, 1780–1800," *Franco-American Review* 1 (1936–37) 215–30; and Beatrice Hyslop, "American Press Reports of the French Revolution, 1789–94," *New York Historical Society Quarterly* (Oct. 1958) 329–48.

fashion, design, quality, and price of incoming cargoes of manufactures; indeed, the populace as a whole, curious to learn what mischief the great powers were up to that might touch their livelihoods or their new nation's wellbeing.

Britain's easy success in dominating this country's perceptions of Europe came as no surprise to those who knew how heavily Americans relied on British journals for their overseas news. When the French journalist, Joseph Nancrède, launched his *Courier de Boston* in April 1789, he gave as one reason for the enterprise his hope to free Americans from the "moral slavery" they had fallen into from constant exposure to newspapers arriving from England. The American, he wrote, "has become, without wanting to, the partisan of a rival nation whose interests are directly opposed to his."[53] Such efforts to counter the influence of the British press failed for several reasons. In Nancrède's case, the *Courier* died from want of subscribers within six months.

The failure of such individual undertakings, however, could scarcely obscure the mounting difficulty France encountered merely to keep open the Atlantic channel of communication. First, in 1789, came the French Navy's discontinuance of regular packet service between L'Orient and New York. Announced as an economy measure, this decision evoked cries of dismay from French officials here. Many felt that at best the "paquebots" had never met the need for reliable communication. Then, with the onset of war in 1793, British naval operations further reduced the flow of intelligence as British warships increasingly intercepted and removed mail from both French and American merchantmen. War in the Atlantic, more than any other factor, put the final seal on Britain's monopoly of news from Europe, and left no doubt in the minds of French analysts that by 1795 France had irretrievably lost the battle for access to American public opinion. This breakdown in trans-Atlantic communication, as Joseph Fauchet later observed, was "one of the principal causes of all our misfortunes."[54]

---

[53]*Courier de Boston: Affiches, Nouvelles & Avis. Prospectus*, 6. See also Barthold, "French Journalists," 219–20.

[54]Fauchet, "Mémoire sur les Etats-Unis d'Amérique," *Annual Report of the American Historical Association for the Year 1936* (Washington 1938) 118. For the communications breakdown in the Atlantic, see Fauchet and the Commissioners to CMC, Philadelphia, 21 brumaire, an 3 (11 November 1794), série BB^3, doss. 64, ff. 150–51, ANF; Fauchet to CRE, Philadelphia, fructidor, an 3 (18 August–16 September 1795), AECPE-U, 2e série (supplément), 31: 42; Létombe to CRE, Philadelphia, 24 frimaire, an 4 (15 December 1795), CC (Philadelphia), Tome 3, 395–95vo; and "Extrait d'une Lettre du Consul [Mozard], Boston, 14 vendémiaire, an 5 (5 October 1796)," AF III, carton 64, doss. 262, ANF.

By and large, until war crowned their worst fears of resurgent British influence, French officials could reasonably believe that Americans of the 1780s were still emotionally and politically in the French camp. Despite periodic alarms, they perceived no sustained or systematic threat from London on the diplomatic front. Americans may have begun to evince doubts as to France's goodwill toward them, but the claims of gratitude were heard often enough to keep the fear of British influence subliminal. Not until that gratitude failed the test of renewed great power warfare did France's failure to capitalize on American goodwill become apparent. By then, it was too late.

III
LOSING TO BRITAIN IN THE ATLANTIC

In New World endeavors French statesmen of the 1780s met their sorriest defeats in the field of commerce. Neither the limited trade they broached to Americans in their West Indies nor the unlimited opportunities they expected from a direct and profitable exchange with the United States bore the fruit they desired. The openings they accorded in the Antillean trade invariably met with demands for more concessions which, when withheld, Americans seized anyway, mounting a contraband trade in sugar and coffee that mocked their best efforts to suppress. Equally disheartening was the spectacle in the Atlantic where, as they watched helplessly, British merchant vessels, swarming into familiar sea lanes, reclaimed a pre-eminence in America's European trade that seemed hardly interrupted by either war or American independence and, moreover, appeared to be unchallengeable.

As to Britain's recovery of the Atlantic carrying trade, the recorded views of French officials generally fell into three separate but often related questions. First and recurrently, they asked themselves *why* the British had been able to make this comeback. Second, what obstacles had made it so difficult for French merchants to contest them successfully? And finally, because ministers and consuls were expected to take a positive attitude toward adversity, what actions might France take to overcome these obstacles?

Why Britain dominated the Atlantic carrying trade evoked a variety of explanations. Statistics bore out the fact, however, and no one questioned the deleterious effect of that domination on the French economy. Ironically, the wartime years seemed to promise an ample share of carriage for French vessels and a major outlet for French manufactures. During the last three years of the war, French exports climbed to an annual average value of eleven million livres. These exports included high quality textiles and hardware, as well as wines and foodstuffs, and their arrival reportedly inspired American firms to send buyers to France looking for other consumer items. Moreover, a low wartime level of American exports gave France a comfortable balance of trade in her favor. For the entire wartime period, 1775 to 1783, her receipt of specie totaled more than thirty-two million livres. However auspicious, these statistics proved only that French carriers and French products could compete successfully under favorable circumstances, in this case created by French government loans, subsidies, and expenditures for military operations. What the statistics also revealed was that Americans, even in wartime, continued to carry on the bulk of their commerce with Britain, either directly or through British West Indies ports. At the height of the war in 1781, despite French gains, Britain's exports to the United States were still double those of France.[1]

The postwar era brought no improvement in France's commercial position. Indeed, two successive shifts in Atlantic trade patterns spelled near disaster. First came a rapid and engulfing upsurge of British exports. With stunning swiftness American consumers returned to old habits of "buying British." To oblige them, British warehouses backlogged with commodities for the postwar market disgorged their contents wholesale into American port cities. Although commodity prices fell and bankruptcies followed, British exporters emerged from this selling spree firmly entrenched as Americans' principal suppliers of manufactures. A second development, partly the result of the first, created a serious problem for France. While Americans steadily bought fewer and fewer French products, their sales to France gradually increased. Traditional export items — tobacco, rice, indigo, fish, lumber, etc. — came to be augmented by shipments of grain and flour. The balance of payments so favorable to France during the war years reversed itself. By the end of the decade, 1787–89, the value of American exports to France and her Caribbean possessions reached an annual average of more than twenty million livres, whereas the value of French exports to the United States fell to a yearly average of only 1.8 million. Buying American products at more than ten times the value of goods she was able to sell in return meant that France and her colonies suffered a yearly cash outflow of more than eighteen million livres. This drain of specie, serious enough in peacetime, took on tidal wave proportions when France, hit by wartime food shortages, began in 1793 to step up her purchases of American grain. During the next two

---

[1]French trade balances and marketing problems for this period are summarized by Jacques Godechot, "Les relations économiques entre la France et les Etats-Unis de 1778 à 1789," *French Historical Studies* 1 (1959) 26–39. Also useful is Edmond Buron's research in ANF, série F^{12} (Commerce et Industrie), doss. 501^A, published in "Notes and Documents: Statistics on Franco-American Trade, 1778–1806," *Journal of Economic and Business History* 4.1 (November 1931) 571–80.

years, her excess of purchases over sales cost France 202 million livres, or roughly $30 million.[2]

Mortified enough to believe that any outflow of cash weakened the French economy, French leaders angrily resented the use to which Americans put it. Clearly, that cash was being used to settle American merchants' accounts with Britain. The imbalance in Franco-American trade had its reverse counterpart in Anglo-American trade. With Americans chronically unable to cover the cost of their purchases from Britain with value enough in raw material exports, the trans-Atlantic cash flow took on a circular pattern, draining specie from France to the United States and thence to the British Isles. Small wonder that French statesmen chafed at the spectacle of France's loss becoming Britain's gain, with Americans as guilty intermediaries.

As early as 1786, Consul Jean Toscan grumbled at the irony that Boston merchants so recently engaged in privateering against British shipping "now send their vessels to England taking to their manufacturers the gold and silver France spent in America . . . to help them win their independence." Nor did it escape Moustier's notice two years later that "it is with our money that they pay England for the merchandise they buy from it." Somewhat more vividly, the French economist Arnould wrote in 1791: "The Americans procure for themselves from France a balance of money with which they smelter British industry." Taking this quotation from Arnould as his rubric, the French journalist Tanguy de la Boissière in the late 1790s penned an 82-page analysis of the disjunctures in Franco-American commerce. In describing the cash flow, Tanguy metaphorically depicted the United States as "a basin that continued to fill," and France as a basin "that did not cease to empty." Those closest to the phenomenon wrote with greatest fervor. Former Boston consul Antoine Duplaine wrote angrily in the summer of 1794: "The Americans, one will say, have brought provisions to France; does anyone believe this

---

[2]See Godechot and Buron, and for contemporary awareness of France's steadily worsening trade position: Tanguy de la Boissière, *Mémoire sur la situation commerciale de la France avec les Etats-Unis de l'Amérique depuis l'année 1775, jusque & y compris 1795* (Paris 1796); Ambroise Marie Arnould, *De la balance du commerce et des relations commerciales extérieures de la France* (Paris 1791) 3 vols.; and an anonymous 12-page survey entitled "Extrait d'un Mémoire sur la Situation Commerciale de la France avec les Etats-Unis d'Amérique," 6 nivôse, an 5 (26 December 1796), AF III, carton 64, doss. 261, ANF. Occasionally the consuls in their year-end reports dealt at length with local manifestations of the trade imbalance. See, for example, Petry to Montmorin, No. 48, Charleston, 30 January 1788, and Létombe's "Etat du Commerce D'importations & Exportations des batimens français avec Boston Pendant l'année 1788," documents Nos. 9 and 23, respectively, in série B[7], doss. 461, ANF.

was done as a favor? . . . if anyone has such an idea, I would tell him that it was because they found higher prices in France than elsewhere. Have they bought [in return] items of our manufacture and production? no, they have had themselves paid off in good specie which has fed the manufactures of our cruelest enemy, England!"[3]

While some, like Duplaine, charged Americans with base ingratitude for neglecting France as a supplier of manufactures, most observers hardly blamed them for turning to Britain. La Luzerne, for example, early foresaw that gratitude alone was unlikely to dissuade American merchants from doing business with British factors with whom their experience of satisfactory dealings stretched back to colonial times.[4]

"Royalist neglect," a favorite theme among later revolutionaries, offered an alternative explanation. Indeed, the *ancien régime* did seem loathe to bestir itself, perhaps because the American market seemed unpromising. Marbois, writing in the spring of 1783, warned French businessmen against exaggerating its importance. Americans, after all, numbered only two and a half million persons, and with their ports now open to all nations, France could expect only a modest share of that market. Even Joseph Fauchet, looking back more than a decade later, expressed no surprise at the royal government's inattentiveness to trade matters. Quarrelsome states, disordered finances, a central government without authority had all conspired to induce French statesmen of that period to "look on the United States only with pitying eyes." To counter the first signs of growing British domination, the monarchy had contented itself, far too complacently, he thought, by making minor commercial concessions to Americans in French home ports and in the Antilles. Beyond that, he wrote, "the cabinet of Versailles was interested only in preventing the United States from acquiring an energetic form of government . . ." Like Fauchet, Talleyrand saw neglect mixed with ideological overtones. If the monarchy had lost early opportunities to enhance its commerce at Britain's expense, it was because Bourbon Paris, fearing America's "principles of

---

[3]See, respectively, Toscan's "Mémoire du Consulat de Boston pour 1785," April 1786, AECPE-U, Mem. et doc., vol. 9, 53vo; Moustier to Montmorin, No. 1, New York, 8 February 1788, "Correspondence of Moustier," *American Historical Review* 8 (1903) 716; Tanguy, *Situation commerciale*, 6; and "Notes sur le Commerce de la France avec les Etats Unis d'Amérique . . . par A.C. Duplaine," August 1794, AECPE-U, Mem. et doc., 9: 200.

[4]See La Luzerne to Vergennes, No. 369, Annapolis, 1 March 1784, AECPE-U, 27: 184vo–86vo, but also Duplaine's "Notes sur le Commerce," 200; Delaforest to MMC, No. 331, New York, 6 June 1791, CC (New York), 910: 344–44vo; and Rochambeau's "Sur les rapports avenirs des Etats unis de l'Amérique septentrionale avec la France," 25 November 1794, AECPE-U, Mem. et doc., 9: 211–12.

independence," had discouraged Frenchmen "from all connection with that country."[5]

Whatever responsibility for failure Frenchmen, then or later, placed on the *ancien régime*, all agreed that Britain possessed certain inherent advantages. When La Luzerne characterized British sellers as being satisfyingly familiar to their American buyers, he touched on a recurrent theme. "The taste and long-established preference of Americans for English things," wrote Tanguy, was too little understood as an obstacle to French marketing. "Habitude," as he called it, "is perhaps the most redoubtable enemy of French commerce in the United States." Even so astute an observer as Barbé-Marbois seemed puzzled at the wartime inability of French hardware manufacturers to compete with the British. "Americans are firmly persuaded," he wrote, "that the English [hardware] is superior to ours even at the same price." Price, but also quality, it turned out, Americans could not be sure of when dealing with French suppliers. A French consul at Baltimore put his finger on the problem when, having examined a recently arrived French cargo in the fall of 1782, he reported finding goods of strikingly inferior quality. Such cargoes were not infrequent, and the lesson to be drawn was sobering. Americans would soon be buying European goods in a completely open market. They would inevitably compare the price and quality of every item and buy accordingly. French imports would flag, he warned, unless his countrymen showed the same kind of "good faith which alone inspires confidence" and which Americans invariably received from their British suppliers.[6]

Familiar with American tastes, but also trusted in matters of price and quality, British businessmen had an edge. Not even the recriminations attending the business failures and bankruptcies of the mid-decade price collapse seemed to diminish British pre-eminence in these respects.[7] In the aftermath of that debacle, Martin Oster, French consul at Norfolk, noted the two-way benefit British merchants enjoyed from their familiarity with local conditions. Not only did they profit from the trust and confidence in which they were held by their American customers, but

---

[5]See, respectively, Marbois to MMC, No. 31, Philadelphia, 20 May 1783, CC (Philadelphia), 945: 309vo; Fauchet's "Mémoire" (1796) 90–91; and Talleyrand, *Mémoire sur les Relations commerciales des Etats-Unis avec Angleterre* (Paris 1799).

[6]Tanguy, *Situation commerciale*, 15; Marbois to MMC, No. 9, 30 December 1781, CC (Philadelphia), 945: 172vo; and D'Annemours to same, No. 17, 25 September 1782, CC (Baltimore), Tome 1, 24–25vo.

[7]See testimony of Létombe to MMC, December 1782, CC (Boston), 209: 127–27vo; Delaforest to same, No. 160, 13 June 1786, CC (New York), 909: 156; and Moustier to Necker, New York, 12 May 1789, AECPE-U, 34: 95–97.

also, as creditors, they were virtually the only foreigners then able to collect debts in the state of Virginia. Because state laws shielded Virginia debtors from prosecution by foreigners, Oster explained, defrauding one's foreign creditors had become widespread, except in the case of the British who could count on collecting what was owed them because of "their former ties with the better inhabitants and by the knowledge they have of commerce and of the country."[8]

Despite the American buyer's occasional fraud and more frequent default, Frenchmen who analyzed British business practices frankly admired the readiness of London suppliers to extend credit, especially long-term credit. Such willingness to accept deferred payment, they believed, gave them a marked competitive advantage over the French who preferred, indeed usually insisted, on cash payment for goods on delivery. As Martin Oster observed in 1788, French suppliers found it difficult to compete with British merchants who could wait three months for payment and imposed a credit charge of only 5 percent in Virginia dollars.[9]

Easy credit appeared all the more remarkable in view of the American reluctance to make good on debts pending from the colonial period. Although the Treaty of Paris stipulated that American authorities would put no "lawful impediment" in the way of British creditors' efforts to collect those prewar debts, state courts and legislatures had been so successful in frustrating collection as to make this issue one of the major complaints George Hammond brought to Jefferson's attention in 1792.[10] Still, French analysts who had mixed feelings about urging their own merchants to emulate British credit practices doubtless accepted the dictum of Lord Sheffield that long-term credit went far to explain Britain's continued domination of American commerce. Sheffield, known principally for his influence in persuading British ministries to keep American vessels out of Britain's postwar trade lanes, also had something to say about credit. Estimating that four-fifths of Britain's sales to the United States were made on credit, he went on to boast: "This credit, so necessary to Americans, can only be found in England; the French who have given it to them have all gone bankrupt: the French businessman cannot offer long credit."[11] It remained for Tanguy de la Boissière, however, to discern the importance of an already long-established interdependence. Debts still

[8]"Questions Répondues sur la Population, L'Agriculture, Le Commerce et Les Finances de Virginie," 26 November 1788, enclosed in Oster's No. 61 to MMC, 5 December 1788, CC (Norfolk), 927: 212.

[9]Ibid., ff. 212–12vo.

[10]Hammond to Jefferson, 5 March 1792, *ASP,FR* 1: 193–200.

[11]Sheffield, *Observations*, 173–74.

owing from the prewar period, he felt, furnished powerful impetus to both sides to continue: the British because they hoped to recover those earlier debts, Americans because they wanted access to new credit.[12]

How well this Anglo-American credit structure would weather the storms of economic depression remained to be seen. Curiously, the first price dip in 1783 was ascribed not to over-supply, or "dumping," but to incoming cargoes badly selected. This was Sheffield's opinion, and Barbé-Marbois, who was an eye-witness to the price slide, confirmed it. The latter reported in mid-1784 that both British and French vessels, arriving in large numbers, often discharged cargoes for which there was little demand. After their initial losses the British, he felt, showed "more intelligence as to assortments." Writing a year later to describe what was, by then, a major price collapse, Louis Otto shunted aside such fine distinctions. Sheer British impatience, he wrote, had destroyed the American market for everyone. They "poured a prodigious quantity of merchandise into the continent; this abundance and the bad faith of their commission agents ruined them." Amid recriminations over unpaid accounts, he reported that bankruptcies "followed one another with astonishing rapidity." Commerce dropped to a near standstill.[13]

Signs of economic recovery inevitably raised speculation as to whether the British credit structure had survived. Moustier thought not. Writing from New York in May 1789, he thought he saw Americans entering an era of cash transactions. British creditors badly stung had become so chary of extending credit that any nation, he felt, could challenge their grip. Now that Americans had been broken of the "credit habit," anyone could sell them goods on cash terms. French consuls, however, closer to the scene, reported British merchants continuing to bail out their debtors with additional extensions of credit.[14] Throughout the depression, no matter how severe their losses, they showed a determination to retain their customers that was ultimately rewarded. Martin Oster painted a vivid picture of the business cycle in Virginia. In mid-1785, Virginia debtors hard pressed to settle their British accounts as prices plummeted lost almost everything, specie, tobacco, even slaves and real estate. Despite the transfer of assets, prices sank so low as to wipe out nearly all British creditors; it was not uncommon for incoming British cargoes to be sold

[12]Tanguy, *Situation commerciale*, 14.

[13]Sheffield, *Observations*, 9n, 220; Marbois to MAE, No. 385, Philadelphia, 14 July 1784, AECPE-U, 28: 33vo–34; and Otto's "Mémoire remis par le Sr. Otto," f. 289.

[14]Cf., Moustier to Necker, New York, 12 May 1789, AECPE-U, 34: 36; Delaforest to MMC, No. 19, 7 October 1784, CC (Charleston), 372: 43vo; and Chateaufort to same, No. 12, 12 September 1785, ibid., ff. 134–34vo.

at public auction. Two years later those same British creditors, wary but ubiquitous, were back in business. British trade in Virginia had climbed to an annual value of fifteen million livres, while French commerce remained virtually non-existent.[15] A few months before Moustier thought he saw Americans being broken of the "credit habit," Consul G.J.A. Ducher, whose intensive study of American commerce gave him a broader knowledge of business conditions than his insignificant post would suggest, was reporting from Wilmington, N.C., that Britain still controlled two-thirds of America's external commerce, and that much of it still rested on credit. Other consular reports confirmed that throughout the depression years British merchant-creditors had persevered.[16]

Then and later, French reactions ranged from chagrin to barely suppressed admiration. Looking back from the year 1793, an unnamed memorialist described the recovery period as one in which the British had taken bold initiatives "while our merchants remained in a stupor." The British, he told the Committee of Public Safety, had known "how to put their commerce on a durable footing, while we thought only of our interests of the moment." Antoine Duplaine, too, chafed at the memory of resilient British merchants who "had not been discouraged by their losses." Nor could the foreign office have drawn much comfort from Otto's observation, in 1791, that although Americans traded more voluminously with Britain, they did so on the basis of credit and ought, therefore, to value their trade with France more highly because French merchants paid in cash.[17]

Meanwhile, in that larger realm where governmental policy was seen to have a part, French officials marveled at how unhandsomely London managed to treat its former colonies and still retain its hold on their commerce. Or, perhaps for that very reason, Britain's narrow mercantilism helped to explain why she continued to prevail. It disturbed those officials to compare the generous concessions Louis's government had extended to American shipping, both in the Antilles and in the home ports, with Britain's tight, unrelenting adherence to the closed principles of her navigation system. Britain's intent to keep that system closed manifested

---

[15]Cf., Oster to MMC, No. 9, Williamsburg, 27 July 1785, CC (Norfolk), 927: 73vo–74vo, and his "Questions Répondues" to Moustier, 5 December 1788, ibid., ff. 189–89vo.

[16]See Ducher to MMC, No. 27, 19 December 1788, CC (Wilmington), Tome 1, 56vo–57, and for similar assessments, Delaforest to same, No. 11, 24 July 1784, CC (Charleston), 372: 23–24; Chateaufort to same, No. 12, 12 June 1785, ibid., f. 142vo; and Delaforest to same, No. 160, 13 June 1786, CC (New York), 909: 156.

[17]The unsigned, undated memorandum is in a carton labeled "Marine Archives, BB 7/9," Archives de la Marine Française, Château de Vincennes. See also Duplaine's "Notes sur le Commerce," f. 200vo; and Otto to MAE, No. 61, Philadelphia, 25 May 1791, AECPE-U, 25: 356vo.

itself most sharply on 2 July 1783, when London announced that thereafter only vessels of British registry would be permitted to carry goods in either direction between American and British West Indian ports. Americans having opened their ports to the trade of all nations, wrote Marbois, were furious at not being allowed the "reciprocity" of trading with British possessions in their own vessels.[18]

Both the consul general and La Luzerne foresaw the likelihood of American retaliation. Just how they would vent their wrath appeared uncertain, but there was talk of state laws being enacted to prohibit such favored British carriers from entering American ports. Feeling ran high enough for some to suppose that even Congress might rouse from its torpor to make the prohibition uniform. In the end, only Massachusetts and New Hampshire saw fit to close their ports to British shipping, and Massachusetts soon retreated under the threat of British reprisal. North Carolina and Virginia, to be sure, put discriminatory levies on British vessels and cargoes, but full-scale commercial warfare, unless it could be coordinated, was out of the question. State lawmakers, mindful of their constituents' need for transit facilities, especially for export items, were reluctant to tamper with traffic patterns.[19]

Nor did Congress rise to the challenge. That body failed repeatedly to establish even minimal control over commerce, far less to legislate a retaliatory response. Anger at British constraints gradually subsided into sullen acquiescence. By 1786 Antoine Delaforest detected a pervasive sense of helplessness. The British islands were being provisioned by British vessels, he wrote, with Americans left to nibble at that trade as best they could by registering their ships under names borrowed from British business associates.[20]

Were France to grant concessions in her Indies of the type Britain denied, some thought she might win back lost ground in the Atlantic. This was never more than a fleeting supposition, however. When, in 1784, France did open her islands to a limited American traffic, her motives had more to do with the islands' need for American foodstuffs. Secon-

[18]To MMC, No. 46, 23 September 1783, CC (Philadelphia), 945: 377. For the Order-in-Council of 2 July and two othets of 4 May and 6 June 1783, also restrictive of the British West Indies traffic, see *Acts of the Privy Council, Colonial Series, 1766–1783*, 527–32.

[19]Marbois to MMC, Nos. 46 and 55, of 23 September and 5 December 1783, CC (Philadelphia), 945: 377, and 400–402, respectively; La Luzerne to MAE, No. 363, Annapolis, 15 January 1784, AECPE-U, 27: 48–48vo. For state commercial legislation of this period, see Merrill Jensen, *The New Nation: A History of the United States During the Confederation, 1781–1789* (New York 1950) 293–301.

[20]To MMC, No. 181, 24 November 1786, CC (New York), 909: 201–201vo.

darily, Paris hoped that by allowing Americans to carry away a small variety of Indies goods they might be deterred from smuggling. When asked "what favors could we obtain from the United States" in return? Marbois replied that he saw "no object of compensation to be expected from them." Americans, he wrote, were too fully committed to free trade to devise navigation laws favorable to France. Paris must consult its own self-interest.[21] In 1784, that self-interest was clear enough: the islands needed American grain, and the American penchant for dealing in contraband needed to be appeased.

To encourage trade in the Atlantic, France employed stratagems that seemed to offer too few enticements and, worse, did more to stimulate imports than exports. The monarchy at first appeared to believe that it had furnished stimulus enough in opening Marseille, Dunkerque, and later, L'Orient as "free ports" and by granting Americans exemptions from certain tonnage duties. Later in the decade, it encouraged Americans to import whale oil and fish, and made a not inconsiderable effort to facilitate imports of American tobacco by curbing the monopolistic powers of the Farmers General. This emphasis on easier access for imports, however, did virtually nothing to serve France's greater need: an American market for her exports that would reverse the unfavorable balance of trade.[22]

By the end of the decade Frenchmen could only speculate that Britain had fared better than France because she had adhered more rigorously to mercantilist precepts. The contrast invited such speculation: Britain had conceded nothing; France had been as generous as self-interest would permit. French ministers and consuls, however, perhaps out of loyalty, seldom credited Britain's adherence to the "system" to explain her continuing commercial pre-eminence. Even later critics of royalist commercial policies rarely made this connection. They were less sure that France by yielding concessions to Americans had improved Britain's hold on the American market than that those concessions had simply been costly and weakening to France.[23]

Even so, no one could mistake the commercial success of Britain's closed-door mercantilism. Louis Otto counted sixty-seven British vessels

---

[21]To same, No. 33, 3 June 1784, CC (Philadelphia), 945: 311–12.

[22]See Nussbaum, *Commercial Policy*, 173–78, and by the same author, "American Tobacco and French Politics, 1783–1789," *Political Science Quarterly* 40 (December 1925) 499. Contemporarily, Delaforest was among the first to discern this misdirection of French commercial policy, first in his No. 232 to MMC, 9 May 1788, CC (New York), 910: 53–54vo, and again in his "Mémoire sur la situation actuelle des Etats Unis relativement à l'industrie et au Commerce Etranger," New York, 18 February 1789, série B^7, doss. 461, 7–8, ANF.

[23]See, for example, Tanguy, *Situation commerciale*, 23–27; Fauchet, "Mémoire sur les Etats-unis," (1796) 90–91.

(and only seven French) putting into New York harbor in the year 1786. Some of these British arrivals he ascribed to that country's larger direct trade, but many of them, en route to the British islands, were loading American cargoes which American carriers were forbidden to export.[24] A year later, the Comte de Moustier wrote in exasperation:

Without making any sacrifice, without seeking the friendship of a people bereft of principles, of system, of government, [Britain] sees herself in possession of nearly all its active and passive commerce; she reserves to herself the right to carry from the Americans all that is indispensable to her Colonies, and brings to them all the goods she can. . . .[25]

Reluctant to believe that Britain had succeeded in capturing the American market except through some contributing defect in France's rival efforts, French officials also looked for explanations closer to home. Studiously they examined the contemporary business practices of French commercial houses. With equal care they weighed and analyzed the aims, procedures, and actual consequences of government policies affecting commerce. What they uncovered, with dispiriting frequency, was a congeries of commerce-related handicaps and incapacities that seemed to be fixed by immutable circumstance or ingrained in practices and policies not easily changed.

Amid the many hazards to navigation, however, there appeared one more fearsomely obstructive than perhaps all the others combined. Having to do with neither practice nor policy, but rather institutional in nature, its removal, it was believed, would clear the sea lanes to American markets as would no other act within the power of government. With near unanimity, ministers, consuls, and other close observers early concentrated their fire on what they saw as the overridingly obstructive presence of that venerable French corporate institution known as the Farmers General. Created by the French government in 1721 to collect certain kinds of taxes, the Farm subsequently grew in the size and scope of its monopolistic enterprises. Among them was the exclusive right to import tobacco. Not only did France absorb annually about one-quarter of all American tobacco grown for export, but these purchases also comprised the principal item of French import from the United States. From taxes collected on this item alone, the Farmers General by the end of the 1780s was returning revenues to the French government in the amount of more

----

[24] To MAE, No. 79, New York, 16 February 1787, AECPE-U, 32: 198.
[25] To same, No. 13, New York, 29 May 1788, ibid., 33: 180.

than thirty million livres a year.[26] Such abundant returns, gathered with no administrative expense to Paris, obviously gave the royal government good reason to allow the Farmers General to continue its monopolistic operations unimpeded. Only clear evidence that it was choking off larger opportunities for French commerce could outweigh the importance of the tax-collecting service it performed so handsomely.

Although free traders had long taken pot-shots at it, the Farm's tobacco-buying monopoly came under blistering attack when in the spring of 1785 it jumped the Atlantic and landed in the hands of the American financier, Robert Morris. The organization's Receiver General at La Rochelle gave Morris a million livres and a three-year contract. The latter was to buy tobacco directly from the growers and to furnish the Farm with 20,000 barrels a year at a constant price of thirty-six livres per quintal. For its part, the Farm agreed to buy its American tobacco only from Morris.[27]

Economic historians agree on one point: the Morris contract forced American tobacco growers to accept lower prices. The average price for the 1785 crop fell by nearly 50 percent, then rose again the following year when the French government stepped in to modify the contract. Because tobacco prices were already high, however, some question remains as to whether the planters suffered as severely as their angry outcries suggested. Men closest to the scene, like Oster in Norfolk and Delaforest in New York, while they reported great hardship to independent French tobacco buyers in Maryland and Virginia, felt the growers had little to complain of. Both officials believed that planters were still making profits from what they sold to Morris and his associates. Delaforest thought they were sulking less about prices than about being exposed to the whims of a monopolistic organization whose profits they suspected exceeded their own.[28]

---

[26]See Nussbaum, "American Tobacco and French Politics," 497–516; Brigham Duncan, "Franco-American Tobacco Diplomacy, 1784–1860," *Maryland Historical Magazine* 51 (1957) 273–301; and Richard K. MacMaster, ed., "The Tobacco Trade with France: Letters of Joseph Fenwick, Consul at Bordeaux, 1787–1795," ibid., 60 (1965) 26–55.

[27]A printed copy of the Morris contract is in AECPE-U, 30: 50–50vo.

[28]See Delaforest to MMC, No. 129, 25 November 1785, CC (New York), 909: 203–204; and Oster to same, No. 16, Williamsburg, 24 December 1785, CC (Norfolk), 927: 112–13. A detailed account of the Morris operation is contained in Jacob M. Price, *France and the Chesapeake: A History of the French Tobacco Monopoly, 1674–1791, and Its Relationship to the British and American Tobacco Trades* (Ann Arbor 1973) 2: 743–56. Price ascribes the decline in prices to the bumper harvest of 1785, and agrees that planters' price complaints were exaggerated, ibid., 755–56. For concurring views, see Nussbaum, "American Tobacco and French Politics," 503; Duncan, "Tobacco Diplomacy," 275; and MacMaster, "Tobacco Trade," 27.

The outcry from the American tidewater served principally to draw attention to the more extensive mischief the Farmers General had visited on Franco-American commerce throughout its operations. The Morris contract, for its part, merely underscored the parlous state of that commerce. Its most immediate effect was to ruin the small independent French tobacco buyers. Some had already bought good quality tobacco at a higher price than Morris's agents would pay to take it off their hands. Others, for whom tobacco was a medium of international exchange, suddenly found they could obtain little or no tobacco with which to "pay" for incoming cargoes of French commodities. Morris's agents had bought it all up, moving so swiftly that some suspected a deliberate campaign to put French buyers out of business.[29]

Worse, from the standpoint of France's already unfavorable balance of trade, the Farmers General traditionally paid with cash, not with French exports. Nor did anyone seriously expect the Farm—whose only American concern was tobacco—to take over and conduct the import-handling function of the French traders it was forcing into bankruptcy. Ironically, then, at a time when France needed more American customers, if only to stem her loss of specie, the Farmers General was ruining the same small businessmen who had made a livelihood of cultivating a consumer demand for French manufactures. This anomaly did not pass unnoticed.[30]

Not only did the Farm's mode of buying without selling accentuate an unfavorable trade balance; its fixed-price experiment of 1785 also induced American growers to turn to British and Dutch markets where prices were higher. Such a shift predicted still further losses of American outlets for French commodities. Ships laded with tobacco for British and Dutch ports would return with British and Dutch cargoes. France's competitive position would deteriorate accordingly.[31]

Incensed at the havoc wrought by the Morris contract, the Comte de Vergennes and the French Controller-General Charles Alexandre de Calonne called for an inquiry. They asked the American Minister Thomas Jefferson, the Marquis de Lafayette, and the heads of several prominent French business houses to investigate and make recommendations. This

---

[29]Oster to MMC, No. 16, Williamsburg, 24 December 1785, CC (Norfolk), 927: 112–13; Otto, "Mémoire remis," f. 283; and Delaforest to MMC, No. 140, 30 January 1786, CC (New York), 909: 111–14vo.

[30]Same to same, No. 232, New York, 9 May 1788, ibid., ff. 53vo–55. Jefferson made the point forcefully in a warning letter to Vergennes, Paris, 15 August 1785, in Julian P. Boyd, ed., *The Papers of Thomas Jefferson* (Princeton 1953) 8: 385–89.

[31]Ibid.; Delaforest's No. 129, CC (New York), 909: ff. 204vo–205; Oster's No. 16, CC (Norfolk), 927: f. 113; "American Committee" to Vergennes, untitled memorandum of 28 February 1786, AECPE-U, 31: 151vo; and Nussbaum, "American Tobacco and French Politics," 500.

so-called "American Committee," relying in turn on ministerial and con-sular dispatches, went beyond the Morris contract to denounce the whole concept of monopoly. Although it stopped short of urging an end to this monopoly, the Committee did succeed in persuading Paris to modify the Morris contract so as to require the Farm to buy at least some of its American tobacco from independent traders. The Farm at first refused to do so, but gave way gradually when it became clear that Morris could not deliver tobacco in the quantity contracted for.[32] Thereafter, free trade advocates sniped periodically, convinced that the giant agency continued to cast a pall over prospects for expanding French markets.

In casting about to explain why France failed to develop her full market potential, experienced observers could recite the sins of the Farmers General and, dark though they were, know that they constituted only one of many somber passages in the long litany of unhappy self-discovery. They recounted other reasons for failure as well.

The persistently shoddy quality of French export items offered one such explanation. Beginning with the first wartime shipments to arrive from France, complaints about poor quality recurred with monotonous regularity. Of this early period, the French economist Ambroise Arnould mused: "Our merchants seemed to believe that everything that could not be sold elsewhere was still too good for America." French consuls in American port cities had reason to agree. From Boston in the late war years, Philippe Létombe twice remarked on "the bad quality of merchan-dise which comes here from France." In some instances, cargoes had been returned to France or sold at loss. Their prices had been set too high, he thought, but poor quality had also figured. In the postwar year 1784, with little improvement in sight, Saint-John de Crèvecoeur expressed no surprise at the sales resistance to French wines and brandies recently landed in New York. The wines, he wrote, had arrived sour or almost sour. With becoming Gallic sensitivity, he adverted to the possibility that they were the "delicate victims" of exposure to the unaccustomed rigors of the American climate. More likely, he thought, uncaring exporters had simply paid no heed to quality. In 1785, Consul Chateaufort at Charleston observed drily that if French imported goods did not improve in quality,

---

[32]For the Committee's stinging attack on the Farm, see "Propositions pour le Commerce des Etats-Unis" to Vergennes, 23 May 1786, AECPE-U, 31: 368–77. Modifications of the Morris contract were agreed to the next day. See "Résultat du Comité tenu à Berni chez M. le Contrôleur général," ibid., ff. 378–79. The fullest summary of the "Berni" decision is in vol. 2 of Price, *France and the Chesapeake*, 757–87.

Americans could hardly be blamed for using the epithet "French stuff," a phrase borrowed from the British to describe goods of inferior grade. From Norfolk that year, Martin Oster heard complaints about French products from as far west as the Monongahela. Oster, who often sought to enhance his own views by forwarding the like opinions of his merchant constituents, sent Paris a letter he had received from a M. Savary de Valcoulon. Datelined "George Creek sur les bords de la Monongahela," Valcoulon's letter confirmed that poor quality, in part, accounted for the almost complete disappearance of French goods from the western parts of Virginia. Quality may have improved over time, but the reputation took root, doubtless cultivated by repeated slurs from British rivals, that French-made products were either weak, not durable, or defective in some way.[33]

Americans may have been put off by the poor quality of French products, but they also balked at their unfamiliarity. Unless French manufacturers could be persuaded to produce goods of the same size, shape, style, color, texture, etc., that American customers were accustomed to buying from the British, French officials in America despaired of their ever getting a share of the existing market. Some, to be sure, hoped to see France break the old habits of "buying British" by creating a distinctive market for French-style products. If this were a possibility, warned Chateaufort, then "France has no time to lose." From Boston Létombe agreed. James Swan, the New York merchant who later served as purchasing agent for the French Republic and whose trenchant pamphlet on Franco-American trade problems was widely read, foresaw that the accustoming process would not be easy. American buying habits, he wrote, "will long resist the most useful and most reasonable innovations; and it is only by slow and imperceptible means that one can hope to change them."[34]

More reasonably, French manufacturers might have been expected to adapt their products to existing consumer tastes. "It has to be easier to change the practice of manufacturers," wrote Moustier sensibly, "than that of an entire people." From the Virginia frontier Valcoulon echoed

---

[33]See, respectively, Létombe to MMC, No. 12, 14 November 1783; and his year-end report to same, February 1784, in CC (Boston), 209: 262 and 289vo; Crèvecoeur to same, No. 2, 19 January 1784, CC (New York), 909: 6–7; Chateaufort to same, No. 12, 12 September 1785, CC (Charleston), 372: 143vo; Oster's copies of the Valcoulon letter (sent to Vergennes, de Castries, and Lafayette), 15 May 1785, AECPE-U, 29: 248–60. See also Swan, *Causes qui se sont opposées*, 28; and Brissot, *New Travels*, 396.

[34]See, respectively, Chateaufort to MMC, No. 17, 9 June 1786, CC (Charleston), 372: 162; Létombe to same, December 1782, CC (Boston), 209: 127vo–28; and Swan, *Causes qui se sont opposées*, 27.

the thought when he scoffed at French exporters who "seemed to think they could force the inhabitants to be pleased with French tastes," instead of offering Americans the items they obviously preferred. When French shipping came to a standstill in mid-1785, Louis Otto warned that if French trade were to revive, French manufacturers must learn to adjust to American buying habits. As the decade lengthened James Swan saw no change for the better: French manufacturers seemed determined not to produce goods explicitly designed for the American market. Their folly, he recalled, dated from the war when they had sent goods "badly chosen, alien both to our climate and our usage; the colors and designs were equally shocking and defective . . ." Later, he felt, Americans would have liked to express their gratitude to France by purchasing goods of French manufacture, but continued to be offered items whose size, shape, and color they were not accustomed to.[35]

Whether too-high prices also figured in France's declining share of the market found opinion divided. Most observers agreed, however, that British suppliers retained a competitive edge in pricing, at least until the price collapse of mid-decade when that factor temporarily ceased to be relevant.[36] Occasionally, someone like the free-trade enthusiast who memorialized the foreign office in 1784 would argue that anything Americans were accustomed to buying from the British they could buy more cheaply from France—if only the French government would abolish its taxes and restrictions on commerce. The items he listed, however—toiles, silk, ribbons, etc.—spoke to a luxury market that was all too small and had little parallel in the British trade.[37] Still, the French government's "unnatural taxes" (Lafayette's phrase) undeniably exerted an upward pressure on the prices of French exports. The marquis, soon to join the "American Committee," argued that less interference from government would put French exporters back in business because the prices on most

[35]See, respectively, Moustier to Montmorin, No. 1, New York, 8 February 1788, "Correspondence of Moustier," *American Historical Review* 8 (1903) 717; Montmorin to Moustier, No. 1, Versailles, 23 June 1788, ibid., 729; Oster's dispatch of 15 May 1785, AECPE-U, 29: f. 251vo; Otto to MAE, No. 3, New York, 26 August 1785, AECPE-U, 30: 248; and Swan, *Causes qui se sont opposées*, 28, 103.

[36]Awareness of Britain's competitive price advantage extended through the decade and beyond. See, for example, Marbois to MMC, No. 31, 20 May 1783, CC (Philadelphia), 945: 303–309vo; Létombe to same, No. 12, 14 November 1783, CC (Boston), 209: 261–62; Crèvecoeur to same, No. 3, 15 July 1784, CC (New York), 909: 11; Duplaine, "Notes sur le Commerce," f. 200vo; and Lucien Hauteval, "Mémoire," Paris, 6 thermidor, an 6 (24 July 1798), AECPE-U, Mem. et doc., 10: 146vo.

[37]"Réflexions problématiques proposées à Philippe Mazzei par un Seigneur Français," AECPE-U, 27: 229vo–32.

British goods stood only slightly higher than those on the comparable French product.[38]

If French prices were as close to being competitive as Lafayette suggested, the reduction of tax levies on exports ought to have been a major focus of consular recommendation. Perhaps reticent to propose a reform that would cost their government revenues, but more likely because they saw export taxes as merely one of many trade-inhibiting factors, few consular officials took aim in that direction. Shortly after Yorktown Marbois casually suggested that certain French textiles might usefully be exempted from export duties. And Martin Oster four years later warned that such taxes made French exports "much too expensive to be sold in a foreign country where there is competition, and where the cheaper price always has preference."[39] By and large, however, French officials spread their fire across the broader field of governmental interference.

Goods crossing the Atlantic in both directions met with more government-created impediment than either French or American officials could keep track of from month to month. The crazy-quilt of American state tariffs and tonnage duties had their French counterparts in mystifying forms, fees, and port regulations, not to mention the uncertainties of dealing with the Farmers General. An anonymous French merchant lamented, in 1787: ". . . . the regime of our duties, the complicated forms . . . the variety of our tariffs, the restrictions placed on the majority of our manufactures . . . have in many respects destroyed the effects of the reciprocal goodwill between the two nations."[40] More significantly, such obstacles caused American merchants to think twice before dispatching cargoes to French ports. Such avoidance had an obvious, adverse implication for France's export trade. As Jefferson pointed out, that trade depended heavily on U.S. carriers. Americans more frequently sent cargoes in their own ships than did Frenchmen go to fetch them. Thus, anything that discouraged American vessels from entering French ports meant fewer bottoms for return cargoes.[41]

---

[38]"Observations sur le Commerce entre la France et les Etats Unis," série B[7], doss. 460, doc. 54, ANF.

[39]Marbois to MMC, No. 9, 30 December 1781, CC (Philadelphia), 945: 171vo; Oster to same, No. 16, Williamsburg, 24 December 1785, CC (Norfolk), 927: 113vo.

[40]"Rapport sur le Commerce des Etats-Unis de l'Amérique avec la France, fait à Monsier le Contrôleur Général," 15 October 1787, AECPE-U, Mem. et doc., 9: 110vo.

[41]To Vergennes, Paris, 15 August 1785, AECPE-U, 30: 221. Vergennes received similar warnings from Jean Jacques Bérard, "Mémoire sur le commerce de la France avec les Etats Unis," Paris, 10 January 1786, ibid., 31: 35vo; also from the "American Committee," 28 February 1786, ibid., ff. 150–50vo; and from Otto's No. 49, New York, 20 May 1786, ibid., ff. 322–22vo.

Delay ranked first among American shipowners' complaints. The voluminously informed James Swan spelled out how and why delays occurred. French port officials, he noted, persisted in the absurdity of requiring incoming vessels to wait their "turn" before unloading, irrespective of perishable cargoes or leaking holds. Waiting one's "turn" in an unprotected harbor like Le Havre could even be dangerous; it was always costly. He compared delays of a week or more in French ports with American harbors where unloading could begin the day after entry and upon submission of a cargo manifest. Equally ridiculous, French customs officials required incoming articles to be separately packed or wrapped—stockings, gloves, etc.; he doubted Americans would long put up with such nonsense. To fall into the clutches of the Farm could bring disaster. He told of captains who had landed cargoes of tobacco only to have an agent of the Farmers General offer them too low a price and then forbid them to reload and leave. To Swan this was "intolerable brigandage." To Lafayette French customs procedures were equally capricious. American captains, wrote the marquis, "float between [twin] fears" in declaring the value of their cargoes. Too low an estimate, if challenged, could lead to confiscation. Too high an estimate left the seller without a profit. No wonder, he wrote, that Americans preferred to market their tobacco in London or Amsterdam.[42]

Defensive at being regarded as arbitrary and obstructive, French officials of the 1780s laid as much blame as possible on the Farmers General. Still, French officialdom as a whole seemed irrepressibly eager to scrutinize vessels and cargoes and to milk them for whatever advantage their complex regulations would permit. They admitted causing frustration, delay, and hard feelings, but they also believed that Americans in their eagerness for profits would tolerate a good deal of portside regulation. In this respect, the best that could be said of the *ancien régime* was that its revolutionary successors outdid it in sheer petty officiousness. At that later time, Americans showed how gun-shy they had become. During the great grain convoys of 1794, at a time when France desperately needed American foodstuffs, it was perhaps predictable that the French Commissioner Jean-Baptiste Petry should alert Paris of American shipowners' fears of being delayed on arrival in French ports. Before they sailed, they were demanding assurances of per diem recompense for every day they might be detained beyond a reasonable period for offloading. If word got back to the United States of any unwarranted delays, he warned, the entire grain shipping operation might break off.[43]

---

[42]See Swan, *Causes qui se sont opposées*, 69–74; also Sheffield, *Observations*, 78; and Lafayette, "Observations."

[43]To MAE, No. 7, 24 prairial, an 2 (12 June 1794), CC (Norfolk), Tome 2, 13.

Whatever price France ultimately paid for regulatory excess, her commerce also suffered from the bewildering complexity of American state tariff and tonnage laws. The Confederation Congress, unable to impose uniformity, left foreign merchants at the mercy of state legislatures whose efforts to protect local interests created a kaleidoscope of fees, taxes, duties, and prohibitions. Because most of these efforts were overtly intended to disadvantage the British, French officials muted their protests. Marbois and Otto, keeping a close watch on these state enactments, nevertheless occasionally had reason to be apprehensive. Navigation acts devised by Massachusetts and New Hampshire, and subsequently by Pennsylvania, North Carolina, and Virginia, in some instances came close to violating certain articles of the Franco-American commercial treaty. When reminded of these articles, however, nearly every state legislature either made British carriers the explicitly designated object of discrimination or accomplished the same thing by exempting from the laws' effects the vessels of nations with which the United States had commercial treaties. One can speculate that had France's export trade in the 1780s shown any signs of sustained vigor, these tariff and tonnage exemptions might have given her the edge she needed to undersell lower-priced British goods. As it was, they merely stood as painful reminders to Frenchmen of the 1790s that the later federal Congress did not intend to show comparable favors.[44]

American commercial legislation, though confusing in its state to state variations, generally favored French shippers over British. Such passive encouragement might have nudged French businessmen more fully into American markets had it not been for the massive shove backward exerted by the awesomely adverse business depression that began as early as 1783 and lasted in some American port cities as late as 1787. The downcycle began when European exporters "dumped" commodities on the postwar American market in larger quantities than buyers could absorb. Frenchmen recounting later what had transpired reviled those French, British, and other European sellers who, in their greedy haste to cash in on high prices for goods in short supply during the war, misgauged the purchasing power of American buyers, causing shops and warehouses to fill with goods that ultimately could not be sold at any price. Sellers and buyers alike brought ruin on themselves. As prices fell, Americans paid with what they had, which proved not to be enough. Gold and silver quickly departed, followed by "return cargoes" often of insufficient value to offset the value of imports. Paper money, an indifferent medium in the

---

[44]For the Marbois and Otto reports on the vagaries of commercial legislation in 1785–86, see their dispatches in AECPE-U, 30: 212–12vo, 237vo, 274vo, 345, 469–69vo; 31: 52, 81–83; and 32: 3–3vo.

best of times, was often forced on European creditors who could plow it back into American public securities, but had no use for it back in Europe. Lines of credit stretched and broke, leaving the frayed ends of financial embarrassment to irritate French creditors and American defaulters to the end of the decade.

Like weathercocks swinging fitfully in the lull before a squall, French consuls reported a contrariety of business indicators in 1781–82. As military operations began to wind down after Yorktown, their assessments grew increasingly optimistic. Barbé-Marbois, who as consul general was centrally placed to give an accurate overview, thought market conditions by late 1781 merited a full-scale assault. To be sure, a lingering British naval presence in the Chesapeake kept insurance rates high, but on the bright side Americans seemed to have been cured of their paper money addiction. Such currency, he reported, "is almost entirely abolished," and what remained in circulation no one was being forced to accept. Moreover, French exporters could now count more readily on obtaining return cargoes of grain, tobacco, salt meat, etc. Given these favorable circumstances on which the British were already capitalizing, Marbois said he saw no reason for French businessmen to hold back. Other consular officials testing the winds confirmed Marbois's optimism.[45]

The storm French officials were about to witness, when it came, struck the port cities not all at the same time nor with equally destructive force. Consular descriptions of its whirlwind descent, however, conveyed back to Paris beginning in the spring of 1783 a bleak picture of business conditions suddenly very much changed for the worse. The effects of "dumping" began to be noticed almost at once. More vessels were arriving from Europe than anyone had expected, Marbois wrote in May. As commodity prices tumbled, he described chaotic scenes in Philadelphia: jubilant buyers, merchants caught with over-priced inventories, still-laden vessels being re-routed to other ports where, it was hoped, the "abundance" was not so great; and as wartime accumulations of specie began to disappear, there was renewed talk of introducing paper money.[46]

A few months later, Létombe painted a grim picture of maritime New England, its merchant fleet reduced to 400 vessels (compared with 2800, prewar), shops closed, commerce at a standstill, and paper currency

---

[45]Cf., Marbois to MMC, No. 9, 30 December 1781, CC (Philadelphia), 945: 169–70vo; Létombe to same, No. 13, 18 July 1782, CC (Boston), 209: 252–52vo; and D'Annemours to same, No. 17, 15 September 1782, CC (Baltimore), Tome 1, 26.

[46]To MMC, Nos. 31 and 46, 20 May and 23 September 1783, CC (New York), 945, 307–10vo and 375–78vo, respectively; and to MAE, No. 385, Philadelphia, 14 July 1784, AECPE-U, 28: 33–33vo.

fluctuating so wildly that estimates of its value made in the evening had to be amended next morning. Twenty French ships arrived in Boston in 1783, but only four the following year, a decline he ascribed to New England's inability to furnish return cargoes. Her usually flourishing fisheries, he wrote, stood at a quarter of their prewar levels, "her distilleries were deserted, her furs were very rare."[47]

Arriving in New York in the fall of 1784, Marbois estimated the presence of a three-year backlog in French and British goods, and thought it fortunate that French exporters, having learned of saturated market conditions, were no longer sending cargoes. A year later Otto confirmed the nullity of French commerce, not only in New York but everywhere, and ventured that several years would elapse before French goods would again be saleable. Further south the high postwar price of tobacco delayed the drain of specie, but failed to attract French carriers. As Martin Oster explained, the Farmers General preferred to ship their purchases of tobacco in foreign vessels. The only French ship to put into Norfolk in the first six months of 1786 was "a little boat coming from Martinique." From Charleston, Chateaufort noted a similar slackening in French shipping. Even though South Carolina's bumper rice crop of 1785 had been well publicized in France, not a single French carrier had appeared. He was not surprised: rice cargoes lacked value enough to pay for higher-priced French goods, and Carolina buyers had not enough specie to make up the difference. If the British still managed to eke out profits, it was because they charged less for carriage and were still willing to extend credit.[48]

Against this dreary backdrop, patchy but nonetheless indisputable signs of commercial revival began to appear in 1786–87. They gave cold comfort, however, to those who hoped to see France restored to a favorable balance of trade profitably carried in French bottoms. Tentatively at first but gradually gaining confidence in their assessments, consuls reported the clearing skies. Commodity prices rose as market surpluses were bought up. Banknotes and state issues of paper money held to near face value as hard-cash alternatives began to reappear. And as American farms and fisheries produced more fully, incoming shipmasters no longer lacked for return cargoes.[49]

---

[47]To MMC, No. 12, 14 November 1783, CC (Boston), 209: 260–63; and "Mémoire des Affaires du Consulat de France à Boston pendant l'Année 1784," ibid., f. 379vo.

[48]See, respectively, Marbois to MAE, No. 395, New York, 23 September 1784, AECPE-U, 28: 246–46vo; Otto to same, No. 3, New York, 26 August 1785, ibid., 30: 248; Oster to MMC, No. 23, Williamsburg, 15 July 1786, CC (Norfolk), 927: 122–22vo; and Chateaufort to MMC, No. 12, 12 September 1785, CC (Charleston), 372: 142vo.

[49]See, for example, Otto to MAE, Nos. 37 and 67, 12 February and 25 October 1786, AECPE-U, 31: 92, and 32: 117–18vo, respectively; and Delaforest to MMC, Nos. 152 and 160, 15 April and 13 June 1786, CC (New York), 909: 143vo and 157–57vo, respectively.

While Americans welcomed the rebirth of traffic in the Atlantic, French consuls more often remarked on its lopsidedness and despaired of the meager role French carriers seemed to play in its re-emergent configuration. Not only did outbound cargoes greatly exceed the returns from France, but also too few vessels of French registry carried goods in either direction. Their year-end reports underscored both phenomena. In the South, Jean-Baptiste Petry estimated that for the two years, 1786–1787, Charleston exported to France goods three times the value of those it imported, an unfavorable balance that cost France 1,164,512 livres. In New England for the single year, 1788, Létombe reported an even greater imbalance: combined imports–exports carried by French vessels he valued at less than 170,000 livres, but the 258 American vessels he and his vice consuls had officially cleared for French ports carried away cargoes worth nearly six times that figure. Reports from New York, Philadelphia, Norfolk, and other port cities told essentially the same tale of unfavorable balances and few arrivals of French-flag merchantmen.[50]

Despite its appearance of full recovery, the American business scene obviously stirred little entrepreneurial zeal among France's merchant-exporters. Moustier thought he understood their lethargy: French exporters still remembered the shattering losses they had suffered during the American price collapse. The bad debts and bankruptcies he blamed on their own ignorant and disorganized rush to skim profits in the immediate postwar period. What concerned him more, in 1789, was that French businessmen still brooded over those losses when they should have been adapting their export goods to the new opportunities for meeting American consumer needs. Like Moustier, James Swan lamented the bad experience that seemed to have put a permanent damper on French export activity. Bitterness remained because American business houses still owed large sums to French suppliers, debts forever beyond hope of recovery. British exporters might have been somewhat too reckless in continuing to extend credit through the depression period, but French exporters had been too quick to withdraw it. Their rancor, he felt, blinded them to the fact that now, at the end of the decade, American buyers were much better credit risks.[51]

[50]Cf., Petry, "Etat des Importations de France dans le Port de Charleston & ses Exportations de ce Port en France Pendant L'année 1787," enclosed in his No. 48 to MAE, Charleston, 30 January 1788, série B^7, doss. 461, doc. 9, ANF; Létombe, "Etat du Commerce D'importation & Exportation des Batimens français avec Boston Pendant l'année 1788," loc. cit., docs. 23, 24; Delaforest to MMC, No. 232, 9 May 1788, CC (New York), 910: 53–54; and Oster to Moustier, 5 December 1788, CC (Norfolk), 927: 189–89vo.

[51]Moustier to Jacques Necker, New York, 12 May 1789, AECPE-U, 34: 93vo–97; Swan, *Causes qui se sont opposées*, 58–59, 91–95, 102.

Swan's mention of credit underscored a telling difference between traditional British and French business methods. British factors accustomed to wait for payment, sometimes as long as eighteen months, were thought to possess an advantage in dealing with American retailers that more cautious French businessmen seldom dared risk. Urging more of his countrymen to come and do likewise, Marbois singled out credit in 1783 as the principal "secret" of Britain's marketing success. The few French firms still prospering in the fall of that year were doing well, he believed, because they were willing to extend credit over periods of two to eight months. He warned that successful credit arrangements required intimate knowledge of a buyer's reliability, but for those firms unafraid to tie up capital there existed a time-tested "chain" of transactions beginning with "sales on credit, payment, new sales again on credit and so forth." Better this than the too frequently practiced French mode of consigning cargoes to sea captains who knew no English, were unknown to buyers, and tried to quick-sell their cargoes, usually in an atmosphere of uncertainty and distrust.[52]

A year later the consul general did an abrupt about-face: French merchants, he warned, would be ill-advised to follow British practice. A drop in commodity prices, the reappearance of paper money, but, above all, the disappearance of specie militated against any credit transactions whatsoever. He wrote: "If the scarcity of specie proves on the one hand that Americans need long-term credit, it also demonstrates that it is not in the interest of foreign nations to extend it to them." He foresaw, moreover, that Americans would doubtless look for credit elsewhere, now that British suppliers were drawing back. French houses must be warned, he wrote, that whatever the merit of long-term credit for regularizing commerce under normal conditions, now was not the time for it. Louis Otto confirmed Marbois's prediction. From L'Orient where he awaited passage Otto reported that American businessmen had besieged local merchants with requests to be sent consignments of goods, to be paid for one or two years later. The latter had wisely refused, even though Americans were offering to put up "very considerable security."[53]

Nor did it escape notice, even as the business outlook brightened in

[52]Marbois to MMC, No. 50, 15 October 1783, CC (Philadelphia), 945: 392–94. Marbois summarized this dispatch in his "Supplément au précis remis à Fontainebleau de toutes les dépêches d'Amérique concernant le commerce des Etats-Unis avec nos colonies et avec le Royaume," série B⁷, doss. 460, doc. 1, ANF. General Rochambeau (the younger) also criticized French business practices in his "Sur les rapports avenirs," f. 211vo.

[53]Cf., Marbois to MAE, Nos. 395 and 402, 23 September and 17 November 1784, AECPE-U, 28: 245vo–46 and 393–94, respectively; and Otto to same, No. 1, L'Orient, 30 June 1785, ibid., 30: 73–73vo.

the late 1780s, that British firms, usually so generous with credit, showed extreme caution. This British chariness, combined with earlier consular warnings, plus their own "sad experience" (as Otto called it), doubtless reinforced French exporters in their disposition to sell for cash only. Moustier and Swan might vouch for the improved credit ratings of American buyers and hail the dawn of new opportunities for a credit-based expansion of French export sales, but few French businessmen were listening. Louis Otto perhaps voiced most accurately the perception of most French exporters when he wrote that among the mercantile community at L'Orient "the name American has everywhere become the signal for fear and distrust."[54]

Animated by their countrymen's inability to contest well-favored British merchants for a reasonable share of the American market, French officials seldom lacked for advice or recommendations, and sometimes made elaborate proposals for improving the odds in their favor. Curiously, it was George Washington, a man who admitted his unfamiliarity with mercantile matters, who put his finger unerringly on the three major "problem areas" these officials themselves most frequently identified. France, Washington told Moustier, could expect to increase her exports only if she were to match the British in furnishing long-term credit, providing warehouse facilities, and in emulating the latter's ability to adapt to consumer preferences.[55]

Because credit of any kind was unlikely to be forthcoming from the private sector, Moustier and others not surprisingly looked to government to play a compensatory role, especially in those other two areas of British challenge: warehousing and consumer adaptation. From whence came the idea of establishing a "*grande maison*," or (as some suggested) a complete chain of government-financed warehouses for each major port, remains a matter of conjecture. The idea was already well developed when James Swan made it a centerpiece of his *Causes qui se sont opposées aux progrès du commerce entre la France et les Etats-Unis*, published in 1790. Most likely, French officials came by it spontaneously from observing British practice, and from the corresponding anguish they felt watching the helter-skelter arrivals and disposals of French cargoes. Whatever its origin, nearly every French consul, witness to such disorder, voiced the

---

[54]Ibid., f. 73vo.
[55]Washington to Moustier, Mount Vernon, 26 March 1788, *Writings of Washington* 29: 448; Moustier to MAE, No. 10, New York, 21 April 1788, "Correspondence of Moustier," 727.

need for permanent onshore storage facilities—places where cargoes arriving out of season could be held at modest expense to be sold later by competent business agents. Without such facilities, French sea captains worked under enormous pressure to offload cargoes, sell them, and relade as quickly as possible lest profits be eaten up by seamen's wages. Hasty transactions, unsettling to both buyer and seller, usually yielded profits so low as to discourage French exporters from repeating the venture.[56]

Where commission agents made their services available, the results were seldom better, often worse. How to identify reliable middle-men, or whether to use them at all, found opinion divided. La Luzerne felt that these agents' fees added too much to the selling price, and recommended that American merchants be encouraged to deal directly with French manufacturers. His consul general, Barbé-Marbois, urged French houses to send out their own representatives. Not only did American agents often have conflicts of interests, but they also aroused wariness among American buyers who suspected their wares of having passed through too many hands to have come to them at a fair price. For French exporters to entrust their business to these "worthless adventurers," he felt, was the height of folly. He knew of agents who had accepted a consignment, then bought it at a loss under a false name, and later sold it for their own profit when prices rose. When some French firms did send their own agents, Crèvecoeur saw little improvement. He characterized them as mostly "young men" who had no language facility and often neglected business for pleasure—an assessment confirmed by others.[57]

Besides criticizing dubious agents, Crèvecoeur in his concern for the broader problems of French marketing produced one of the earliest proposals for structural innovation requiring government initiative. Particularly solicitous for the reputation of French wines, the New York consul urged Paris in 1784 to establish in the United States a "*caveau national*"—a government agency that would pass on the quality of incoming wine shipments before allowing them to be sold to American consumers. Only by turning back wines of inferior quality, he believed, could France create a reliable clientele for one of her proudest exports. So that American con-

---

[56]See, for example, Marbois to MMC, No. 50, 15 October 1783, CC (Philadelphia), 945: 393–93vo.

[57]See, respectively, La Luzerne to MAE, No. 376, Philadelphia, 4 May 1784, AECPE-U, 27: 233–34; Marbois's No. 50, 15 October 1783, CC (Philadelphia), 945: 392–94; also his Nos. 9 and 31 to MMC, Philadelphia, 30 December 1781 and 20 May 1783, ibid., ff. 175–75vo and 308–309vo, respectively; and Crèvecoeur to same, No. 3, 15 July 1784, CC (New York), 909: 11. Three years later Delaforest saw little improvement in the quality of French commercial agents. See his No. 198, New York, 4 April 1784, ibid., ff. 254–55.

sumers would have confidence in such an agency, he recommenced that the "*caveau*" be supervised by an "honest American."[58]

When, that same year, tobacco magnate William Alexander vigorously urged France to build warehouse facilities in Virginia, the idea of having the French government take a more direct hand in marketing operations began to gain momentum. Alexander currently held a one-year contract to furnish the Farmers General with Virginia leaf which meant that he spoke with some authority on matters of Franco-American commerce. Specifically, Alexander saw warehouses as a means to undercut the credit structure by which the British had thus far prevailed. Americans were wedded to long-term British credit, he explained, because it permitted them to carry on business operations four or five times larger than their capital investment; they paid back what they owed only after they had sold off what British factors had brought them. The average interest cost on such credit, however, ranged up to 25 percent. France, he argued, could easily undersell the British by bringing in goods and storing them for gradual release on to the cash market. Sales from warehouses, moreover, would help reverse the balance of trade. Alexander promised that within three years the Farm's heavy cash outlays for tobacco could be replaced: that is, the tobacco paid for, instead, with French export goods passing through the warehouses into the American consumer market. The Farmers General, he thought, could properly be asked to share with the French government the cost of building these storage facilities.[59]

As time went on, the warehouse concept suggested still other advantages to its advocates. Savary de Valcoulon, for example, envisioned a "*grande maison*" at Norfolk becoming not only a distribution center for high quality French products, but also as a place from which French and American buyers spreading out through the interior would gather up the major products of the continent for export to all of Europe. If, as he projected, a great entrepôt of this sort succeeded in making France mistress of the Atlantic traffic, it might assist her in recovering her Antilles trade

---

[58]To MMC, No. 2, New York, 19 January 1784, ibid., ff. 6vo–7.

[59]Member of a prominent Edinburgh family firm, Alexander set up in Richmond in 1783–84, where, under contract with the Farm and in secret partnership with Robert Morris, he suffered financial reverses when the immediate postwar price of tobacco remained high longer than he expected. Following his own contractual default, and again when the Morris contract fell into disrepute, Alexander put forward the warehouse idea as an alternative to the cumbersome and chancy operations of the Farm. See his "Memorial on the Trade with Virginia and the other United States," Richmond, 7 September 1784, AECPE-U, 28: 188–90vo; and his "Quel est le système que l'on pourrait substituer au Contract de M. Morris," enclosed in Oster's No. 9 to Moustier, 26 November 1788, CC (Norfolk), 927: 241–44. See also Price, *France and the Chesapeake*, 742–47.

as well. Success depended, however, on the government's willingness to take the necessary initiatives. Paris must invest about a million livres to launch the enterprise, he wrote, and to assure its growth, lift internal restrictions on French manufactures and repeal taxes on exports.[60]

Just as Crèvecoeur and Valcoulon regarded "quality control" as a function of government supervision, so too did the Sieur de Chateaufort, French consul at Charleston. Thinking along separate but similar lines, Chateaufort believed that a single strong commercial house established in South Carolina could best serve France's export interests by enforcing standards of high quality on French suppliers. Such a house, richly endowed with capital and easing gently into the American market with only the finest French products, would surely win the confidence of American consumers. For Jean Toscan, writing from New England in 1786, it was enough that a "*grande maison*" would familiarize consumers with the best wares France already had to offer. Give Americans a closer look at the range and quality of French products, and they would buy. To that end, he proposed "establishing in Boston a vast store filled with all our manufactures, wines, brandies and other comestibles . . . everything [to] be sold on the account of His Majesty."[61]

Not to be outdone by his consuls, the Comte de Moustier put a somewhat different twist on current proposals. His, like the others, however, recognized the central dependence of any plan's success on the backing of the French treasury. Rather than put money into building warehouses, Moustier called for a more fully coordinated mercantile effort in France itself. He urged Paris to rouse, organize, and underwrite the activities of groups of "patriotic" merchants throughout the major port cities. In proposing a collective enterprise of "merchant associations," he showed how well he knew his countrymen. Individual exporters too often tried for one-time, fat-margin profits from sales of luxury items, whereas "associations" of exporters, he hoped, could be motivated by patriotism and the assurance of government support to settle for small but sure profits.[62]

Also distinctive was Moustier's curious but essentially logical insistence on reversing the priorities of market planning. His "merchant associations" must first decide on what they could agree to import. Americans, he explained, because they lacked specie, were not likely to

---

[60]"Extrait d'une lettre," ff. 255vo–59.

[61]Cf., Chateaufort to MMC, No. 12, 12 September 1785, CC (Charleston), 372: 141–44; Toscan, "Mémoire du Consulat de Boston pour 1785," to the Controller General, April 1786, Mem. et doc., 9: 53vo–54.

[62]To Necker, New York, 12 May 1789, AECPE-U, 34: 98vo–102.

buy French exports unless first assured of a French market for their own products. Thus, the merchant associates would have to look more closely at some of the other American products they had heretofore ignored and determine whether they could be sold in France or re-exported profitably to some other market. If the British could take profits from buying American lumber, salt meat, cotton, potash, linseed, and tar, so could France, he argued. Starting with cash payments for most of their initial purchases, the associations would gradually be able to substitute French goods for French cash. These goods must, of course, take into account American tastes, but Moustier believed that French manufacturers need not go "too far" in imitating British-style exports. More important were packaging, decoration, and a durable finish. As for financing the venture, he suggested either the royal treasury or Dutch bankers as a source of capital.[63]

As Moustier soon learned, entertaining Paris with proposals that would cost money sat ill with a government whose efforts to resolve its financial problems had taken on unexpectedly revolutionary overtones. From Jacques Necker, the regime's controversial director of finance, came praise for Moustier's "very instructive" proposals. But, added Necker, with an eye to events, "our general circumstances cast a chill on great enterprises of commerce."[64]

When James Swan in 1790 published his famous *Causes qui se sont opposées*, he seemed to sense that no French government would likely spend money to improve Franco-American commerce as long as the Revolution went forward. With this in mind, Swan blended the "*grande maison*" and merchant-association ideas in a project which he promised would not "risk a sou." Paris need only exert itself, he wrote, to bring together and pool the resources of French merchants who had an interest in the American market, charter this group as the "Compagnie du Nord et de l'Amérique," and let it sell stock with which to finance the construction of "houses or shops" in every major port from Boston to Charleston. Staffed by persons of ability and trust, these company shops he envisioned being constantly replenished with items of French manufacture, its French agents assuring that only goods suitable to American tastes were shipped out, its American agents having authority to buy American products on the company's account. If the company succeeded in keeping prices low, it would build enough customer confidence to capture the American market. Pushed from sight first by revolution and then by war, Swan's proposed

---

[63]Ibid., ff. 102vo.–105.
[64]To Moustier, Paris, 16 October 1789, ibid., f. 294vo.

"Compagnie," along with other like schemes, disappeared into that compost heap of disappointed hopes already piled high with frustrations.[65]

Equally frustrating to those who urged it was the failure of government and private enterprise to enhance French exports by engaging in market research. At the time Washington told Moustier that French manufacturers must adapt to American tastes, little progress had been made to that end. The perceived need for such accommodation, however, was already well developed. Philippe Létombe was probably the first to see it. As early as 1782, he suggested the Navy recall him to France so that he might effect a liaison between his business acquaintances in Boston and the principal merchants of France's port cities. Shortly thereafter, his request refused, Létombe urged that the government at least send out agents to identify American consumer needs. By Moustier's time (1788–89), the problem of matching goods to tastes persisted, but the foreign office showed only mild concern. Montmorin wrote Moustier in 1788 that the government would do what it could to encourage producers of export goods to adapt their products to American tastes, but his assurances were couched in such general terms as to leave doubt that any action was taken. Sporadically, the private sector showed interest. In 1791 Delaforest reported that a Frenchman named Simond had recently spent two years in New York studying import–export possibilities, and an American named Barret had just returned from France where he had counseled a group of Paris investors who planned to open shops in Boston, New York, and Philadelphia.[66]

The most elaborate and systematic proposal for market research came from the pen of Girondin ex-consul Antoine Duplaine. Writing at a time when British blockades were already choking off access to American ports, Duplaine put forward plans for a full-scale government undertaking to begin as soon as hostilities ceased. Paris, he wrote, should send four or five market experts to the United States "to procure samples and models of everything which the English send there." These investigators should note whether goods were sold "in gross, by the dozen, piece, bale, barrel or ton, according to quality and type." They were also to record "the forms, weight, and dimensions of all objects for which they cannot send

---

[65]Swan, *Causes*, 286–95. For evidence that Swan's influence was felt both before and after he published in 1790, see Toscan, "Mémoire du Consulat de Boston pour 1785," f. 54; Létombe to MMC, No. 7, 1 March 1787, CC (Boston), 210: 150vo–51; Mangourit to MMC, No. 9, 26 November 1792, CC (Charleston), 372: 411; and Brissot, *New Travels*, 396.

[66]See, respectively, Létombe to MMC, December 1782, CC (Boston), 209: 128–28vo; Montmorin to Moustier, No. 1, Versailles, 23 June 1788, "Correspondence of Moustier," 729; and Delaforest to MMC, No. 341, 20 October 1791, CC (New York), 910: 251vo–52.

back models. . . ." In addition, they should "discover the quantity consumed in each state annually, the freight rates, the insurance . . . the customs duties and other expenses." Never implemented, Duplaine's memorandum stood as a reminder of all the things left undone in the field of intelligent marketing over the preceding decade.[67]

Although French manufacturers failed to tailor their output to American tastes, French consuls sometimes thought they saw markets for goods already in production. Of these wares, usually more suited for a small "luxury" market than for general consumption, Marbois, Oster, Duplaine, and later Arnould all made similar observations: French silks, linens, and high-grade cottons were competitively priced; so, too, were good-quality wines and brandies. To the more optimistic, only the American market for rough cottons and hardware need be yielded to the British. How to persuade Americans to buy what was already on the shelves, so to speak, depended (they felt) on furnishing them with reliable price-lists, and giving them some assurance that goods they wished to exchange would find a market in France.[68]

As to the first, consuls persistently entreated French chambers of commerce to send out price-lists, and to do so well in advance of shipping the goods they intended to sell. Létombe even dug into his own pocket to make sure New England newspapers published these lists. As Delaforest explained, however, conveying price information required some skill. He was pleased, he wrote (in April 1787), to have a price-list of Languedoc fabrics from the Montpélier chamber of commerce. Then he told why he did not intend to have it published, as he had other such lists. In this instance, fabrics were described in ways unfamiliar to American buyers. Some few might understand, but it was not the sort of thing to be printed in the public press. Rather, he planned to ask his consuls to transmit the list to local merchants with appropriate explanations.[69]

Offering American buyers a return-sales market in France occurred not only to Moustier, but to others as well. Lafayette, in his "Observations," argued that if France expected Americans to buy French wines, it must make it easier for Americans to sell their own products in France. The marquis's colleague on the "American Committee," a French merchant named Bérard, made essentially the same point: Americans could

---

[67]"Notes sur le commerce," ff. 206–206vo.

[68]Cf., Marbois to MMC, No. 45, Philadelphia, 1 September 1783, Archives de la Marine, série B^7, doss. 460, doc. 2; Oster to Moustier, "Questions Répondues," ff. 219–20; and Duplaine, "Notes sur le Commerce," f. 201.

[69]Létombe to MMC, No. 6, 16 February 1787, CC (Boston), 210: 137; Delaforest to same, No. 198, 4 April 1787, CC (New York), 909: 253vo–54vo.

not be forced to buy French goods, but if they were encouraged to bring in articles of their own production, they would soon be lading cargoes of French production for their return voyages. Others agreed, urging the need to keep Americans regularly informed of changes in French port formalities and of the fluctuations in French market prices for American goods.[70]

Although French officials often identified certain American products that France might have use for, they seldom seemed to envision those products becoming articles of popular consumption. Their thinking usually ran, instead, to naming items useful to naval construction or to some larger national purpose. Consuls particularly, as was perhaps natural to Navy employees, often mentioned the availability of live oak "knees," masts, tar, pitch, and turpentine.[71] Or, like Martin Oster who saw American charcoal as a valuable energy source for French industry, and Antoine Duplaine who thought American iron ore worth extracting, they looked to achieving some greater good for the French national economy. Almost always, it seemed, these consular projects called for an activist role by government. Neither Oster nor Duplaine, for example, expected private enterprise to undertake the charcoal and iron ventures they suggested. Rather, Oster intended that Paris send out French charcoal makers to work on location, and Duplaine thought it expedient for France to try to buy iron-producing lands outright.[72]

With quiet but unmistakable urgency, French officials in America campaigned throughout the decade, hoping to induce their masters in Paris to exercise the powers of government they believed must be enlisted in the commercial battle of the Atlantic if France were to secure markets for exports comparable to those of her British rival. Too nearly insolvent to respond to proposals that required cash outlays and too enervated by financial crisis to furnish the kind of aggressive leadership that was called for, the royal government settled for making concessions piecemeal.

---

[70]See, respectively, Lafayette, "Observations"; Bérard, "Propositions pour le Commerce des Etats Unis," 23 May 1786, AECPE-U, 31: 369vo–70; also Delaforest to MMC, No. 160, 13 June 1786, CC (New York), 909: 156vo; Swan, *Causes*, 274–75; and Moustier to Montmorin, No. 26, New York, 18 November 1788, "Correspondence of Moustier," 90–91.

[71]Delaforest made the fullest, most systematic survey of American natural resources in his 261-page "Mémoire sur la situation actuelle des Etats unis relativement à l'industrie intérieure et au Commerce Etranger," 18 February 1789, série B^7, doss. 461, ANF. See also Létombe's wide-ranging "Mémoire des Affaires du Consulat de France à Boston pendant l'Année 1784," CC (Boston), 909: 22–26; also Otto to MAE, No. 65, New York, 15 October 1786, AECPE-U, 32: 100vo; and Moustier to Necker, New York, 12 May 1789, ibid., 34: 100–101.

[72]Cf., Oster, "Questions Répondues," ff. 233vo–26; and Duplaine, "Notes sur le Commerce," ff. 201vo–202.

Though well intended, these concessions tended to smack more of cosmetics than substance and often evoked more irritation than goodwill. In May 1784, for example, the king's council, reaffirming the "free port" status of Dunkerque and Marseille, graciously announced that American shippers would have similar privileges at L'Orient after 1 July. "This news," wrote La Luzerne, "has made the greatest sensation throughout the continent and has encouraged several firms to prepare ships for France."[73] By the time those ships arrived at L'Orient, a second decree had been issued, so severely restrictive that American captains described it as "incompatible with a free port and causes us much embarrassment." Several weeks passed in confusion before a third royal decree reaffirmed *in toto* what had been expected of L'Orient's free port status.[74] Again, in the fall of 1786, when the royal government proposed what it believed were modest tariffs, Jefferson had to point out to the Controller-General that the duties proposed for American potash, tar, pitch, and turpentine would, in fact, be prohibitive.[75]

Even France's most sweeping concessions—those embodied in the so-called "whale oil decree" of 29 December 1787—were not unmarred by awkwardness. Inspired by suggestions from the American Committee, this decree singularly favored New England fisheries by subjecting American-produced whale oil, as well as dried or salted fish, to the lowest category of French tariffs.[76] Within two months, however, the American Committee had to be called back into session to draft clarifying language. As Montmorin explained to Otto, the 29 December decree needed several changes to make its meaning more clear. Then, without warning, the government decided on 28 September 1788 to prohibit all importations of whale oil from foreign sources. An astonished Jefferson told Montmorin he could scarcely believe that France intended to snatch away a favor so recently granted. Surely, he continued pointedly, the king meant only to exclude whale oil from European sources. While Jefferson impor-

---

[73]La Luzerne, "Résumé des affaires de l'Amérique du 17 mars au 27 avril, 1784," AECPE-U, 27: 315vo. For the decree itself, see "Arrêt du Conseil d'Etat du Roi, portant confirmation & établissement de Ports francs dans le Royaume," 14 May 1784, *Extrait des Registres du Conseil d'Etat.*

[74]"Copy of a letter written to M. Franklin by some American Captains of the date of August 7, 1784," AECPE-U, 28: 93–94, shortly followed by an angry protest from L'Orient merchants themselves, ibid., ff. 95–125. For the text of the second, highly restrictive decree, see "Arrêt du Conseil d'Etat, portant règlement sur la franchise de L'Orient," 26 June 1784, ibid., 27: 464; and the text of the third decree conveyed by the Controller General Charles-Alexandre de Calonne to Vergennes, Paris, 13 September 1784, ibid., 28: 199.

[75]Jefferson to Calonne, Fontainebleau, 22 October 1786, ibid., 32: 114vo.

[76]A translated text of this "Act of the King's Council of State, for the encouragement of the commerce of France with the United States of America," is in *ASP,FR* 1: 113–14.

tuned the foreign office, Montmorin hoping to contain the damage gave Moustier permission to spread the word among Americans that although the prohibiting decree was still under discussion, his majesty's ultimate decision would almost certainly "favor" a restoration of whale oil imports from the United States.[77] Moustier predicted correctly: two months later, in early December, the king's council moved to exempt from the prohibition "the oils of the whale & other fish, as well as the whale bones, produced by the fisheries of the United States."[78]

Considering France's well-recognized need for a greater export market, the whale oil decree offers an interesting study in misdirection. Seven of its thirteen articles spelled out either entrepôt or import procedures. The latter, to be sure, lowered to gratifying levels the duties on a wide variety of American products. Similar tax relief for French exports, however—at least of the scope that many believed would make French wares competitive—received only scant attention. Except for lifting export duties from paper products, including books and wallpaper, and reducing to virtually nil the export taxes on arms and gunpowder, this major commercial decree of the 1780s revealed how unwilling Paris was to relinquish sources of revenue even in a good cause. That the government felt pressures to go further appeared dimly in Article XI. Therein the king reserved "to himself" the right to encourage certain other exports. Hardware and textiles were mentioned as possible candidates for tax relief, but in the future.[79]

Clear-eyed as usual, Consul General Delaforest remarked ruefully that whatever else it accomplished, the whale oil decree missed out as a stimulant to Americans to consume French goods. He urged Paris to look next to measures more explicitly aimed at providing such stimulation.[80] In reply to similar urgings from Moustier, the foreign office closed the door to anything that resembled further concessions. France had already gone as far as it should in that direction, Montmorin wrote in mid-1789. Any new commercial arrangements must await the advent of the new American government; only then could France gain a clearer idea of what

---

[77]See, respectively, Montmorin to Otto, Versailles, 26 February 1788, AECPE-U, 33: 112vo; Jefferson to Montmorin, Paris, 23 October 1788, ibid., ff. 303–304; and Montmorin to Moustier, No. 3, Versailles, 21 November 1788, ibid., f. 343vo.

[78]Published with the title *Arrêt du Conseil d'Etat du Roi qui excepte de la prohibition portée par l'arrêt du 28 septembre dernier, les Huiles de Baleine & d'autres Poissons, ainsi que les fanons de Baleine, provenant de la pêche des Etats-unis de l'Amérique, du Décembre 1788* (Paris 1789).

[79]*ASP,FR*, 1: 113–14.

[80]To MMC, Nos. 232 and 234, New York, 9 May and 6 June 1788, CC (New York), 910: 53vo–54 and 63vo, respectively.

else might be worked out to the reciprocal advantage of both parties.[81]

By encouraging imports rather than exports, the 1787 decree served merely to tilt the balance of trade more heavily against France. Moreover, its potential for this effect was soon accentuated by the avalanche of French purchases, especially of American grain, which began with the bad harvest of 1789 and gathered further momentum when food shortages persisted. When the shortage first appeared, Otto remarked complacently that at least it was "showing Americans the way to our ports."[82] Indeed, by the early 1790s, Franco-American traffic was brisk. For American carriers that found their way to French ports, however, the return voyage was often made in ballast or after an intervening stopover in the British Isles to pick up a return cargo. Clearly, the mounting volume of trade, though it served France's immediate needs for grain and foodstuffs, accentuated her unhealthy trade balance. The French pattern of importing more than she could export—a pattern fixed in the previous decade despite the best efforts of French officials to enlarge markets for French goods—became now enormously one-sided. It cost France astronomical sums in outbound specie rather than outbound cargoes. Nor did Paris need reminding that the money France paid for her swollen imports Americans, in turn, used to make remittances to her "cruelest enemy, England." The cycle of frustration in the Atlantic was unambiguous: France's decade-long quest for offsetting markets in the United States had ended as a lost cause.

[81]Montmorin to Moustier, No. 5, Versailles, 7 July 1789, AECPE-U, 34: 225vo.
[82]To MAE, No. 13, New York, 19 January 1790, ibid., 35: 32.

IV
AMERICANS IN THE ANTILLES

Few other developments in Franco-American commerce so mortified French officialdom in the 1780s as did the brazen Yankee takeover of the French West Indies carrying trade. Helpless, they watched as American ship-masters swiftly engulfed that trade, skimming its profits away from French carriers, setting French customs laws at nought, and in the end, leaving France little but the empty husk of sovereignty. By 1788, only four years after the decision to allow Americans a foot in the door, Dela-forest wrote that "nearly all the profits of freight are in the hands of the Americans."[1]

Lost profits from carriage, however, were only a small part of the mischief. Tanguy de la Boissière, taking stock of other damage done by the American incursion, estimated that France in the nine-year period, 1784–93, lost specie amounting to 283 million livres—thanks to a traffic that was not only illegal but also disfavored the net balance of payments. For the same period, potential taxes and duties evaded by American smugglers cost her another 360 million livres; and the value of West Indies goods re-exported by Americans that should have passed through French hands amounted to 245 million.[2] The total cash loss to France, her government and her subjects, calculated roughly at five francs to the dollar, came to a staggering $178 million. No statistical summary, however, could express the chagrin or do justice to the feelings of impotence Frenchmen experienced as they watched their nation's last major asset in the New World ravaged by the upstart power they had helped to loose on the high seas of commerce and independence.

Explanations, usually edged with recrimination, offered little solace.

---

[1]To MMC, No. 232, 9 May 1788, CC (New York), 910: 55vo.

[2]Tanguy, *Situation commerciale*, 23–29. For confirmation of the size of these commercial losses, see also Buron, "Notes," 571–80; and Létombe, "Extrait d'un Mémoire sur la situation commerciale de la France avec les Etats-unis," Philadelphia, 15 December 1795, Mem. et doc., 9: 247–48vo.

It was easy to charge folly to the government's decision to open the Indies in the first place, or to ascribe what followed to the rapacity of American shipmasters. The consuls, however, put most of the blame on lax law enforcement. Some doubted the wisdom of the decision, and all showed impatience with American lawbreakers, but most of them had faith in the workability of tax and customs laws, provided there were officials willing to enforce them. If American interlopers made damaging inroads, it was because West Indies officials winked at the liberties they took, or followed slipshod procedures. This explanation, for which there was ample evidence, nevertheless spoke to a deeper and more disheartening truth: the islands could never, for long, shake off their dependence on the mainland for much-needed foodstuffs. Whether to feed a slave population too fully used in the growing of sugar to be diverted to food production, or to alleviate the periodic food shortages with which no number of France-based supply ships could cope, this need persisted.

Such need explains why the government in August 1784 opened ports in Martinique, Guadaloupe, and three ports in Saint Domingue to American ships bringing lumber, cod, dried fish, and other foodstuffs. A second decree in December added other fish products and naval stores.[3] American grain, significantly, did not appear on the list. Grain carriage from France touched on the livelihood of too many Frenchmen, farmers, seamen, and shippers, to be yielded to Americans — at least officially. Unofficially, island authorities exercised discretionary powers to admit American grain cargoes whenever shortages made it reasonable to do so.

Because importers expect to lade return cargoes, the two decrees permitted Americans to carry away rum, taffia (a rum of inferior quality), and, curiously, goods of French manufacture. The latter included such items, more likely to be of French than of West Indian manufacture, as arms, powder, paper, cartons, books, and jewelry. How Paris could realistically expect Americans to forgo loading cargoes of sugar and coffee testified only to its bureaucratic optimism. Like the omission of grain from the list of imports, sugar and coffee were omitted from a list of permissible exports. Indeed, the carriage of these two products was exclusively reserved to French bottoms, and France itself remained their only legal destination.[4]

Earlier that year, Vergennes had explored the merits of allowing a limited American traffic. Marbois had warned him not to expect reciprocal concessions; and La Luzerne's opinion, soon to arrive, cautioned against

---

[3]*Arrêts du Conseil d'Etat du Roi*, 30 August and 7 December 1784.
[4]Ibid.

outright prohibition of grain shipments. Not even the British had managed to suppress grain imports; the island peoples connived at it, surveillance was useless. Even to try would evoke "mutual complaints," and the traffic would continue through illicit channels.[5] The Foreign Minister, long aware of American success in smuggling, obviously shared these misgivings. The government, he replied, had not yet decided what might be yielded, but he at least saw the need to appease those Americans who had an interest in the Indies trade. Perhaps by making other concessions France could save for her own vessels the carriage of grain, but unless some concessions were forthcoming, he told La Luzerne, Americans would simply take over the Antilles trade, doubtless with the enthusiastic collusion of the island residents.[6]

Efforts to reserve for French subjects the islands' importing of grain and exporting of sugar and coffee were explicitly set forth. Legally, after 1784, the critical requirements were as follows: *only* French vessels were to supply the islands with grain, and *only* with French grain; and *only* they could take off cargoes of sugar and coffee, and *only* to French port destinations. Detecting violations of these requirements depended on vantage. The consuls, for example, had a clear view of miscarriages in the sugar and coffee trade because they could see the illicit cargoes being off-loaded. They could report less of the illegal grain trade because they had no way of knowing the destinations of outbound vessels carrying such cargoes. France, on the other hand, offered a better vantage for discerning the effects of the 1784 decrees on grain trafficking.

The principal effect, according to French grain merchants, was imminent ruination. Getting wind of the August decree before it was promulgated, more than a hundred Bordeaux businessmen warned Vergennes he was opening the way to an even greater American trade in contraband. "Once the American flag is admitted and recognized in our Colonies," they wrote, "it will be very difficult, even impossible, to prevent the subjects of the United States from pouring in all kinds of commodities. . . ." Hold the line, they begged, and crack down on Antilles officials well known for their laxity. American grain might be cheaper, but the prosperity of the entire Bordeaux region depended on retaining the island market for France.[7]

Within a year such predictions of disaster began to be fulfilled. From

[5]See Marbois to MMC (forwarded to MAE), No. 33, 3 June 1783, CC (Philadelphia), 945: 311vo; and La Luzerne to MAE, No. 376, Philadelphia, 4 May 1784, AECPE-U, 27: 335vo–37.
[6]Versailles, 15 February 1784, ibid., 134vo–35. For Vergennes' earlier concern, see his No. 29 to La Luzerne, Versailles, 23 March 1782, série B[7], doss. 460, doc. 46, ANF.
[7]"Mémoire des Négocians de Bordeaux," 1 April 1784, AECPE-U, 27: ff. 243vo, 244–47.

Dunkerque, in January 1785, came complaints of commercial stagnation and high unemployment among seamen and ship chandlers. From Brittany the Procurer General foresaw the certain ruin of local industry; and from Le Havre, intimations of "frightful consequences just beginning to be demonstrated."[8] Deputies from the maritime cities, when they bore their *cahiers de doléances* to the Estates General four years later, left no doubt that they believed the *ancien régime* guilty of pursuing grievously destructive trade policies in the Caribbean.[9]

French analysts later taking the measure of the 1784 decrees underscored the scope of failed intent. Not only did these measures fail to convince French grain and shipping interests that Paris had acted wisely; they also failed to appease American merchants who, some believed, would not have settled for anything short of complete free trade. Most significantly, however, they failed to stem the swelling flood of American-carried contraband. As Delaforest forecast when he published the decrees in Charleston the following spring, Americans would welcome the newly opened ports from which to enlarge their illegal transport of coffee and sugar to the United States. Nor did he need to remind Paris of what this would mean in terms of lost carriage, lost tax revenues, and lost specie.[10]

The consuls, though they felt helpless, fully understood how temptingly the Indies invited Americans into surreptitious exchanges. The islands needed cheap grain, the mainland offered good prices for sugar and coffee. Marbois, for one, had difficulty blaming either party for trying to profit from the other's need.[11] As for the profits from carriage, American shipowners definitely had the edge. Not only did they use cheaper-built vessels, but also they operated under less surveillance. American ships arriving in American ports brought sugar and coffee that was "contraband" only by French definition. That these cargoes had eluded French authorities at their Antillean point of departure caused no difficulty on arrival. American customs officers cared less that France deemed such cargoes "contraband" than that their owners paid the required import duties. Insofar as the contrabandists were Americans employing vessels of American registry, French consuls could do little but note their arrivals and report them to Paris.

---

[8]Chambre du Commerce de Picardy to Vergennes, Dunkerque, 25 January 1785, ibid., 29: 32–35vo; "Mémoire des Députés et du Procureur Général Sindic des Etats de Bretagne" to Vergennes, 27 July 1785, ibid., 30: 156–63vo; and "Mémoire des Négocians du Havre," (n.d.), ibid., f. 102vo.

[9]Godechot, "Les relations économiques," 25.

[10]To MMC, No. 5, 23 April 1785, CC (Charleston), 372: 102–102vo.

[11]To same, No. 42, 1 August 1783, CC (Philadelphia), 945: 359vo.

French shipowners, hoping to stay competitive, adapted as best they could to the post-1784 regime. Some bought the cheaper-built American vessels. Others, forgoing the trade lanes reserved exclusively for French-flag ships, switched to American registry, or even took out American citizenship in order to put themselves still further beyond French jurisdiction.[12] Those who continued to sail under French colors fell under consular surveillance and if caught importing French-grown sugar or coffee risked having their vessels confiscated. The certainty of punishment in such cases depended, of course, on a consul's being able to prove the cargo's French island origin, as well as on his ability to enlist the cooperation of American law enforcement officials. Still, the risk was great enough to avoid whenever possible. Consul D'Annemours put enough fear into French contrabandists to report that when they approached Baltimore, they waited for their friends on shore to signal whether they should enter the main harbor. If the signal warned them off, they landed their cargoes after nightfall in some out-of-the-way inlet. Efforts to force French captains into those ports where resident consuls could inspect their holds met with little success. Even so, French smugglers were put to inconveniences that their American counterparts were not. Struck by the disparity and considering how freely Americans came and went, Delaforest urged that Frenchmen caught in the act not be punished too harshly.[13]

How much of the incoming sugar and coffee came illicitly from the French islands the consuls could only guess. Few captains, French or American, they noted, would admit to a cargo's being of French origin. They usually claimed to have laded either in the British Indies or at one of the so-called "neutral islands."[14] Documentary evidence to the contrary was hard to come by. Sometimes American customs officials cooperated, sometimes not. A consul like Philippe Létombe who pursued such evidence relentlessly relied on paid informers. Using his authority to hire "agents," Létombe employed as lookouts native Americans well placed to have access to customs records. A militia officer in Newbury, a local judge in Providence, a port captain in Newport, and in Boston the customs director himself were all on his payroll. One of the things he paid them for was "to verify the declarations of French captains arriving from the

---

[12]See, for example, Létombe's year-end report for 1784, CC (Boston), 209: 383–83vo; Delaforest to MMC, No. 17, 7 October 1784, CC (Charleston), 372: 44–44vo; and Chateaufort to same, No. 12, Charleston, 12 September 1785, ibid., f. 141.

[13]See, respectively, D'Annemours to MMC, 3 July 1786, CC (Baltimore), Tome 1, 58vo; and Delaforest to same, No. 11, 24 July 1784, CC (Charleston), 372: 31–31vo.

[14]See, for example, Delaforest to MMC, No. 148, n.d., CC (New York), 909: 122–22vo; Oster to Moustier, "Questions Répondues," f. 214vo; and Létombe to MMC, "Mémoire des Affaires du Consulat de France à Boston pendant l'année 1788," CC (Boston), 210: 335–35vo.

islands under the French flag."[15] That Létombe felt it necessary to "verify" import statistics regularly published by the state governments testified to the belief, widespread among French observers, that the official figures were notoriously inaccurate. Knowing that fraud and even outright smuggling existed on a grand scale, the consuls put little trust in the official record. As Delaforest noted, "all declarations are more or less fraudulent." His colleagues agreed.[16]

As if smuggling and fraud were not damaging enough, the impenitent, even insolent, attitude Americans took toward these freewheeling enterprises left French officials spluttering between shock and admiration. Americans, Marbois explained, "have a horror of any kind of restriction." In their striving to break and enter the island trade, he wrote, "The authority of government, alliances, public welfare, good order, reputation count for nothing. . . . Smuggling is not a shameful crime; monopoly is, and he who enriches himself by breaching it is honored and applauded."[17] It was true, Louis Otto confirmed: Americans "look on our Colonies as a common treasury"; they possess "a profound knowledge of all sorts of interloping and a boldness to try them all. . . ." He doubted whether "the most piercing eye can penetrate all the various maneuvers in a traffic which is regarded in America as legitimate because it is held to justify the supposed rights of freedom of Commerce."[18]

Otto and Marbois made the same observation about Americans wanting trade, not possession. Thinking to underscore this point, Otto recounted an offer once jokingly made by Conrad Gérard. The former minister had reportedly told a president of the Continental Congress, "If you absolutely must have some sugar islands, we will give you one provided we can stay in quiet possession of the others. 'That is not what we need,' the American replied: 'we leave to you the honors of sovereignty without regret, we will be content with the commerce.' " That Americans would come as "hardened contrabandiers," not as conquerors, Marbois had long since decided, although he seemed not to realize that a successful commercial take-over was also a form of conquest. Moustier, too, saw no physical threat but thought it bad enough that in their mastery of smug-

---

[15]Ibid., ff. 330–31vo.

[16]To MMC, No. 11, 24 July 1784, CC (Charleston), 372: 30; also Chateaufort to same, No. 14, 21 May 1786, ibid., ff. 197–97vo; and Oster to same, No. 9, Williamsburg, 27 July 1785, CC (Norfolk), 927: 75–76.

[17]To MMC, No. 45, Philadelphia, 1 September 1783, série B^7, doss. 460, doc. 2, ANF; and later to MAE, No. 438, New York, 29 August 1785, AECPE-U, 30: 254.

[18]"Mémoire remis par le Sr. Otto," ff. 280, 283vo–84.

gling "these people are more enterprising and more intelligent than any other."[19]

Had the contraband trade lacked symmetry, it might have languished. As it was, the splendid profits to be had from smuggling out sugar and coffee were matched in urgency by the islands' need for foodstuffs. Periodic shortages made American grain carriers a welcome sight. Given the slightest color of legality, island authorities tended to wink complacently when the captains of American grain ships bid for return cargoes technically permitted only to French-flag carriers destined to French ports. Meanwhile, few would deny the islands' more or less continuous dependence on mainland grain except, of course, French grain suppliers who argued somewhat callously that the islands had managed to survive on French-grown grain before the days of American interlopers, and could do so again.[20] Most consuls would not have agreed. To them, the exchange of needed grain for profitable sugar was no more stoppable than the diurnal tides. Indeed, when food ran in short supply, the *colons* did not stand on ceremony waiting for American grain ships to arrive. At such times, as happened in the fall of 1784, an unnamed number of island vessels reportedly turned up in Charleston seeking cargoes of "wheat and rice." Once the need was known, Charleston merchants responded promptly. During the first four months of 1785, some twenty-one vessels flying the American colors headed out of Charleston loaded with food for Antilles ports.[21]

Official records, fragmentary and seldom accurate, make it difficult to know how much American grain the French islands actually absorbed. Also, as Delaforest pointed out, the islands' need for foodstuffs varied from year to year. Still, the available records suggest grain exports on a grand scale, and the figures themselves can be assumed to be fairly accurate. That is, shipmasters departing American ports had less reason to falsify their cargoes than did those arriving with dutiable items which they hoped to land at greater profit by "under-declaring" their value. Export statistics, therefore, were more reliable than import statistics, and consuls could forward them to Paris with reasonable assurance of their accuracy. For the larger port cities at least, export activity was measurable. Saint-John de Crèvecoeur, for example, drew up a "tableau" for New York

[19]See, respectively, Otto to MAE, No. 30, New York, 6 June 1790, AECPE-U, 35: 107vo; Marbois to same, No. 437, New York, 28 August 1785, ibid., 30: 252vo; and Moustier to same, New York, 14 February 1788, ibid., 33: 37vo.

[20]See "Mémoire des Négocians de Bordeaux," AECPE-U, 27: ff. 242–47, and a similar complaint from the Chamber of Commerce of Picardy, ibid., 29: ff. 32–35vo.

[21]Delaforest to MMC, Nos. 17 and 5, 7 October 1784, and 23 April 1785, CC (Charleston), 372: ff. 44 and 103, respectively.

that totted up all the city's *entrés* and *sorties* for the five years, 1784–88. While he did not specify the nature of outgoing cargoes — he had no way of knowing how many were of grain — New York's repute as an export center for grain (and other foodstuffs) suggests a booming trade in such commodities from the sheer number of vessels officially cleared for French Antilles ports: 188 in all, over that five years. By contrast, vessels clearing for ports in the British islands numbered 309. This, however, was a traffic reserved to British-flag carriers, whereas nearly all ships leaving for the French islands were of American registry. Had French carriers been permitted to engage in the sort of triangular trade open to the British, the picture might have been different. But because the French islands were supposed to be supplied only with French-grown grain, French vessels missed out on such profitable circuits as from, say, Bordeaux to New York to Cap Français. Thus, not only did the French West Indies absorb a large quantity of American foodstuffs, including forbidden American grain, but they also received it from the hands of American merchants who pocketed the profits from sales and carriage.[22]

Grain shortages hurt most whenever France herself had a poor harvest. Foreseeing a shortfall of exportable grain in 1789, Paris took the unusual step of opening the island ports to the "free importation of flours and biscuits." American suppliers learned of their opportunity in late November. Now unvexed by the flimsiest of restrictions, they lost no time dispatching cargoes. The results were startling. By mid-February, Otto reported the islands so fully provisioned that they were re-exporting grain to Europe. He added, ironically, that just as American merchants had earlier grumbled about the restrictions, now they complained about the price-depressing effects of the glut.[23]

Besides a poor harvest in France, the turn of the decade foreshadowed two other developments soon to deepen the islands' dependence on American foodstuffs. The first was the possibility of war in Europe over the Nootka Sound affair, the other a flaring of civil disturbances in the islands themselves. Though the Nootka crisis loomed unexpectedly from a British challenge to Spain's exclusive claims in the Pacific Northwest, had war come in 1790 France could scarcely have left Spain to fight alone. In that event, France's Caribbean possessions would have risked the twin perils of conquest and starvation. While the crisis still brewed, Antoine

---

[22]For Crèvecoeur's "tableau," enclosed to MMC, No. 10, 29 December 1788, see CC (New York), 910: 83vo–94.

[23]To MAE, No. 18, Philadelphia, 15 February 1790, AECPE-U, 35: 53; Létombe also reported the surfeit, to MMC, No. 4, 19 May 1790, CC (Boston), 210: 401–401vo.

Delaforest set himself the task of reassuring Paris that the islands would be well fed because Americans were both able and eager to cash in on the profits of wartime carriage. Then he voiced a truism that many begrudged: that "the majority of the Antilles have to depend on them [the United States] for subsistence, in peacetime and even more in time of war." Unless Britain seized American port cities, he wrote, American supply ships, sailing singly, never in capturable groups, would stream forth to feed the islands. Nor had he any doubt, he added, little knowing how fully his prediction would be borne out when war did come in 1793, "that England, France, and Spain will all admit them."[24] For France the walls tumbled resoundingly when the National Convention voted on 19 February 1793 to open "all the ports of the French colonies . . . to the vessels of the United States."[25] Meanwhile, the Nootka crisis sounded a warning of vulnerability.

If the prospect of war had left any doubt as to the islands' dependence on mainland food supplies, those doubts were already being blown away by the revolutionary winds that began, as early as 1790, to break the islands' heavily race-structured social entity into warring factions. First to give way was any semblance of law enforcement respecting contraband. The "confusion" in Saint Domingue, as Otto called it, broke through all trade restrictions. "All the goods of the United States are admitted there," he wrote, "and I have reason to believe that colonial goods are being exported from there with the same facility."[26] Then came a series of acute food shortages. When the new French minister Jean de Ternant arrived in mid-1791, he found himself almost wholly taken up, not with preserving some share of the grain trade for French carriers but with laying his hands on enough money to buy and ship the American grain that would save the strife-torn islands from imminent starvation.[27] War with maritime Britain, when it came in 1793, merely put a seal on the fact of dependence. American foodstuffs—no matter how sorely it troubled Frenchmen to admit it—figured critically thereafter as a matter of life and

---

[24]To MMC, No. 311, New York, 2 November 1790, in Dépêches des consuls aux Ministre de la Marine, puis des Relations Extérieures, 1790–1813, AECPE-U, 5: première série (supplément), 12–21.

[25]"Loi relative aux Denrées exportées ou importées par les vaisseaux américains dans les Colonies ou en France," Lois et Actes du Gouvernement (Paris 1806) 6: 424.

[26]To MAE, No. 39, New York, 28 September 1790, AECPE-U, 35: 179.

[27]Beginning with his dispatch to MAE, No. 16, 17 November 1791, Ternant's preoccupation with provisioning Saint Domingue dominates his official correspondence. See CFM, 72–200, passim.

death to the island peoples and, moreover, gave vital sustenance to France's military operations in the Caribbean.[28]

Not surprisingly, French officials often dwelt on the possibility of replacing the United States as a food provisioner with some other nearby source. Louisiana came frequently to mind. Spain's Mississippi holding, once French and still possessed of a sizable French-speaking population, conjured up bright visions that if it could be recovered, the islands might be relieved of their dependence on foodstuffs from Anglo-America. Although serious diplomacy aimed at "retrocession" would await the mid-1790s, the seed of the idea took root in the preceding decade. Moustier is generally credited with having planted it. In a long memorandum dated January 1789, the count projected the advantages, political as well as economic, France might derive from recovering her lost colony. Not the least of these, he noted, would be to make Louisiana the breadbasket of the Antilles.[29] Some years later, Joseph Fauchet lamented the neglect the *ancien régime* had shown toward Moustier's trenchant arguments. Like his predecessor, Fauchet underscored the political as well as the economic leverage such a "continental establishment" would place in the hands of a highly motivated French government. For France to be positioned at the mouth of the Mississippi, he wrote, "would allow us to compete with and contain American power at the same time it would diminish the dependence of our insular possessions on [Americans] for provisioning them."[30] In the 1780s, retrocession remained an idea whose time had not yet come, but already whenever Frenchmen spoke of France's destiny in the New World, their ruminations turned instinctively to those other Frenchmen, ostensibly pining in the wilds of Louisiana to see the French colors flying once more over New Orleans. Even Talleyrand despondently enduring his American exile could joke with his bookseller friend, Moreau de St. Méry, that one day they would move to Louisiana and become its governors.[31] Little did he know the part that he and Barbé-Marbois would later play when Bonaparte put his mind and muscle to the project. Until then, beyond the pipe-dream stood the humiliating reality of French islands fed from the holds of American supply ships.

---

[28]See, for example, General Rochambeau's bleak assessment of 8 June 1794, to the Conseil Exécutif, série BB 7/9, Archives de la Marine (Château de Vincennes).

[29]E. Wilson Lyon, ed., "Moustier's Mémoire on Louisiana," *Mississippi Valley Historical Review* 22 (1935) 251–66.

[30]"Mémoire sur les Etats Unis d'Amérique," 20 March 1796, AF III, carton 64, doss. 260, ANF, published in *The Annual Report of the American Historical Association for the Year 1936* (Washington 1938) (hereafter cited as "Mémoire [1796]) 119.

[31]Kenneth and Anna M. Roberts, *Moreau de St. Méry's American Journey, 1793–1798* (Garden City, N.Y. 1947) 215–16.

Need explained the contraband trade in grain. Greed explained that in sugar and coffee. French perceptions differed accordingly. American grain ships penetrating Antilles ports could be viewed as satisfying a hunger, literally, that in time of shortage bespoke a humanitarian interest outweighing the interests of grain merchants who calculated lost freight charges in Bordeaux or Marseille. Considering the stakes in human terms, Frenchmen closest to the scene tended to look with indulgence on island authorities who admitted American grain ships. They might cavil at a mother country's not being quite able to feed her island dependencies, and resent the Americans who could, but they seemed to recognize necessity as the true mother of contravention.

Island sugar and coffee illicitly outbound for the United States, however, called forth quite different emotions, especially when it appeared that, quantitatively, these commodities so far exceeded Americans' domestic needs as to become part of a thriving and profitable American re-export trade to European markets. As already noted, French officials ranged from expressions of irritation to impatience, even awe, at the way these "hardened contrabandiers" stole profits from French carriers and tax revenues from the French treasury. Also worth examining for what it revealed of their frustration is the question of how the smugglers operated. What, precisely, were the wiles and deceptions practiced by these lawbreakers that led Moustier to describe them as "more enterprising and more intelligent than any other"?

Philippe Létombe made an important distinction when he observed that cargoes leaving American ports "are the secret of the merchant."[32] Not so, incoming cargoes. Except as falsified to evade duties, the nature, value, and volume of imported goods were public knowledge, formally declared to American customs officers when they were offloaded. At this juncture, procedural differences acted to obscure the extent of contraband. Captains of American vessels needed only to report to American customs houses, whereas captains of French vessels were supposed to report to French consuls as well. Consuls began to lose count when faced with what might be called the "double flag" deception. This occurred when shipmasters found it expedient to present French "papers" when calling at an Antilles port, and to show evidence of American registry when they returned. From Philadelphia Consul General Barbé-Marbois noted the "double flag" phenomenon as early as mid-1783.[33] Within a year, French consuls in every port city had remarked on its prevalence as a device for smuggling contraband.

---

[32]To MMC, "Mémoire des Affaires du Consulat de France à Boston pendant l'Année 1787," 20 April 1788, CC (Boston), 210: 265.
[33]To same, No. 37, 10 July 1783, CC (Philadelphia), 945: 321vo.

From Boston Létombe asked the Navy minister, not altogether rhetorically, what he should do. New England ships arrived daily from the French islands with sugar and coffee. The high volume of traffic caused him to suspect that Paris might have relaxed its restrictions on island exports. If so, he thought it best to keep silent. A year later, with copies of the 1784 decrees in hand, he vowed his vice consulates would do all they could to intercept illicit cargoes, but exclaimed helplessly that he could not act against American captains who imported sugar and coffee in their own vessels. Even French vessels evaded his authority. At the height of Shays's Rebellion (which he reported with some anxiety), French captains masquerading with American papers, he wrote, put into New England ports every day. At that moment, two French vessels lay at anchor in Boston harbor, "loaded with molasses, rum, sugar, and coffee. Contraband is daily in my department. The majority of French vessels which arrive here have two captains, two flags, two crew rosters, and almost all their crew is American."[34]

Early in 1786 from his post in New York Antoine Delaforest thought he detected a slackening in the "double flag" abuse. He rejoiced that Antilles officials now took more pains to prevent illicit cargoes from escaping. The results were being felt. He offered in proof that three New York newspapers had become "very violent against us." It helped, too, he thought, that authorities in the British islands had also cracked down on vessels displaying two sets of papers. As acting head of the consular establishment, Delaforest was doubtless tempted to grasp eagerly at any sign of better law enforcement. By year's end, however, he had to admit that his optimism had been premature. With more evidence of continuing leakage, he returned to criticizing the island authorities for their negligence. Until French admiralty officers made it more difficult for smugglers to clear Antilles ports for any other port of their choosing, he wrote, the illegal traffic would persist. Requiring outbound captains to post bond against arrival at their avowed destination, he felt, might be sufficient deterrent. In any event, the "double papers" practice must be attacked where it was most used to deceive—in the islands themselves.[35]

Evidence of contraband entering Baltimore was sketchy. Moustier later judged the French consul there to be one of the least attentive to consular business. The Chevalier D'Annemours probably deserved that

---

[34]See his 1783 year-end report to MMC, February 1784, and to same, No. 2, 27 March 1785, CC (Boston), 209: 292vo and 386vo, respectively; and to same, No. 17, 2 December 1786, ibid., 210: 84vo.

[35]To MMC, Nos. 148 and 187, 2 March and 31 December 1786, CC (New York), 909: 123 and 227vo–28, respectively.

judgment. Not until three years after it first appeared did D'Annemours get around to giving the Navy a detailed description of the "double flag" phenomenon. By this time he, like Delaforest, thought it was in decline. Still, he reported, single vessels in a single voyage had been known to conduct illicit trade under as many as three flags. He said they "usually" sailed from New Orleans under Spanish colors, circulated through the French islands under French colors, and ended up bringing contraband to an American port under American colors. D'Annemours's account sounded faintly as if he had received it second hand. At least, no other consul described such a pattern as being "usual." Typically, contraband ships made their runs directly from and to American ports. One has to assume that either Baltimore received so little French sugar as to be unremarkable, or D'Annemours was too preoccupied with what Moustier suspected were his private business ventures to have paid much attention.[36]

The real experts in deceit were the three consuls who served in Charleston during the 1780s: Delaforest before he was transferred to New York, Avistay de Chateaufort, and Jean-Baptiste Petry. Charleston because it lay so close to the islands witnessed nearly every variation on how to smuggle.

About the same time Létombe discovered the "double flag" deception in Boston, Delaforest was describing its appearance in Charleston. Shipmasters, he wrote, secretly acquired both French and American papers to use in French and American ports as best served their ends. He gave as a classic example a Frenchman, resident in Charleston, who having bought an American-built vessel, had no difficulty getting American registry for it, then sailed to Cap Français where because he was a Frenchman easily obtained French registry as well. After clearing a cargo of sugar, ostensibly for a legal French port destination, he turned up in Charleston, presented his American papers and thus eluded Delaforest's authority altogether.[37]

Charleston in Chateaufort's day (1785–86) saw no slackening of the "double flag" evasion, nor did the consul foresee an end to it until island officials were made to realize that only they could nip it. Clearly, American officials took no interest in where cargoes originated, and he in his consular capacity had little authority over Frenchmen, none over Americans, whose ships' papers met American customs requirements. Chateau-

---

[36]Cf., D'Annemours to MMC, 3 July 1786, CC (Baltimore), Tome 1, 58–59vo; Moustier, "Distributions des Consulats," f. 188.

[37]To MMC, Nos. 11 and 17, 24 July and 7 October 1784, CC (Charleston), 372: 31–31vo and 44vo, respectively.

fort chafed irritably at how completely powerless he was to cope with blatant and widespread offenses. The illegalities "occur so openly here," he wrote, "that it would be impossible for a consul to be unaware of them." One Charleston shipowner, a Frenchman named Sasportas, he found particularly offensive. Sasportas flagrantly operated two vessels "which are alternately French or American." Deeply frustrated, Chateaufort could think of no other way to punish the man than not to invite him to the next meeting of the city's French business community.[38]

If by 1786 Antilles authorities had begun to curb the "double flag" practice, their limited success may explain the new mode of smuggling that Jean-Baptiste Petry began to report later in the decade. This stratagem might be labeled "the false destination." Characteristically, the carrier, either French or American, circumvented the ban on exporting sugar and coffee to an American port by its captain's declaring the cargo to be destined from one French island to another. When, instead, the vessel arrived in Charleston, the captain, if he were French, evaded consular authority by claiming his ship to be of American registry (American port officials scarcely cared), fortifying the deceit by changing the vessel's name. Thus, wrote Petry, the *Victoire* became the *Franklin*, and the *Lucille* metamorphosed into the *Washington*.[39] Even more devious were French shipmasters who combined "false destination" with "false origin." Because French-flag vessels violated no precept of royal decree by carrying sugar from a non-French source, Petry suspected that many of them touched at one of the so-called "neutral" islands in order to hide the fact that their cargo was of French Antilles origin. Thus, for example, a French captain might falsify Bordeaux as his destination in order to secure clearance for a cargo of sugar from Martinique, then put in at the Dutch island of St. Eustacia long enough to get documents which falsified that island as the cargo's place of origin. When these captains subsequently requested Petry to furnish them with passports, ostensibly to return to one of these "neutral" islands, he was certain they intended to sail directly to the French island from whence they had come. "After which," he asked, "is it possible to know the exact state of commerce?"[40]

Although most smugglers favored carrying two sets of "papers" as the simplest way of spiriting illicit cargoes from French to American ports, some Frenchmen who dealt in contraband found themselves at a

---

[38]To MMC, No. 12, Charleston, 12 September 1785, ibid., f. 142.

[39]To same, No. 5, 29 March 1789, ibid., ff. 342–43; see also Petry to MAE, No. 69, 1 September 1789, ibid., ff. 365vo–66.

[40]Ibid., f. 366; see also Létombe's year-end report for 1788, n.d., CC (Boston), 210: 335–35vo.

disadvantage when they were unable to secure American registry. For these, the "stress of weather" pretext became an alternate form of deception. In such instances, contraband goods entered American ports on board French vessels ostensibly crippled by storms en route to France and forced to make a landfall, usually at Charleston or Wilmington. Anything from torn canvas to smashed rudders, parted rigging, or provable leaks could gain them "legal" entry under the recognized exigencies of *"relâches forcées."* Lacking the American "papers" that would shield them from consular inquiry, they chose a southern port near enough to regular shipping lanes to make the pretext credible. Many a French captain sold cargoes of sugar and coffee in Charleston to pay for "repairs." Barbé-Marbois first noticed large numbers of unseaworthy French carriers in late 1783. Vessels from the Antilles, he wrote, pleading stress of weather, were landing forbidden cargoes in southern ports and carrying back rice. A year later Delaforest confirmed the phenomenon in Charleston.[41] By mid-1785, Chateaufort was able to give detailed descriptions of the deception, now widely practiced. Captains and crews of French vessels limping into Charleston typically presented him with sworn statements testifying to storm damage. The captains then sold more than enough sugar and coffee to pay for repairs. Exactly what quantity of forbidden imports they disposed of, he could not be sure. They often told Charleston customs officials they were selling salt, not sugar, to avoid paying the higher import duties. Nonetheless, Chateaufort put more trust in customs declarations than in his own rough guesses. Port officials who inspected cargoes at first hand, he explained, were less likely to be deceived. He also expressed a muted note of compassion for French smugglers who pleaded "stress of weather." The "double flag" deceit, he thought, gave much more latitude to those bent on violating the 1784 decrees. Americans who took out dual registry and those Frenchmen who emulated them ran smoother and more profitable operations.[42]

Because the 1784 decrees permitted American carriers to enter at least some of the island ports, the principal concern of officials in the Antilles was to prevent them from making off with sugar and coffee. If a captain showed French registry and managed to persuade them that his outbound destination was a French port, he could get away with relative ease. Not

---

[41]Cf., Marbois to MMC, No. 46 (23 September 1783), as summarized in "Supplément au précis remis à Fontainebleau de toutes les dépêches d'Amérique concernant le commerce des Etats Unis avec nos Colonies et avec le Royaume," série B^7, doss. 460, doc. 1, ANF; Delaforest to same, No. 17, 7 October 1784, CC (Charleston), 372: 44.

[42]To MMC, Nos. 4 and 14, 16 July 1785, and 21 May 1786, ibid., ff. 129–30 and 197–98, respectively.

all port authorities, however, could be gulled. Circumvention sometimes became a shell game of sorts. American carriers often arrived bringing empty barrels, and left with them. Once offshore, they would lie-to while small boats brought out sugar to fill the barrels for the voyage home. Létombe, though he knew no sovereign remedy for this sort of chicane, believed it to be widespread and recommended last-minute inspections of the holds of departing vessels. To make sure that casks and barrels contained what they were supposed to, Delaforest urged officials to weigh them.[43] The consuls, for their part, rarely saw evidence that their suggestions, these or any others, were ever taken to heart. Indeed, despite the care with which they watched and tried to prevent it, the traffic in Antillean contraband flourished and grew without serious interruption throughout the 1780s.

Ministers and consuls often suggested to Paris various ways France might respond to the contraband problem. Their suggestions illustrated, at least, how formidable the difficulties inherent in trying to pit the forces of government against the inexorable interplay of supply, demand, profit, and convenience. Many who talked of remedies thought the disease incurable. Others believed in the remedies but doubted the ability of government to apply them. All who made suggestions, whether they hoped for a cure or not, conveyed to Paris an increasingly jaundiced view of Americans who fed parasitically off France's colonial empire and invited renegade Frenchmen to follow their example.

Consular prescriptions fell into several broad categories. Most important, they all agreed, was to tighten the export controls at the island end of the traffic. On this score, consuls tended to be free with advice. Some merely found fault with the laxness of island authorities; others eagerly proposed tightening the existing procedures and volunteered to cooperate more fully. Still others, like Marbois and Moustier, envisioned structural changes: a measured yielding to economic forces, a relaxation of certain restrictions, coupled, however, with taxes, licenses, and other safeguards designed to retain for France her essential stake. Finally, nearly all French officials in America looked fervently to the day when the consular convention, so long under negotiation, would expand their powers to the point where they could deal summarily, at least with those smugglers who were Frenchmen.

With a certain degree of smugness the consuls placed most of the

---

[43]Cf., Létombe to MMC, No. 2, 27 March 1785, CC (Boston), 209: 396vo–97; Delaforest to same, No. 187, 31 December 1786, CC (New York), 909: 227.

blame on the shoulders of the island port authorities. Whether from slackness, indifference, perhaps even connivance, they believed, the latter appeared not to be doing all they should or could to prevent illicit cargoes from escaping their jurisdictions. To be sure, such cargoes escaped from both ends of the traffic, but the contrast in authority to stop it gave the consuls a feeling of moral superiority. They, after all, could do nothing on American soil to prevent grain ships from leaving American ports, but surely French officials having full authority over the island end of the shipping lanes could stop sugar and coffee from departing.

Most proposals for better law enforcement smacked of a bureaucratic faith in better record-keeping. Not surprisingly, men who spent their careers certifying to the truth of the written word clung to the belief that fuller documentation would rout those who transgressed by lying. To the extent that contraband was a tripartite problem, the consuls had "paper" solutions for each part. If, for example, every shipmaster arriving at an island port were required to show a consular "passport" certifying his vessel's registry as either French or American, the problem would be one-third solved. Certain as to the ship's true registry, island officials would know not to clear the vessel for return to an American port if she were French, or to a French port if she were American. As it turned out, requiring Indies-bound vessels to have consular "passports" proved to be one of the few consular proposals the Navy Ministry saw fit to act upon. As a check to contraband, however, it was incomplete.

A second part of the problem arose from the failure of enough French-flag vessels to arrive yearly from France to meet the islands' need for carriers. Because only vessels of French registry could legally lade sugar and coffee, when too few showed up to take the island crops to market, officials did not inquire too closely of others who offered to fill the need. Newly arrived captains who asked to be furnished with French registry usually were not turned away. As long as growers needed transport and carriers came from the mainland to oblige them, these officials continued to wink at shipmasters who acquired two sets of papers, not caring whether the sugar they laded sailed to Bordeaux or Baltimore.

Such laxity persisted, Delaforest thought, partly because there was no law against using two registries. This explained why the island governments "had no interest at all in pursuing" those who used French registry to lade illicit cargoes and American registry to land them. Not all consuls voiced such fatalism, however. What island officials so negligently permitted Martin Oster thought might be curbed by taking remedial action at the American end. He proposed that Frenchmen who bought American vessels, if they wanted French registry, be required to seek it immediately from the nearest French consul, and then be required to sail the vessel directly to France. As for disciplining Americans, Oster hoped that the state governments might be encouraged to follow the example of North Carolina which had enacted legislation to confiscate any vessel apprehended with two sets of papers. The idea of the states taking a firmer hand came also from Jean-Baptiste Petry. Earlier, from Charleston, Petry had ventured the possibility that Congress might be pressed at least to "recommend" to the states that they emulate North Carolina's crackdown. Nor would it be amiss, he added, if officials in the Indies also confiscated vessels operating under double registry. Unfortunately, only North Carolina saw fit to act against the double-flag abuse; and the long-awaited consular convention, when it issued in final form, in no way authorized consuls to register and send to France American carriers purchased by French citizens within their jurisdictions. Thus, for want of counter-measures, the "double flag" deception continued to facilitate the swift and massive trade in contraband.[44]

To resolve the first part of the problem, then, meant making sure that a vessel possessed only one registry when it left an American port; second, to ascertain whether it still possessed only one registry when it returned. Coping with "false origin" constituted a third part of the problem. Here, what the consuls most needed was a sure means to detect the illegal (i.e., French) origins of sugar and coffee which incoming captains claimed to have brought from one of the "neutral" islands. Although the consuls found it nearly impossible to come by proof, one way or the other, they repeatedly voiced the hope that a more scrupulous attention to paperwork—at both ends—might document at least one certainty: that cargoes laded in the French islands were, in fact, the same that arrived in the United States. Requiring bond seemed most likely to accomplish this end. Delaforest, especially, urged Paris to consider whether shipmasters, before they cleared an Indies port, ought to be required to post bond recoverable on arrival at their declared port of destination. That island officials did not, generally, require bond doubtless spoke to the islands' urgent need for American carriers and to a reluctance to discourage their comings and goings. Moreover, the few references to bond having been required suggest that a determined smuggler could readily evade its intent.[45]

---

[44]See, respectively, Delaforest to MMC, No. 136, 6 January 1786, ibid., f. 93; Oster's "Articles à soumettre à l'Examen de Monsieur le Comte de Moustier," enclosed in his No. 60 to Moustier, 18 October 1788, CC (Norfolk), 927: 177; and Petry to MMC, No. 11, Newbern, N.C., 18 January 1786, CC (Wilmington), Tome 1, 15vo–16.

[45]Delaforest to MMC, No. 187, 31 December 1786, CC (New York), 909: 227vo. One of the few references to bonding having been required appears in Ducher to MMC, No. 32, 27 March 1789, CC (Wilmington), Tome 1, 59vo–60.

Beginning in 1786, the consuls had thrust into their hands the device known as the "consular passport" — the only major innovation in enforcement procedures to be tried throughout the decade. Passports thereafter became the principal weapon, albeit a weak one, in the consular establishment's never-ending battle against deception. Quite possibly, it was the Charleston consul, Avistay de Chateaufort, who could claim credit. Writing in September, 1785 to Navy Minister Maréchal de Castries, Chateaufort said he saw no end to the fraudulent traffic conducted under *"doubles pavillons et doubles papiers"* unless both he and officials in the Indies kept a more systematic watch on ship movements. French consuls on the mainland, he wrote, must establish a "regular correspondence" with officials at Cap Français. Specifically, no vessel, French or American, should be admitted to a French island port unless its captain bore a consular passport verifying the ship's registry as being either French or American. On return voyage, incoming shipmasters should bring letters from the islands certifying the nature of their cargoes.[46]

Up to this time, perhaps not wanting to criticize their island counterparts from whom the abuse flowed, consuls had been reticent to propose ways to stop the double-flag practice. Létombe, describing the phenomenon in his year-end report for 1784, thought the solution would require a subtlety of legislative enactment that he would not presume to suggest. Delaforest, too, deferred to Paris as an authority that would know better than he what to do about such "abuses."[47] Chateaufort's explicit proposal, then, may have been what the Ministry, long aware of the problem, had been waiting for. In any event, de Castries issued orders on 31 March 1786 that passports be instituted, and that both mainland and island officials correspond regularly on cargoes and registries.[48]

Flaws in the passport system surfaced almost immediately. Chateaufort's own experience typified its shortcomings. Though pleased that de Castries had acted on his proposal, the Charleston consul related a disappointing sequel. On the positive side, the passport requirement had forced an increasing number of Indies-bound shipmasters to make an unequivocal choice between claiming French or American registry. Most opted for French registry because it facilitated their lading of sugar and coffee once they arrived. In the past, American registry had been principally useful when, on their return to Charleston, they used it to evade

---

[46]No. 12, 12 September 1785, CC (Charleston), 372: 141vo.

[47]Cf., Létombe's year-end report, CC (Boston), 209: 386; and Delaforest to MMC, No. 17, 7 October 1784, CC (Charleston), 372: 44vo.

[48]Chateaufort reported having had de Castries's orders published in Charleston newspapers in his No. 23, 20 June 1786, ibid., f. 206.

the authority of the French consul. Now, when they returned, they increasingly claimed to have shipped their cargoes of sugar and coffee from a "neutral" island, and thereby, if not evading the consul's attention, at least came before him with ostensibly clean hands. Indeed, requiring passports had as its major consequence to shift the mode of deception: from double registry to false declarations of neutral origin. Moreover, captains who claimed such origin brought back none of the confirmatory documents that French island officials were supposed to endow them with. Chateaufort noted uncomfortably that he was more certain his passports arrived at their destinations than he was of getting back papers that clarified what transactions had taken place in the interim.[49]

Finding a reliable means of communication proved to be a problem in itself. Antoine Delaforest, who anticipated the passport system by several months, discovered how vexing it was to try to run a documentary check on vessels plying between the islands and New York. "I experience the greatest difficulty," he wrote, because ". . . the lines of communication are more generally established through American vessels. They refuse to take our letters, or they destroy them." He had begged administrators in Martinique, Saint Domingue, and Guadaloupe to send him the address of "a correspondent who would not be suspect," so that he could write in secrecy. He doubted, however, that even secure channels of communication would produce proofs of fraud sufficient to apprehend individual smugglers. The "fraudeur," he wrote, "will escape prosecution by never returning to the same Antilles port more than once under the same name."[50]

Question also remained as to how seriously American captains regarded the consular passport as a requisite to entry. That Létombe in 1786 found it necessary to warn Boston shipmasters, repeatedly, not to sail without a passport suggests that some relied instead on the well-known laxity of island officials to assure a welcome at the other end. Even so, Létombe proudly announced having issued fifty-seven such documents to American vessels during a six-month period in 1788, an increase of twenty-two over the comparable period of the preceding year. He added ruefully, however, that he had uncovered statistical discrepancies that showed it was "very easy for Americans to make false declarations in our colonies."[51]

---

[49]Ibid.

[50]To MMC, No. 136, 6 January 1786, CC (New York), 909: 93.

[51]See his Nos. 17 and 9, 2 December 1786, and 10 October 1788, CC (Boston), 210: 84vo and 316–17, respectively. Delaforest two years later recounted his struggle to make the passport system effective, in his "Raport demandé par M. le Comte de Moustier," enclosed in No. 255 to Moustier, March 1788, CC (New York), 910: 30.

Passport controls moved toward complete collapse during the food shortage of 1789 in the islands. With the islands desperately in need of American grain—and the prohibition temporarily lifted—Petry reported from Charleston that grain ships were being held up because some of the ports of Georgia and the Carolinas from which they were ready to sail had no resident consular official empowered to issue passports. He was improvising to assure their departure, he wrote, but the message was plain: no Indies port would likely turn away a grain carrier simply because it lacked papers from consuls on the mainland.[52] What remained of the passport system soon vanished entirely amid the exigencies of revolution at home, and in the islands as well.

As the battle against contraband lengthened without perceptibly staunching its flow, some of the king's officials began to speculate on what profitable corners of the traffic France might retain were she to alter the patterns of her Antillean trade to accommodate some of the more insistent forces of supply and demand. Proposals in this vein were risky, sure to be rejected, if they hinted at any further concessions. Officials who dared suggest any yielding to economic imperatives took care to wrap their suggestions in assurances that it was only France's self-interest they had in view. For one thing, they understood the tenacious hold exerted by the central precept of mercantilist theory: that a closed commercial system was always better than an open one. They knew, too, the misgivings already aroused by the violence done to that precept by the royal decrees of 1784. There could be no turning back, however, because the islands had to be fed, and only the Americans could assure a steady supply of food. Still, they could argue, if the concessions of 1784 had solved the supply problem, perhaps they had not been imaginative enough to realize France's full potential for exploiting a complicated trade pattern.

Obvious differences in station made ministers and chargés, rather than consuls, more frequently the proponents of structural change. The latter doubtless found it safer to uphold the laws that came to them than to brace Paris with proposals that might be deemed presumptuous. From the upper reaches of the hierarchy, however, suggestions flowed freely enough but unevenly, depending on circumstance and personality. La Luzerne, for example, by mid-1784 had more interest in securing his own recall than in shaping a contraband-proof commercial system. Moreover, from what he knew of American smugglers, the wartime minister tended to view almost any restraint as being either unenforceable or likely

---

[52]To MMC, No. 5, 29 March 1789, CC (Charleston), 372: 341–41vo.

to provoke serious controversy.[53] The self-confident Barbé-Marbois, as consul general and later as chargé d'affaires, thought differently. To Marbois, the pattern of smuggling suggested several ways of turning a profit for France, and he told how this might be accomplished. Louis Otto, who succeeded Marbois as chargé, remained curiously indifferent to innovation. Knowledgeable but not bold, and more narrowly watchful of politics than of commerce, Otto seemed content to try to hold the lines set down by the 1784 decrees. Remarkably, it was the Comte de Moustier, whom historians often dismiss as a fussy, overly punctilious cipher, who ultimately produced the only full-scale blueprint for rethinking the opportunities still open to France in the Caribbean.

Marbois, who had a good bureaucrat's finely honed instinct for new sources of revenue, seemed drawn to the idea that what government could not prevent it should at least tax. This was the expedient he proposed in 1783 when no fewer than seven French vessels, all cleared from France for ports in the Indies, turned up instead in Philadelphia. Their captains in each instance pleaded either adverse winds or storm damage to explain their arrivals. The cargoes they requested to sell off, he noted wryly, were of the type obviously never intended for the island market. For reasons of profit, these captains had laded goods for American as well as Indies buyers, and would doubtless proceed to their originally authorized destinations with whatever additional cargoes they could pick up in Philadelphia. In short, French shipmasters, like so many before them—and Americans, still—had discovered more profit to be taken from a triangular trade than from a linear one. Not unsympathetic, and pointing to the American example, Marbois urged Paris to accord French carriers the same degree of latitude. He voiced confidence that, once the temptation to fraud had been removed, the French government could devise taxes and draw revenues from its leniency. On the matter of revenues, Marbois spelled out the opportunities even more explicitly with respect to incoming West Indies contraband. Rather than try to dam the leakage of French sugar and coffee to the United States, he counseled his masters in Paris to bless that traffic with an export tax levied at the island source.[54]

How much Moustier owed to Marbois for his thought on commercial rejuvenation can only be inferred. Although nearly three years separated their respective tours of duty, Marbois had left behind a written record in the copies of his dispatches, and Moustier said that he had read them. The Count also worked closely with Antoine Delaforest who, having served

[53]To MAE, No. 376, Philadelphia, 4 May 1784, AECPE-U, 27: 335vo–37.
[54]To MMC, Nos. 39 and 42, 24 July and 1 August 1783, CC (Philadelphia), 945: 335–38 and 359vo, respectively; and to same, No. 44, 26 August 1783, série B⁷, doss. 460, doc. 3, ANF.

both men, may have been the filter through which Marbois's suggestions became Moustier's roundly pronounced recommendations. Nor, after all, was it unlikely that Moustier should reach similar conclusions from personal observation. By whatever process, Marbois's idea of opening the Indies more fully to imports and exports heretofore restricted was reborn in Moustier's lengthy memorandum.[55]

Although he focused primarily on ways to stimulate trade in the Atlantic, Moustier did not neglect changes he believed would also profit France in the Indies corridor. Two of his proposals took dead aim at the most central—and therefore most troublesome—purposes of the 1784 dispensation: the twin efforts to regulate the islands' imports of grain and to control their exports of sugar and coffee. Moreover, in their explicitness, Moustier's proposals bespoke a particular soreness at Americans for having battened on the carrying trade. Indeed, few could miss the irony of French trade restrictions that failed to prevent American shipmasters from feeding richly on the profits from carriage denied to law-abiding Frenchmen. This concern for French freight carriers gave Moustier his dominant motif. On one hand, he would lift the 1784 ban to permit the islands to import American grain, but couple the concession with encouragements to French vessels to enter that trade as principal carriers. Conversely, he would permit the islands to export sugar and coffee to the mainland but, again, in prospect that these commodities would be transported in French bottoms. To accomplish these ends he recurred to Marbois's proposed incentive: that of permitting French merchantmen to make their voyages triangular. Thus, French wines and brandies would make their way to the East Coast cities, American grain, fish, and salt pork to the islands, Indies sugar and coffee back to the States, and finally, return cargoes of tobacco to France. Moustier's vision plainly took as its model the pattern American merchants had shown to be most rewarding.[56]

Mindful of the vested interests Paris had sought to protect in 1784, Moustier made a number of reassuring observations. He believed, for example, that French growers and exporters of grain could be kept competitive in the Indies market by levying duties on grain imported from the United States. Duties stiff enough to erase the American growers' advantages of lower costs and greater proximity would serve to keep a share

---

[55]Moustier's opus, entitled "Extrait d'un Mémoire du Cte. de Moustier sur le Commerce des Etats Unis," was enclosed in his No. 20 to Montmorin, New York, 2 July 1789, AECPE-U, 34: 221–24, and was foreshadowed in his No. 3 to same, New York, 12 February 1788, "Correspondence of Moustier," 8: 724.

[56]"Extrait d'un Mémoire," ff. 221–21vo. Like Moustier and Marbois, Delaforest had also suggested more flexible routing for French carriers. See his letter to Montmorin, New York, 20 November 1787, série B^7, doss. 461, doc. 14, ANF.

of the market in French hands. As for island exports, sugar and coffee in particular, Moustier's reassurances were a shade more problematical. Again, he emphasized the importance of carriage. As long as Americans seemed determined to have much of their sugar and coffee from the French Antilles, perhaps as much as two-thirds of all they consumed, he thought it proper that French carriers should earn the freight. The danger remained, of course, that Americans would re-export to Europe any surpluses, as they had done in the past, and thus continue to deprive French merchants of this opportunity for profit. Moustier postulated, however, that if this design were acted upon, France by recapturing the carriage of sugar and coffee would effectively shut out American re-exporters.[57]

Moustier's proposals, though tightly reasoned and well informed, evoked a negative response from Paris, perhaps because that city was already transfixed by stirring events in the newly assembled Estates General. Given more favorable circumstances, French shipping interests, could they be separately distinguished from the mercantile community as a whole, might have welcomed Moustier's proposals for enlarging the permissible channels of carriage. Not so, certainly, France's merchant-dealers in grain and sugar. Had the latter learned of Moustier's plans for allowing these commodities to flow more freely between islands and mainland, they would surely have repeated the campaign of protest they had directed against the initial relaxations of 1784. Montmorin, in his reply to Moustier, indirectly revealed the government's wariness of changes likely to rouse the ire of this group, as well as its opposition to any change that resembled unrequited concession. Despite Moustier's effort to portray his design less as a yielding to lawlessness than as a plan for breathing new life into France's ocean-going carriage, Montmorin insisted on seeing concessions. He admitted that the island trade "is as delicate as it is embarrassing," but in his view, France had already conceded to the imperatives of the island-mainland traffic all that it reasonably could. Thus, while Parisians prepared to storm the Bastille, the royal government set its face firmly against any reordering of that traffic. Moustier's memorandum went quietly to the archives.[58]

Revolution and war completed the American takeover. Made more dependent on the United States, now for military supplies as well as for

---

[57]"Extrait d'un Mémoire," ff. 221–22vo. Otto later concluded that the volume of re-exported sugar had long been exaggerated. He pointed to the more accurate trade statistics of the new federal government as evidence that Americans consumed nearly all the sugar they imported. To MAE, No. 61, Philadelphia, 24 May 1791, AECPE-U, 35: 349vo.

[58]Montmorin to Moustier, No. 5, Versailles, 7 July 1789, AECPE-U, 34: 225vo.

food, the islands succumbed to inescapable needs. They survived, literally, on the boldness of American shipmasters risking capture and confiscation to feed them, to arm them, to dispose of their exportable sugar and coffee, acting always from profit, but nonetheless meeting the requirements of survival that France had never met well and, once at war with Britain's navy, could scarcely meet at all. Among French observers, wartime exigencies deepened their ambivalence of attitude. American interlopers still sought forbidden cargoes, but they brought sustaining cargoes in return. Without them France would be hard put to retain her islands or even defend them, but the American presence signaled, more than before, the heavy price France would pay in lost economic benefits.

The instinct to persevere died hard. Old tenets of mercantilism died even harder. The grain trade might be lost to France, but perhaps not the carriage of sugar and coffee. When in February 1793 the National Convention opened all Antillean ports "to vessels of the United States," it merely recognized in a posthumous way the much earlier demise of restrictions on grain imports. Indeed, France herself needed American grain. The gates were already down. The Convention merely hoisted the flag of surrender.[59] Nothing short of revolutionary optimism, however, could have led the remakers of all things French to believe they could preserve for French vessels a major portion of the carrying trade in sugar and coffee. Little more than a month after it cleared the way for grain imports, the Convention turned to the sugar and coffee question and must have thought itself generous in the sop it threw to Americans. American vessels departing the islands were to be permitted to lade "a quantity of coffee equal to $\frac{1}{50}$ of the(ir) tonnage" and amounts of sugar "equal to $\frac{1}{10}$ of the(ir) tonnage."[60] Such meager allowances led Jefferson to ask Genet if an error had been made in translation. In fact, Genet did find a clerical error in what he had transmitted to the State Department, but not in the percentage figures. One is tempted to conclude that, like so much revolutionary devising, the absurd limitations on sugar and coffee were the gestures of men determined to wage war, even against iron necessities. The plain fact was that the islands needed large quantities of American foodstuffs which would not be delivered unless paid for. They could pay in cash or in sugar. Tanguy's later statistics showed what the choice had been.

To have lost to the Americans the cream of the trade in the Antilles rankled even the most dispassionate of French officials. Royalist and revolutionary alike learned the same bitter truth. No mere act of legislation, no decree, no feasible means of enforcement could break the headlock the

---

[59]"Loi relative aux Denrées," *Lois et Actes* 6: 424.
[60]"Loi qui admet en exemption de tous droits . . .," 26 March 1793, ibid., 471.

interlopers had thrown around the island traffic. Frenchmen might blame their loss on nature for having placed the islands too close to the mainland, and having coupled proximity with economic dependence. Or they might blame one another for complacency, incompetence, or indifference. But no Frenchman could ignore the crucial part played by the interlopers themselves. Lawless, greedy, aggressive Americans were, after all, the principal agents of France's colonial ruin. And the memory of their depredations, still fresh, must be counted among the threads of anger and frustration that wove themselves into the fabric of French antagonism in the years ahead.

Meanwhile, throughout the 1780s and well into the following decade, French statesmen turned increasingly to the idea of rallying French commerce by means of a new commercial treaty. The notion early took root that the old treaty of 1778 had not gone far enough to assure France the kind of exclusive, or even reciprocal, advantages to which her wartime services entitled her. The restructuring they had in mind would, they hoped, show France the favor she deserved that she might better contest Britain for commercial ascendancy in the Atlantic, and perhaps also serve to restrain Americans from making further inroads in the Antilles. How to formulate, and then secure, these compensatory privileges posed one of the great contemporary challenges to French diplomacy. Ministers and consuls alike took up the gage, earnestly debating new treaty clauses which, if agreed to, would put France on the road to commercial resurgence. How indifferently they fared in this endeavor, and with what additional feelings of frustration, merits some systematic examination.

V

THE SEARCH FOR RECIPROCITY

When French officials spoke of "reciprocity," they meant that Americans had it within their power — and should have felt obliged — to extend some very important favors to French commercial interests. Clearly, however, Americans were perceived to have withheld deliberately the bestowal of such favors both with respect to French commerce in the Atlantic and in the Caribbean. This lack of "reciprocity," they believed, had deprived French exporters of the means to compete successfully for American markets, and had left their Antilles open to unrestrained trafficking in contraband. Whatever the label — reciprocity, favor, or gratitude — French officialdom regarded it as France's due. Her wartime services and her subsequent openings to Americans, both in home ports and in the Indies, deserved requital. In that light, Americans should have been moved by a decent respect for their ally and benefactor to show special legislative favor to French ships, French exports, and French colonial interests. Instead, wherever they looked they saw Americans ungrateful, indifferent, and seemingly unaware of their sins of omission.

Whether by threat, cajolery, or appeals to gratitude Americans could be brought to give France the compensatory leverage she needed to deploy her commerce to better advantage remained, for nearly two decades, a question French officials found intensely absorbing. The quest for reciprocity led them first to contemplate diplomatic, then legislative, remedy. At the outset, they pinned their hopes on negotiating a new commercial treaty, a treaty more singularly favorable to France than that of 1778. This hope persisted even when diplomatic efforts met with bad timing, ill circumstance, and, not infrequently, what they felt to be outright evasion. When these efforts flagged, there remained the alternative of trying to extract concessions by enacting coercive legislation. What Americans would not yield through friendly negotiation might still be squeezed from them by legislative sanction, a recourse not requiring their concurrence. In the end, neither diplomacy nor legislation succeeded in redeeming the promise of what so many French officials referred to as a "true reciprocity."

Discontent first stirred when French statesmen discovered how little effect the Franco-American commercial treaty of 1778 had on postwar trade patterns. Their hope that French commerce would derive special advantage from that document soon disappeared amid baffled disappointment. Nor, it appears, did Congress have in mind to confer such favor. The American treaty commissioners, acting on that body's famous "Model Treaty Plan of 1776," intended no more than to assure France an equality of treatment, that is, the same access to American ports and markets as that accorded to other nations. This was the dispensation they wrote into Articles 2, 3, and 4 of the treaty and, unlike their French counterparts, they fully expected that Britain, also having equal access, would likely continue to be their country's principal trade partner. Although neither great power acquired any advantage over the other, the habits, traditions, and benefits of "trading British" were expected to reassert themselves after the war. France and other nations found themselves fending as best their ingenuity and aggressiveness would allow in a field where the equal access principle applied to all.[1] After 17 years of watching this principle unfold, Philippe Létombe remarked that not once had France secured a commercial preference which had not immediately lost its preferential quality by dint of being extended to other nations.[2]

For their sense of failed expectation French officials often blamed the treaty itself, some of whose clauses they seemed either to misunderstand or misconstrue. Article 2 created particular confusion, the more perplexing because that article set forth a most favored nation arrangement originally designed by the French foreign office itself.[3] Favors claimable therein were made conditional, that is, neither party could claim a favor that the other had extended to a third party unless it rendered the same *quid pro quo* that caused the favor to be extended.

By Montmorin's day, French officials had to be reminded of this subtlety. When, for example, the United States exchanged certain treaty favors with Prussia in 1785, France could claim those favors only if she were to match them. Or perhaps some of the entitlements were already claimable. Delaforest scrutinized the Prussian treaty closely because he had received an interesting inquiry from Jean Toscan. Létombe was on

---

[1]For a recent analysis of this expectation, see James Hutson, *John Adams and the Diplomacy of the American Revolution* (Lexington, Ky. 1980) 29–31.

[2]"Extrait d'un Mémoire sur la situation commerciale de la France avec les Etats unis de l'Amérique," 24 frimaire, an 4 (15 December 1795), AECPE-U, Mem. et doc., 9: 245–46vo.

[3]Vernon G. Setser, "Did Americans Originate the Most-Favored Nation Clause?" *Journal of Modern History* 5 (1937) 319–23.

congé, and Toscan, acting as consul in Boston, had written to ask whether he should petition the Massachusetts legislature to accord to French vessels forced in by stress of weather the same privilege of reduced duty payments for offloaded cargoes as had been accorded to Prussian vessels similarly distressed. Delaforest told Paris that he had counseled Toscan not to enter a claim of right, not yet. France, he thought, because she, too, remitted certain fees to vessels forced into her ports, could claim the Prussian privilege under Article 2, but until a Prussian vessel had actually claimed the reduced duties, he thought it best to wait. He also thought it unlikely a Prussian vessel would ever test the clause. It amused him that two nations with so little prospect of significant commerce should shower each other with "great liberality of principles."[4]

Article 3 also disappointed. On its face, this article protected French cargoes from discriminatory import duties: French subjects would pay "no greater" duties in American ports than would the subjects of other nations. By giving the same assurance to other treaty powers, however, the United States had destroyed its potential usefulness to France. Had Americans truly wished to favor France, they might have construed "no greater" to mean that French commodities ought to be taxed at much lower rates. This was Létombe's view, and others shared it. As Létombe pointed out, equal levies on imports effectively favored the British; this, because British importers already had the advantage of traditional ties with American customers. To Létombe, a proper "reciprocity" would have bound the United States to admit all French products duty-free for a period of fifteen to twenty years.[5]

The ingenious and effervescent journalist, Tanguy de la Boissière, published another suggestion, albeit in hindsight. Article 3, he wrote, might have been framed so as to leave control over duty levels at France's disposition. Suppose Americans had agreed to place no higher duties on French imports than those which France imposed on American imports. Thereafter, no matter how high the duties others might pay in American ports, France could always restrain the level of duties on her own exports by keeping down the duties on American products entering France. Tanguy did not explain what would be the presumed equivalencies, for tax purposes, between such unlike commodities as incoming tobacco and outgoing wine, but his proposal at least showed how diligently Frenchmen sought that elusive thing called "reciprocity."[6]

---

[4]To MMC, No. 158, 26 May 1786, CC (New York), 909: 151–52. Cf., Article 2 of the French treaty and Article 9 of the Prussian treaty in Miller, *Treaties*, 2: 5 and 168, respectively.

[5]Cf., Létombe, "Extrait," f. 246vo; and Tanguy, *Situation commerciale*, 15.

[6]Tanguy, ibid., 16.

Similarly, from the one-time Girondin consul Antoine Duplaine came a scheme for bending American commerce to France's will that, unlike Tanguy's speculation on lost treaty opportunities, proposed recourse to the more forceful expedient of legislative coercion. Duplaine urged the National Convention to place a refundable duty on "all foreign vessels" entering French ports. Foreign shipmasters, presumably most of them American, would qualify for the rebate if, on departure, they laded "products of French manufacture up to the same value of the goods they imported." Duplaine's proposal squarely addressed the most serious defect in Franco-American commerce: the reluctance of Americans to buy French produce and the resulting outflow of French specie. If Americans still refused to take French cargoes, at least France could use the tax receipts to subsidize French shipping in the face of the American retaliatory measures he had to admit would be a likely response. To angry men like Duplaine, legislative recourse, despite its perils, offered a means of forcing from Americans the "reciprocity" they would not freely give.[7]

Treaty disappointments aside, French observers also bridled at the reality that Americans did not wish to extend favors to French commerce, saw no reason to, and indeed may not have had it within the power of their Confederation Congress to do so. Marbois expressed bitterness toward a people who would rather receive commercial concessions than grant them and had little sense of reciprocal obligation. In the same vein, when the "American Committee" was lobbying in Paris, Delaforest thought it scandalous that "while M. Jefferson and his friends ask the government for favors respecting exports from the United States, not one of them offers privileges by way of compensation to French merchandise." Nor, he added, could a powerless Congress be expected to reciprocate. The only way to deal with such people, wrote Martin Oster, was to "act toward them as they act toward us, always disposed to exchange favor for favor, nothing more." Implicitly, Antoine Duplaine concurred. American "indifference," he felt, grew in direct ratio to French concessions. Nor was their ingratitude new to him. "Since 1789," he wrote, "I have not ceased to write that one can neither trust nor count on Americans." They had been impervious to "what gratitude should have dictated to them."[8]

Inevitably, the passions roused by war, beginning in 1793, inspired

---

[7]"Notes sur le Commerce," ff. 208vo–09.

[8]See, respectively, Marbois to MAE, No. 433, 14 August 1785, AECPE-U, 30: 212–12vo; Delaforest to MMC, No. 232, 9 May 1788, CC (New York), 910: 53; Oster to MAE, No. 3, 1 messidor, an 4 (19 June 1796), CC (Norfolk), 927: 318vo; and Duplaine, "Notes," f. 209.

French officials to pick out, more clearly than before, the sinister influence they believed Britain and her partisans exerted on trade matters. That American neutrality bore the stamp of London, in a broad sense, few Frenchmen doubted. Logically, then, in the narrower matter of commercial reciprocity, or lack of it, the same suspicion prevailed. The high duties on French wines that Oster called attention to had certainly been "calculated by a Brittanic hand to prevent [Frenchmen] from establishing a permanent commerce in the United States." Another French official, describing the "English faction" that directed the American government, thought it hardly necessary to add that this group also controlled "almost all of its commerce." The son of the famous Rochambeau, who mingled a naval career with political punditry, also saw British influence at work. How else could one explain that "French vessels have not had any preference over those of the British in American ports," and with the result that British tonnage entering those ports was sixteen times that of France? "This monstrous partiality will cease to surprise," he wrote, "when one learns that the American government is English."[9]

Such fevered exaggerations left little room for argument among Frenchmen locked in battle with an ancient foe. Those same Frenchmen, as revolutionaries, fought other enemies as well, not least their royalist predecessors on whom they were wont to pile evils of even greater antiquity. To the world-changers, few acts or policies of the former regime stood in the light of approval. So it was with the late king's failure to extract reciprocity from his American protégés. In disdainful hindsight, the *ancien régime's* effort in this respect was seen to have been either neglectful to the point of nullity, mistaken in its sporadic generosity, or ill favored in its *modus operandi*.

Those who charged "neglect" held up the *ancien régime's* supposed apathy to explain how Americans had escaped their obligations. A less sluggish government would have found means to convert a flourishing wartime trade into a permanent commercial hegemony. Instead, the king's inattentiveness had permitted his erstwhile allies to swing back into Britain's commercial orbit. As to what they would have done differently, these revolutionary critics rarely went beyond the hindsightful suggestion that they would have required Americans to admit French manufactures duty-free. They made clear their conviction, however, that

---

[9]See, respectively, Oster's No. 3, CC (Norfolk), 927: ff. 319vo–20; Pautizel, "Mémoire sur l'Etat Politique des affaires de la République française dans les Etats-Unis de l'Amérique," 1 ventôse, an 2 (19 February 1794), AECPE-U, Mem. et doc., 10: 52vo; and Rochambeau, "Mémoire sur la situation de l'agriculture et du Commerce des Etats-unis," Philadelphia, 5 December 1794, ibid., 9: 225vo.

the Republic's more zealous pursuit of reciprocity would bring Americans to know, in short order, what was expected of them.[10]

While charging "neglect" obviously gratified those who sought to discredit the *ancien régime*, the possibility that Americans themselves felt neglected put an interesting twist on the question of commercial give and take. Moustier discovered this perception when he arrived in New York in 1788. Americans, he wrote, expected him, as France's representative, to declare his government's support for the new Constitution, then in process of being ratified. As noted earlier, Moustier was bound by his instructions not to do. He squirmed even more uncomfortably at having to report a widespread view that France had sought no more than to detach the colonies from Britain, but not to see them prosper. No less a figure than the American foreign secretary confirmed this view when he assured Moustier that his countrymen had long regarded France as indifferent, even passively hostile, to their welfare. John Jay even questioned whether the Franco-American alliance still existed. To Moustier's astonishment, Jay remarked that the alliance had served its principal purpose, that of securing American independence, and might now be regarded as having lapsed.[11]

Reports of Jay's strictures, when they reached Montmorin, brought flaming denials — and on both counts. The French foreign minister insisted that Jay be told to re-read the text of the alliance treaty to remind himself that its obligations were "perpetual." Nor should Jay be allowed to mistake for indifference France's proper restraint from meddling in American affairs. Moreover, considering how much France had freely conceded to American commerce, Montmorin said he had to conclude that France had shown its indifference only in its failure to demand reciprocal favors.[12]

Montmorin's last point was precisely the focus of later critics. Since 1784, and by Moustier's time, France had opened both West Indian and metropolitan ports to American traffic in ways that defied the wisdom of mercantilist economics. Island necessity explained the first; Jefferson's importunings had much to do with the second. That France had been badly served by these concessions found critics in strong agreement. Why,

---

[10]For a sampling of views of those who charged "neglect," see Rochambeau, "Sur les rapports avenirs des Etats-unis de l'Amérique septentrionale avec la France," 25 November 1794, ibid., f. 211; Mangourit, "Mémoire sur la Situation Politique de la France avec les Etats-unis," an 3 (22 September 1794–22 September 1795), ibid., 10: 70vo; Fauchet, "Mémoire" (1796), 90–91; and Talleyrand, *Mémoire sur les Relations commerciales des Etats-Unis avec l'Angleterre* (Paris 1799) 1–2.

[11]To MAE, No. 3, New York, 12 February 1788, "Correspondence of Moustier," 8: 723–24.

[12]To Moustier, No. 1, Versailles, 23 June 1788, ibid., 727–29.

at such cost, royalist France had neither sought nor obtained compensatory benefits puzzled those who, like Joseph Fauchet, marveled at what he called the *ancien régime's* "blind generosity." Revolutionary critics wondered not so much at royalist departures from mercantilist practice (for Girondin and Jacobin, too, differed in their respective views of protected trade systems) as that so little had been demanded in return.[13]

In fact, though unrequited, the concessions made to American commerce in the 1780s spoke less to any flaw in royalist diplomacy than to the near impossibility of extracting "returns" from an American government that was scarcely seen to exist. Thus, while Americans on the high seas constituted a dangerous and demanding presence — and one that Paris could not ignore — the American Congress clearly lacked the power to offer restraints and reciprocities of the kind that characterize the traditional give-and-take of diplomatic intercourse. This perception of American impotence, persistently conveyed to Paris by French diplomats close to Congress, created there a reduced level of expectation that in retrospect may too easily have passed for negligence. To contemporaries, however, impotence was a frustrating reality.

Official testimony on this score was voluminous. French officials watching Congress at close hand seldom failed to remark on that body's constant disarray. They seemed unsure whether they were witnessing tragedy, comedy, or farce. La Luzerne reported in early 1784 that members, once they had ratified the peace treaty, appeared unconscionably eager to disband. They began to trickle away, he wrote, ". . . one was obliged to go home to take care of a sick child, another to get married; a third had very pressing personal business; someone I met told me that his wife had recalled him." When it came time for Congress to reconvene, Marbois, now chargé d'affaires, noted the absence of a quorum and remarked with barely concealed amusement that some members were refusing to come to Philadelphia until they heard that a quorum had been achieved.[14] Marbois's successor, Louis Otto, so often predicted an end to the Union that when Congress refused to die, he felt compelled to apologize to Montmorin for confusing him with vacillating assessments. Montmorin replied soothingly. He understood why Otto might think

---

[13]Cf., Tanguy, *Mémoire*, 21–22; unsigned "Extrait d'un Mémoire sur la Situation Commerciale de la France avec les Etats-unis d'Amérique," 25 frimaire, an 5 (26 December 1796), AF III, carton 64, doss. 261, ff. 11–12, ANF; and Fauchet, "Mémoire" (1796), 91. For Jefferson's role in securing concessions for Americans in French home ports, see Merrill D. Peterson, "Thomas Jefferson and Commercial Policy, 1783–93," *William and Mary Quarterly* 3rd ser. 22.4 (1965) 584–610.

[14]Cf., La Luzerne to MAE, No. 367, Annapolis, 13 February 1784, AECPE-U, 27, 130–30vo; and Marbois to same, No. 403, Philadelphia, 20 November 1784, ibid., vol. 28, 397.

his dispatches misleading, but reassured the chargé that he knew how difficult it was to report on an anarchic situation. Each state, he ruminated, would doubtless soon complete its independence from the others. "This development will do us no harm," he thought and then, as if to confirm the view of French indifference that Jay would later express, he added, "we have had no other purpose than to remove this vast continent from Great Britain."[15]

Otto's pessimism because it was so often repeated undoubtedly deepened the bleak assessments made in Paris. His depictions of Congress confirmed the worst: that it was a body without essential powers, often lacking a quorum, and always eager to postpone serious decisions. Sectional divisions between North and South, he wrote, posed "an insuperable obstacle" to the prospect of permanent union. Still, he took particular pains to differentiate between political weakness and commercial vigor. Americans might suffer from lack of sovereign governance, but they must not be thought impoverished. "The states and individuals," he wrote, "have ample means for the most expensive and difficult enterprises." American merchants were among the world's wealthiest, he remarked, adding significantly, "it is not that the citizen is stripped of cash, but that the government does not yet have the solidity it needs to get into the citizen's pocket." Optimistic for Americans on most other counts, Otto remained darkly prophetic as to the durability of their union."[16]

Moustier, when he arrived, did little to relieve the perception of impotence and impending dissolution, although he regarded the latter with a certain measure of equanimity. Should the Constitution fail of ratification and the Union dissolve, he wrote, France would have to deal with thirteen governments instead of one. Collecting the wartime debt owed to France would thereby be complicated. But on the commercial front he anticipated that the newly ratified consular convention would adequately afford the legal controls France had long sought to establish over her ships entering American ports. Nor were solutions to the larger problems of Franco-American commerce contingent on the Union's survival. Quite independently of American political conditions, Moustier already had in mind to propose unilateral French action to stimulate French exports.

---

[15]For Otto's apologia, see his unnumbered dispatch to Montmorin, New York, 19 May 1787, AECPE-U, 32: 263; and the latter's response, No. 4, Versailles, 30 August 1787, ibid., ff. 250–50vo.

[16]Quotations are from his Nos. 39 and 67, 16 February and 25 October 1786, AECPE-U, 31: 122vo, and 32: 117vo–18, respectively; but see also his Nos. 11, 43, and 91, dated 1 October 1785; 11 March 1786; and 10 June 1787, ibid., 30: 321–31; vol. 31, 179–79vo; and vol. 32, 276–80, respectively.

Such would be the thrust of his later "memorandum on commerce."[17]

Only gradually, as hopes brightened for the new Constitution, did the French minister begin to consider what fresh opportunities a new and stronger American government might present for obtaining trade benefits bilaterally agreed to. The ever-alert Delaforest anticipated him. In May 1788, the consul general urged Paris to watch the American political scene very carefully. Whether Americans renewed or dissolved their government, he warned, France must be prepared, in either eventuality, to negotiate "duties based on reciprocity."[18] Moustier took up Delaforest's urgent refrain when, the Constitution ratified, though uncertainties remained, Americans seemed determined to establish the government that document envisioned. "The present moment is critical," he wrote in November, ". . . but too long a delay might possibly cost us an opportunity that may not return with the same advantages." A month later he cautioned that any sign of French indifference "would be the source of the most alarming evils." At worst, he feared, Britain might by granting timely commercial favors steal a march on France. Whatever Paris now spent on "policy," he promised, would be "returned with interest on commerce." By February 1789, with the first federal Congress soon to convene, Moustier was writing frantically for instructions. Again stressing the importance of timing, he warned that "everything depends on this first moment . . . our influence will either be established or lost forever in the United States."[19]

Curiously, despite his appeals — presumably intended to elicit from Paris a grand gesture of commercial generosity — Moustier shied away from suggesting what that winningly supportive gesture might be. By alerting Paris to the need for action he doubtless felt that, from his side, he had done all that he could. Moreover, he was still preoccupied with putting on paper his own extensive proposals relating to commerce, none of which, however, spoke to the kind of urgent stroke of diplomacy his dispatches called for. When the new Congress met and began to debate revenue measures, Moustier's passion for a grand gesture subsided into quiet watchfulness. Montmorin, meanwhile, dashed any hopes for an initiative from Paris. Although Moustier's appeal to opportunity im-

---

[17]To MAE, No. 8, New York, 16 March 1788, ibid., 33: 153–53vo.

[18]To MMC, No. 232, 9 May 1788, CC (New York), 910: 53.

[19]Cf., Moustier to MAE, Nos. 26, 28, and 3, 18 November and 25 December 1788, and 4 February 1789, to be found consecutively in "Correspondence of Moustier," *American Historical Review* 9 (1903) 89; AECPE-U, 33: 385; and ibid., 34: 22.

pressed him, the foreign minister thought it best to wait "until the new Constitution shall have acquired consistance."[20]

Some years later, Joseph Fauchet ruminated on the effects of bad timing in the conduct of French relations with the United States. New French ministers, he remarked, had always arrived too late to wield their influence at critical junctures. Genet had arrived to find Washington's neutrality policy already formulated. He himself had landed in the midst of congressional debate over the Madison Resolutions which, had he been sooner to work for their passage, would have given French commerce a decided advantage over the British in matters of tariffs and tonnage duties. And Pierre Adet, his successor, had arrived on the eve of, but too late to influence, the critical Senate debate on Jay's treaty. Fauchet also deplored the decision to recall Moustier. He saw it as a woeful break in ministerial continuity that came at a moment when Congress was shaping the all-important framework of a commercial policy.[21] Had he known of it, Fauchet might have cited a further irony: Moustier had asked to be recalled. By June 1789, the Count's sense of urgency had so far abated that he began to find reasons why he should be relieved. His health, he wrote, would suffer if he had to spend another winter in New York. Moreover, he had pressing personal matters to attend to in France. His departure at this time, he thought, would not "inconvenience" the king's interests.[22] A few weeks later, however, Congress belied this judgment — and with a vengeance.

After July 1789, whenever French statesmen sought to define "reciprocity," they usually cited the tonnage duties enacted that month as being illustrative of what was France's due, had Congress, then or later, possessed any shred of gratitude. The tariff and tonnage laws of 1789, though they succeeded magnificently in their principal object, that of raising revenue, infuriated Paris in their failure to show favor to French shipping. Having decided to tax ships and some of their cargoes as the best way of raising money, Congress made the tariff and tonnage laws of 1789 the mainstays of its financial survival. The tonnage provisions, however, provoked the first serious rift between France and the new federal government. Ultimately, disagreement over tonnage duties became a symbol of American ingratitude, a target of French retaliation, and the takeoff point for a decade-long French drive to negotiate a new commercial treaty.

Specifically, the law of 1789 put a tax of 50 cents on each ton of

---

[20]To Moustier, Versailles, March 1789, ibid., f. 51.
[21]*Mémoire* (1796), 102–18.
[22]To MAE, unnumbered, New York, 15 June 1789, AECPE-U, 34: 186–86vo.

burthen of all incoming vessels of foreign registry, while placing only a
6 cents per ton duty on American vessels. Congress obviously had in
mind giving special encouragement to American shipping as well as raising revenue. To Paris, such discrimination instantly raised the question:
why were French vessels not exempted altogether, or at least taxed at a
lower rate than other carriers in the "foreign" category? Equity, gratitude, but especially the most favored nation treatment promised by the
old commercial treaty, should have kept Congress from lumping French
carriers with those of all other nations.

The slight to French interests, displeasing on its face, rankled French
observers still more when they considered some of the attending circumstances, one of which was the reversal of expectation. Moustier blandly
assumed that Congress would tax French vessels at some intermediate
level. He was reassured when the House of Representatives did, at first,
place somewhat lower tonnage duties on the ships of nations having
commercial treaties with the United States. The Senate, however, ex-
punged this intermediate category, and the House concurred. Thus, vessels of all nations, irrespective of treaty status, were to be dutied at the
same high rate of 50 cents per ton. To have this concession snatched away
—and the same thing happened when the law was renewed in 1790—
added chagrin to outrage. The first time it happened, Moustier reflected
bitterly that earlier congresses had lacked the power to make concessions;
this one refused to. He would gladly scourge it with a protest if Paris
gave him permission.[23]

No less exasperating was the recollection of how recently several
state legislatures had freely granted the type of concession the new Congress now withheld. Only a few years before, such states as Massachusetts,
Virginia, and both Carolinas had shown favor, either by imposing lower
tariffs or lower tonnage duties on the traffic of nations having commercial treaties with the United States. Clearly, Congress had a precedent if
it chose to observe it, and Louis Otto, for one, hoped to use it persuasive-
ly. Indeed, with Moustier's departure, it was Otto, the amiable Alsatian
chargé d'affaires, who bore the first burden of trying to regain the lost
ground for the principle of reciprocity.[24]

---

[23]To same, No. 21, New York, 7 July 1789, ibid., ff. 209–30vo. The House passed the tonnage bill on 29 May, debated the Senate's changes on 27 June, and receded from its disagreement
with the Senate on 1 July. See *Annals*, vol. 1, for other elements of debate on the tonnage bill
under the dates of 21 April and 4–7 May.

[24]See, especially, Otto to MAE, No. 37, New York, 12 August 1790, AECPE-U, 35: 157.
For a published summary of southern state laws that favored French shipping, see *Analyse des Loix
avec les tarifs, des Etats des deux Carolines et de la Géorgie* (Fayetteville, N.C., n.d.).

Over time, Otto pieced together an explanation of why Congress had consigned all foreign vessels to the same undifferentiated tax bracket. Members shrank from losing revenue, he wrote, a loss certain to be compounded if Dutch, Prussian, and Swedish vessels, along with French, were taxed at lower rates. Sectional politics also played a role. Northern members, many of whom held government securities, feared the value of their holdings would fall, if Congress foreclosed even small additional sources of revenue. Southerners, for their part, depended on British bottoms to get their exports to European markets. Any concessions to "treaty powers"—Britain not among them—might either diminish British ship arrivals or provoke British retaliation.[25]

Despite its displeasure, Paris was slow to register a formal protest. It hoped, at first, that Congress would accord reciprocity when it reshaped the tariff schedule in 1790. For a time, Montmorin mistakenly thought it had. Otto, meanwhile, prudently awaited specific instructions, unwilling to make a formal *démarche* until authorized. Not until mid-July 1790 did the foreign office decide to register a protest rather than retaliate, although the king's ministers vigorously debated the counter-measures they might take if protest failed.[26]

Otto's meetings with Thomas Jefferson illustrated from the outset how difficult a passage France would weather in her quest for reciprocity, even with the best of goodwill on both sides. In his dealings with Otto, the Secretary of State mirrored the style he had set in Paris. As then, he showed himself, by turns, to be open, friendly, and sympathetic to French concerns, but when pressed, equally capable of evasion and a towering legalistic resourcefulness. When told that France intended to protest, Jefferson "affected to be surprised." He reminded Otto that he had been out of the country when Congress debated the act of 1789. Beyond that, he seemed reluctant to regard the French plaint as a possible treaty violation, and suggested offhandedly that an exemption for French ships would entail, at most, asking Congress to amend the law. Otto was invited to file his government's protest and did so the next day, 13 December 1790.[27]

---

[25]To MAE, No. 28 and 39, New York, 20 May and 28 September 1790, AECPE-U, 35: 96vo–98 and 172vo–75, respectively.

[26]See Montmorin to Otto, No. 1, Paris, 10 July 1790, AECPE-U, 35: 128–29vo; Moustier to MAE, Paris, 24 July 1790, ibid., ff. 142–44vo; Otto to MAE, No. 37, New York, 12 August 1790, ibid., f. 157; Montmorin to Controller General Claude-Guillaume Lambert, Paris, 15 August 1790, ibid., ff. 164–64vo; and Otto to MAE, No. 39, New York, 28 September 1790, ibid., ff. 171vo–72. See also O'Dwyer, "A French Diplomat's View."

[27]Otto reported this meeting to MAE, No. 48, Philadelphia, 13 December 1790, AECPE-U, 35, 234–38vo. A translated copy of his protest is in *ASP,FR* 1: 112.

Otto's note was short and to the point. Article 5 of the commercial treaty had exempted American vessels from paying a 100-sol duty, equivalent to a tonnage tax, at a time when the United States levied no tonnage taxes whatsoever. France, to be sure, had retained another kind of tonnage tax but imposed it only on ships engaged in coastwise traffic. Article 5 accorded the same privilege to the United States. Clearly, Congress had exceeded that privilege when it sought "to lay *any* tonnage they should think proper, on French vessels." If Article 5 meant anything, it restricted American levies on French vessels to a tax similar to the one France imposed only on coastwise shipping.[28]

Three weeks later, Jefferson inquired whether France had exempted all most-favored-nation shipping from the 100-sol duty, or only the vessels of the United States. Otto knew why he asked. If France had made the exemption general, then it conferred no special favor on the United States, and deserved no special favor in return. Reluctantly, he sent the secretary a list of nations to which the exemptions had been granted. They included, most recently, Britain and Russia. He went on to iterate, however, how generous to Americans the French exemption had been in 1778—a unilateral act of goodwill Americans at that time could not reciprocate because they had had no similar tax to forgo. In return for this favor, Article 5 had set unmistakable restrictions: no future tonnage tax was to be permitted beyond the equivalent of the French tax on coastwise shipping.[29]

Jefferson made the administration's reply on 19 January 1791, when Washington sent to the Senate the secretary's closely reasoned analysis of Article 5. Characteristically, Jefferson made a more forceful case for the French complaint than had Otto, whose note was attached. That case was not unassailable, however. The secretary believed that grounds existed, if the Senate chose to stand on them, for rejecting the protest. He would argue, if so directed, that the present tonnage law did not violate Article 5 because the latter, taken in the context of articles that preceded it, merely served to illustrate how the most-favored-nation principle was supposed to operate. Nor did France have cause to complain of inequity. The purposes for which the United States collected tonnage duties had equivalent purposes in French taxes designed to fund the costs of anchorage, buoys, beacons, and lighthouses. Thus, as long as French vessels paid no higher tonnage duties than did the vessels of other nations, no violation of treaty or charge of inequity could be sustained.[30]

28Ibid.
29Otto to MAE, No. 52, New York, 6 January 1791, AECPE-U, 35, 259–60.
30*ASP,FR* 1: 109–11.

For all this, Jefferson barely disguised his hope that the Senate would relent. Having made a case for both sides, he pointed to the practical advantages of yielding. Otherwise, he warned, France might rescind the valuable concessions made in 1787 to American whale oil interests. To exempt French vessels from tonnage duties would constitute a belated *quid pro quo* for those concessions and, if put in those terms, prevent other nations from claiming a similar exemption. As the last line of his report pointedly suggested, the Senate might prefer "to waive rigorous and nice discussions of right, and to make the modification an act of friendship and of compensation for favors received. . . ."[31]

When an unresponsive Senate stood firm, Otto found Jefferson's reaction carefully measured but not altogether pessimistic. Otto might think French vessels exempted from tonnage payments, the secretary told him, "but the Senate has judged it differently and it is my duty to adopt its decision." Jefferson went on, however, to explain why France should resist the urge to retaliate. The tonnage duties, while intended to produce revenue, also had as their purpose to coerce Britain into negotiating a commercial treaty. Once that was accomplished, the administration would be freer to create a system of tariff and tonnage duties that would favor only France. He then disclosed to Otto what he hoped to achieve for France's benefit, if Paris remained patient. His report on American commerce, still in draft, would ask Congress to frame a navigation act favoring nations like France which had opened their ports to American vessels, punishing those which had not. At that time, he intimated, special favors to France might be forthcoming. The lower chamber, as Otto knew, was well disposed to be generous, and the Senate, too, might be persuaded, especially if by legislation rather than by treaty it could close the door to claims of the most favored nation. Meanwhile, Jefferson counselled, Paris should refrain from "impolitic" reprisals.[32]

To Jefferson, Otto loyally upheld his government's reading of Article 5. To Paris, however, he pointed out that British shipping suffered more grievously from the tonnage differential than did French. The edge given to American vessels clearly fell more heavily on a merchant marine whose annual tonnage in American ports outweighed that of France by more than twenty to one. His implication was plain: France had a legitimate grievance but she should not be altogether displeased.[33]

Events in France, meanwhile, conspired to defeat Jefferson's hope

---

[31]Ibid., 111.

[32]Otto was not altogether persuaded. He doubted that the Senate, many of whose members were known to hold U.S. securities, would vote any measure that reduced federal revenues. To MAE, No. 56, Philadelphia, 10 March 1791, AECPE-U, 35, 301–305vo.

[33]To same, No. 52, New York, 6 January 1791, ibid., ff. 262–64.

for an eventual legislative remedy. First, the French National Assembly in March placed a retaliatory tax of twenty-five livres per quintal on tobacco arriving in American vessels, then on 2 June called on the king to negotiate a new Franco-American commercial treaty.[34] Neither measure was destined to elicit "reciprocity."

Critics of the tobacco tax saw little to commend it. American chargé William Short complained to Montmorin that unlike his own country's modest tonnage duties, the retaliatory levy on tobacco was so high as to exclude American carriage altogether. Jefferson predicted that British carriers would be its principal beneficiaries. Meanwhile, Otto thought Americans would probably succeed in circumventing it. He reported that some Senators had expressed regret at not having exempted French vessels when asked to, but the major consequence, he thought, would be evasion. One Philadelphia merchant had already announced plans to "borrow" a French name and ship his tobacco on board a French-made vessel. Otto noted unhappily the presence of more than a few impoverished French businessmen who would gladly lend their names to such enterprises and enough French-built carriers in American harbors to complete the deception. The consuls had been alerted, he wrote, to check the papers of departing tobacco ships, but his tone suggested that he thought the tax likely to be set at nought by Americans well versed in the arts of evasion.[35]

Congress's denial of a tonnage exemption also explained the French push for a new commercial treaty. Efforts to secure that concession, however, found its advocates divided on strategy. In their exasperation, French leaders seemed undecided as to whether it was better to seek the exemption by means of a new treaty, or continue to claim it under the old one. Moreover, as long as hope remained of making the claim under the old treaty, little thought was given to what else, besides a tonnage exemption, France might ask to include in a new treaty. Not once in the years that followed did Paris present the Washington administration with a fully detailed plan for resolving the broader problems of Franco-American commerce. From time to time, French emissaries were reminded of the problems and told to find remedies for them, but always in vague and general terms. No one in Paris ever thought to sit down and draft specific treaty articles. Too much was left to ministerial ingenuity, and too much reliance placed on Americans to respond to generalized importunings.

---

[34]See tobacco decree of 20 March 1791, *Archives Parlementaires de 1787 à 1860 (Assemblée Nationale)* première série, Tome 24, 222; and the decree of 2 June 1791, ibid., Tome 26, 710.

[35]Cf., Short to MAE, Paris, 6 April 1791, AECPE-U, 35: 330–31; Jefferson to Short, Philadelphia, 28 July 1791, in Paul L. Ford, ed., *The Works of Thomas Jefferson* (New York & London 1904–1905) 6: 292 (hereinafter cited as *Writings of TJ*); 6: 292; and Otto to MAE, Nos. 61 and 62, Philadelphia, 25 May and 17 June 1791, AECPE-U, 35: 349–49vo, and 360–64vo, respectively.

Predictably, the failure of France to give explicit form to her commercial needs gave the Washington administration ample pretext not to respond at all.

Had Moustier's advice been taken, a new treaty negotiation might have had some prospect of success. Moustier, at least, had thought through a possible scenario. Once back in Paris, he wrote to Montmorin and several other high-ranking officials in July 1790, proposing a phased series of diplomatic pressures. He would begin by emphasizing to Philadelphia the French view that the old treaty had been violated. The American government would, of course, deny the charge. It would argue that France was being treated no differently from the most favored nations with respect to tonnage duties, and that the old treaty required no more than that. Anticipating the rebuff, Moustier would next have his government create a committee of trade experts whose two-fold task would be to devise a series of retaliatory commercial measures, but also work out the details of a new commercial treaty. He believed that under the threat of retaliation, the United States would negotiate a treaty that would establish a "real reciprocity." While brandishing threats of punishment, however, France must be prepared to proffer treaty clauses that would reverse all the untoward changes that had overtaken Franco-American trade patterns. These clauses could be shaped in such ways, he believed, as to restore to vigor French shipping, swell the volume of French exports in the Atlantic arm of that commerce, and recoup French carriage in the Caribbean as well.[36]

This plan of Moustier's came to nought, and Joseph Fauchet later explained why. Moustier himself had shortly thereafter left Paris, sent on mission to Berlin, and from there chose the self-imposed exile of an *émigré*. All his dispatches and memoranda, including the voluminous data he had collected on commercial matters, were dispersed through various government bureaus and lost to view. Without Moustier's plan to orchestrate a series of threats and blandishments, the French government proceeded instead on impulse. First came the National Assembly's retaliatory tax on tobacco carriers of American registry, not merely threatened but enacted. Then, apparently in response to Short's protest, there followed the offer to negotiate a new treaty. Government strategy, such as it was, envisioned revoking the tax if the United States agreed to treat.[37] What appeared to

---

[36]To MAE (with copies to Finance Minister Jacques Necker and to La Luzerne), Paris, 24 July 1790, ibid., ff. 142–44vo.

[37]The proposal to negotiate a new treaty originated in the ministry. See letter, Minister of Public Contributions to Montmorin, Paris, 18 June 1791, ibid., ff. 363–65. See also Fauchet, "Considérations sur un traité de Commerce avec les Etats-unis," Paris, 28 germinal, an 4 (17 April 1796), AF III, carton 64, doss. 260, ANF.

be a more forceful approach proved instead to be disjointed, the product of parallel but uncoordinated executive and legislative purposes, doubtless further confused by the king's flight to Varennes in late June. Whatever the ministry may have projected by way of treaty specifics was swallowed by the monarch's defection and the quickening of political forces soon to plunge France into the self-preoccupying turmoil of republicanism.

How feeble was the impulse to make a new treaty became clear when Jean de Ternant, last of the king's ministers to Philadelphia, arrived uninstructed as to how to proceed. Without draft articles in hand, Ternant found himself on the defensive, put there first by Alexander Hamilton, but also forced to be no less evasive when Jefferson brought forward his own treaty proposals.

Hamilton's ploy was diverting. Ternant was told he might have a new treaty complete with tonnage exemption if France could show that American vessels were exempt from the French equivalent. The French minister could only reply that French vessels were already entitled to the exemption under the old treaty, the honoring of which must be the *sine qua non* of any new negotiation. Hamilton's precondition nonetheless led Ternant to ask Paris to send him documentary evidence that American vessels were, in fact, currently exempt from French port duties comparable to the American tonnage levy. The reply from Paris, six months in transit, was disappointing. The ministry, he wrote, had not furnished him with the sort of solid "attestations" he needed to prove to Hamilton that Congress's failure to exempt had violated the "principle of reciprocity."[38]

Talking treaty matters with Jefferson produced more frustration. On a visit to Mount Vernon in October 1791, Ternant found Washington and his secretary of state reticent because they expected an overture from France. In light of the National Assembly's call on 2 June for a new treaty, they made clear they anticipated that Ternant would bring concrete proposals. Ternant had none to offer. On the trip north, Jefferson found an occasion to be somewhat more forthcoming when bad weather forced the two men to lodge at the same inn in Georgetown. Here, just before parting, the secretary recurred to a proposal, made earlier to Otto, for a one-article treaty conferring common citizenship on Frenchmen and Americans for purposes of trade and commerce. Though Ternant at the time made a joking reply, he nonetheless reported home that he believed Jefferson sincere in wanting to put both nationalities "on a perfectly equal footing, in the different ports of the two nations in Europe as well as in

---

[38]To MAE, Nos. 12 and 38, Philadelphia, 9 October 1791, and 15 June 1792, *CFM*, 58–59, and 129, respectively.

all other parts of the world."[39] Indeed, this grandly simple device was one of Jefferson's favorite nostrums for cutting through the tangle of mercantilist exclusions. Moreover, it had earlier survived Otto's good-humored rejoinder that France would doubtless welcome such a proposal if the United States owned a sugar island as close to the coast of France as Saint Domingue was to the coast of the United States.[40]

France came close, perhaps closest, to getting the sort of "reciprocity" she sought when on 8 April 1792 Jefferson laid out four specific commercial proposals for Ternant's consideration. In Cabinet the secretary had argued against such *sub spe rati* propositions. Dealing with an uninstructed emissary, he contended, meant offering concessions without being assured of reciprocation. This was the line of objection he had taken with Washington when Hamilton first proposed it. When the president insisted, Jefferson subsequently discovered a Hamiltonian "trap." Hamilton had wanted informal treaty talks with Ternant, not with a view to consummating them, but rather to justify similar informal negotiations with the British minister, George Hammond, who was also uninstructed on treaty matters. Still, to Ternant, Jefferson made a case for treaty negotiations that strongly suggested he was not entirely disinclined to treat informally. He told Ternant with apparent sincerity that he wanted a new treaty to accompany the "Report on Commerce" he planned to submit to Congress the following December. A new French treaty he thought would underscore the benefits of other commercial proposals he hoped would be acted upon.[41]

Ternant, because he had neither powers nor guidelines for a treaty, countered nimbly by suggesting a stop-gap legislative remedy. Congress, he urged, might show its good faith by voting a tonnage exemption as soon as it reconvened. If it needed a motive, the king's generous (whale oil) decree of 1787, thus far unrequited, ought to furnish sufficient grounds. Having voiced the grievance he knew most rankled Paris, Ternant subsided and agreed to transmit any proposals the secretary might wish to tender.[42]

Jefferson, obviously eager to get on, made only a perfunctory defense of the tonnage law. The treaty articles he had in mind would resolve a number of trade problems, including the tonnage complaint. What he

---

[39]To same, No. 13, Philadelphia, 24 October 1791, ibid., 60–62.
[40]Otto to same, No. 48, Philadelphia, 13 December 1790, AECPE-U, 35: 236.
[41]Cf., Jefferson, "Anas," entry of 11 March 1792, *Writings of TJ*, 1: 207–208; Ternant to MAE, No. 31, Philadelphia, 8 April 1792, *CFM*, 109.
[42]*CFM*, 111.

proposed, first, was for both parties to open all ports, those of the United States, France, and the Indies. Incoming vessels would be subject only to those admiralty and tonnage duties which the nationals of each "actually" paid in their own ports. This left unanswered, of course, the question of whether American shipmasters were paying hidden French taxes comparable to U.S. tonnage levies. If they were, this was no promise of tonnage exemption to the French. Nor did Jefferson offer to reduce tariffs. To be sure, he called for the untrammeled exchange of all products of each country's growth and manufacture, subject to duties no higher than each government imposed on its own nationals. Again, however, this was no promise that duties on French goods would be lower. As for the Caribbean, Jefferson put forward a trade-off of benefits which, if enforceable, did stand to favor French shipping interests. American vessels were to carry to the islands only commodities of American origin, and were forbidden to re-export to Europe any commodities they carried away. Thus would French vessels be restored as carriers of the Indies trade with Europe, while Americans could lade sugar and coffee as long as such cargoes were destined in entirety for American ports. Bonding procedures, he surmised, could be formulated to enforce the restraints.[43]

Ternant perforce made no reply. Nor did he presume to assess the merits of Jefferson's proposals except to say to Paris that if it accepted them as a basis for negotiation, there might be enough support in the Senate to see a draft treaty through to ratification. Much hinged, he thought, on the administration's British diplomacy. Whatever came of Jefferson's overtures, the American government was much more intent on extracting commercial favors from London. If a new French treaty served that end, Ternant had no reason to doubt its feasibility. Meanwhile, he promised to try to draw Jefferson out more fully but avoid any pretense at negotiation until he had been formally instructed.[44]

Those instructions never came. Instead there followed what Fauchet later denounced as an interlude of "incredible negligence."[45] Such criticism, however, overlooked the appalling disarray that befell the French government shortly after Ternant's discussions on 8 April with the secretary of state. Summer and fall of 1792 found France staggering from monarchy to republic, the ordinary business of government barely tended. That Jefferson's overtures were not apparently even entertained must reflect the succession of five foreign ministers in France between March

[43]Ibid., 111–12.
[44]Ibid., 112–13.
[45]"Mémoire" (1796), 93.

and August of that year. Moreover, Ternant, despite his promise to get further clarification of Jefferson's treaty proposals, thought better of it when events in the Caribbean began to close in around him beginning in late April.

When Ternant wrote in June that he believed it "not in our interests to provoke any new conversations on this subject," he was doubtless troubled by what had suddenly become the all-consuming embarrassment of his mission. Civil strife and near famine in Saint Domingue had put him under compelling pressures to dun the administration for emergency advances against the balance of the French debt. If ever the Washington regime showed its goodwill, it was in its prompt responses to these requests. For years afterward, whenever French apologists reached for an example of American benevolence, the administration's readiness to help Ternant succor the Antilles with advances on the debt figured prominently.[46] By the same token, however, Ternant now found himself in the role of supplicant, potentially weakened as a bargainer. Not insignificantly, it was just after Hamilton had graciously consented to settle the value of a debt payment well in advance of its due date that Ternant voiced doubt as to the opportuneness of pursuing treaty talks. The burden of gratitude clearly inhibited the sort of stiff-jawed give and take that further demands for commercial reciprocity would entail.[47]

How decisively Philadelphia now held the diplomatic initiative was underscored in September when Ternant brought Jefferson his government's request for a one-article treaty to abolish privateering. Already at war with Austria since April, the French government can hardly have thought to urge this kind of safeguard for merchant shipping in anticipation of war with the United States. More likely, it merely sought to champion the new and more "liberal" view of war that frowned on victimizing private property. In this instance, Paris knew its Jefferson; the secretary warmly welcomed the proposal, reminding Ternant that the United States had already abolished privateering in its treaties with Prussia

---

[46]Advances were accorded to Ternant and Fauchet, but not to Genet. Cf., Ternant to MAE, No. 6, Philadelphia, 28 September 1791, *CFM*, 49; and Fauchet and the Commissioners to same, No. 1, Philadelphia, 1 germinal, an 2 (21 March 1794), ibid., 310. Louis Otto later expressed outrage at charges that the administration had not been prompt, even ahead of time, in meeting debt obligations. See his *Considérations*, 16–17. Indeed, low expectations in Paris gradually gave way to astonishment that U.S. debt payments, once begun, were made with such regularity. Cf., anon., "Mémoire sur la Dette du Congrès envers le Roi et sur les moyens d'en faciliter le remboursement," Paris, October 1788, AECPE-U (Finances), Liquidation de la dette américaine, 1783–1797, 19: 2ᵉ série (supplément), ff. 105vo–107; and François Deforgues, MAE, to Genet, No. 12, Paris, 30 July 1793, *CFM*, 229.

[47]Ternant to MAE, No. 38, Philadelphia, 15 June 1792, ibid., 127.

and Portugal. Then came the rebuff. Ternant reported home on 17 October that although the administration seemed eager to end privateering, it would do so only in the framework of an entirely new commercial treaty. Once more, Ternant asked for instructions, again in vain.[48]

For neglecting its treaty opportunities the dying monarchy stood deservedly impeached. Not so its Girondin successors who thought they saw opportunities where none existed. The Girondin emissary Edmond Genet, principally remembered for his spectacular breaches of American neutrality, must also be placed in the continuum of French diplomats in quest of "reciprocity." In Genet's case, unfortunately, both his instructions and his controversial activities tended to obscure, as well as impede, the "commercial" objectives of his mission. On treaty matters his instructions verged on the lurid. Heavily charged with high-flown promises, intermittent bluster, political gropings, and emotional appeals to republican solidarity, they would have frightened off all but the most ardent francophile. Moreover, by calling for a more tightly knit alliance—something they fervidly referred to as a "national pact"—the Girondins created a political context certain to alarm the administration and thereby reduce their chances for a purely commercial negotiation. The warmly embracing language of Genet's instructions took on even more distressing overtones when the bearer made plain that little short of recall could prevent his behaving as though France and America were already locked in *casus foederis.*[49]

Considering the damage he did to Franco-American goodwill, Genet's inability to conclude a commercial treaty might be ranked as the least of his failures, just as commercial matters were the least well articulated purposes of his mission. Unpromisingly instructed to combine a new treaty of commerce with one of alliance, he was to pick up on Jefferson's proposals to Ternant and expand them into a "national pact." That the Girondins intended to forge political as well as commercial ties appeared in the two *sine qua non.* Genet was at once to fashion a new and more binding version of the territorial "guarantee," while securing "unreservedly" a complete exemption for French vessels from payment of tonnage duties. The first envisioned strengthening the obligation each party had undertaken under Article 11 of the old alliance treaty to defend one another's

---

[48]To same, Nos. 56 and 57, Philadelphia, 11 and 17 October 1792, ibid., 161 and 162, respectively; see also Jefferson to Ternant, Philadelphia, 16 October 1792, *Writings of TJ*, 7: 164–65.

[49]For the progressive embellishment of Genet's instructions, see the decrees of the Conseil Exécutif Provisoire, 4 and 17 January 1793, A. Aulard, ed., *Recueil des Actes du Comité de Salut Public* (Paris 1889) 1: 393n and 478, respectively; and *CFM*, 201–11.

New World possessions. And the second, characterized as being "of the greatest importance," iterated the now familiar claim to reciprocity. Both demands were baited with enticements to American self-interest, cast in terms that were rancorously anti-British. Genet was to impress on the administration that a refurbished "guarantee," though of little consequence to France, would place the United States under France's powerful military and naval protection and "shelter them from all insults"; and the tonnage exemption, by encouraging French ship arrivals, would "reduce the too great influence of English shipowners in their ports."[50]

On the grander scale of self-interest, Genet was to dangle the prospect that once in "intimate concert" with France Americans could move quickly "to liberate Spanish America, open the navigation of the Mississippi to the inhabitants of Kentucky, deliver our former brothers in Louisiana from the tyrannical yoke of Spain, and perhaps return the beautiful star of Canada to the American Constellation." What was missing from such evocations of fraternal bliss was a practicable modus. Although those who bade Genet to negotiate a "national pact" knew that he would encounter timidity among American leaders and an ingrained American reluctance to do anything that might offend Great Britain, they all too casually brushed them aside in anticipation that Americans would respond fulsomely and from the heart once they learned of the support and sacrifice a republican France was prepared to make in their behalf.

When it came to spelling out articles for a commercial treaty, Genet's instructions were strangely silent. The tonnage exemption, which in any event Congress could confer without treaty, doubtless figured as an item to be negotiated because Congress had thus far refused to legislate it. Beyond this, the Girondins seemed disposed to rely on Americans to consider certain past and present instances of French generosity—each glowingly catalogued—and to respond in the same spirit. For instructional purposes, far more detailed attention centered on making sure Genet understood the wartime importance of requiring Americans to observe those articles of the existing treaty which allowed French warships to bring captured prize vessels into American ports and forbade the like privilege to her enemies.[51]

Failing adequately to instruct its emissary was not the only flaw in Girondin diplomacy. When Genet told Jefferson he was ready to nego-

---

[50]"Supplément aux instructions données au Citoyen Genet," ibid., 209–11. Some of the commercial proposals were doubtless inspired by Ducher's contemporary pamphlet, *Nouvelle Alliance à proposer entre les Républiques Française & Américaine* (Paris 1792).

[51]Cf., *CFM*, 208; Miller, *Treaties*, 2: 15–19.

tiate a "true family compact," he also enclosed a copy of the National Convention's decree of 19 February. Jefferson must have read the latter with satisfaction. At one stroke, France had freely accorded to the United States nearly half the concessions he had thought to bargain for. To Ternant the previous April he had suggested that both parties agree, by treaty, to open all ports to the trade of each other's nationals. Now he read that France had unilaterally gone so far, at least, as to open all her ports in the Indies. Doubtless he also recalled having broached to Ternant the idea of establishing equality of tariffs, that is, that all imports and exports be subject to no higher duties than each government imposed on its own nationals. Again, the February decree was explicit: "all commodities exported or imported by the American vessels, shall pay . . . only the same duties as are levied on those which are carried in French vessels."[52]

Only the Convention's apparent inability to distinguish tariffs from tonnage duties prevented a clean sweep. The February decree missed the mark when it authorized its Executive Committee to seek from Philadelphia "a reduction of duties similar to that which is granted by the present law." Inasmuch as American tariffs already fell equally on all imported goods irrespective of the nationality of the carrier, this can only be seen as a bid for exemption from the quite dissimilar American levy on the ships themselves. Read literally, this article proposed to swap French equality of tariff treatment for French relief from American tonnage duties —not quite the sort of parity Jefferson had had in mind. Most striking, however, was the National Convention's disregard for the most elementary component of diplomacy: the assurance of receiving a *quid pro quo*. Having made concessions unilaterally, they left no reason—except that of gratitude—for Congress to reciprocate. Indeed, the only leverage Genet retained thereafter was the threat to revoke these concessions unless reciprocation was forthcoming.[53]

Genet did brandish this threat, albeit diffidently, when in September, after a lapse of four months, he again sought out Jefferson for a negotiation. In Genet's second round of approaches American leaders once more heard the familiar refrain. As the French minister rehearsed it, Franco-American commerce, never more than "very slender," was costing France valuable specie which invariably ended up in the pockets of the

[52]See Genet to Jefferson, Philadelphia, 23 May 1793, enclosing a copy of the Convention's decree of 19 February, in "Correspondence Relative to the Renewal of Treaties between France and the United States of America," *The Correspondence between Citizen Genet, Minister of the French Republic, to the United States of North America, and the Officers of the Federal Government* (Philadelphia 1793) 11–13.

[53]Same to same, New York, 30 September 1793, ibid., 17.

British; moreover, past favors, far from being reciprocated, had met with "a most exorbitant tax on tonnage." Despite this ingratitude, wrote Genet, his government had conferred still more commercial favors and now asked only for "a just equivalent." Genet was not optimistic. As he suspected it would, his appeal came to nought. From what was known of the situation in the Antilles the case for gratitude had a hollow ring. Americans, he knew, looked on the open-port and tariff privileges less as acts of magnaminity than of wartime desperation. Given the Indies's now nearly complete reliance on American foodstuffs, any favors shown to American shipping spoke more loudly to the islands' needs than to French generosity.[54]

For his failure to negotiate a treaty Genet put less blame on the administration than did others. He seemed to accept without cavil Jefferson's scruple, ostensibly constitutional, that a treaty negotiation must properly await the reconvening of the Senate. How deceitfully thin this pretext for delay Joseph Fauchet later derided at length. Genet's successor pointed scornfully to the record. From its own published correspondence the administration showed how often it had sought to treat with London, irrespective of the Senate's being in session or even aware that a negotiation was being attempted. Indeed, had Fauchet thought to note it, Jefferson himself had pressed Ternant with treaty proposals during a senatorial hiatus, even urging the expediency of having a completed treaty in hand before the Senate reconvened.[55]

In September, Genet heard and accepted the reasonableness of a much fuller Jeffersonian explanation of why a new treaty was likely to encounter difficulty. The major obstacle was the French requirement of a tonnage exemption. Members of Congress feared that other treaty partners would also claim the exemption under the most favored nation principle. The resulting loss of federal revenue would threaten the government's credit. Against such entrenched and vital interests Genet seemed persuaded that appeals to gratitude would carry little weight.[56]

By the time Jefferson reported Genet's overture to Congress in December, the French emissary was himself discredited and his recall imminent. This plus political turmoil in Paris gave the secretary reason enough to put off recommending a negotiation. As one apologist for

[54]Cf., ibid, 15–16; and Genet to MAE, No. 17, New York, 5 October 1793, *CFM*, 259.
[55]Cf., Jefferson to Gouverneur Morris, Philadelphia, 23 August 1793, *Writings of TJ*, 8: 5; Fauchet's "Mémoire" (1796), 102; Fauchet to CSP, No. 3, Philadelphia, 20 germinal, an 3 (9 April 1795), *CFM*, 630–32; and Ternant to Lessart, No. 31, Philadelphia, 8 April 1792, ibid., 109.
[56]Genet to MAE, No. 17, 5 October 1793, ibid., 258–59.

Genet complained, the overture "was scarcely heard"; he fumed that Jefferson had dared "to insinuate that the present state of France did not permit treating with that power."[57] Herein, however, lay another explanation for the failure of revolutionary diplomats to negotiate a new commercial treaty. Though it infuriated French revolutionaries to admit it, the increasingly bloody aspect they presented to the world hardly inspired confidence.

France's American diplomacy by 1793 had two objectives: to exploit the language of existing treaties to France's fullest wartime advantage, and to increase that advantage by negotiating a new treaty. In demanding treaty rights already stipulated, French diplomats could ignore what Americans thought of their revolution, but as supplicants for a new treaty, they came to realize how much depended on projecting a deserving republican image. They learned how difficult it was to win the sort of confidence that would be conducive to treaty-making when events in Paris portrayed them as agents of transient factions scrambling for power over the dead bodies of their rivals. French officials, roused to self-justification, were able to allay some of the discomfiture by arguing plausibly that they were merely repulsing the attacks of bloodthirsty aristocrats. They found it almost impossible, however, to dispel the idea that by executing the king they had condemned France to perpetual civil disorder. American disapproval touched sensitive nerves. It disturbed Paris deeply, for example, to hear the rumor that Washington wore mourning for "Capet and Antoinette," and to learn that Americans in general resisted drawing a parallel between this and what their English forebears had meted out to the second Stuart.[58]

In Fauchet's view, the execution of the king, together with Lafayette's fall from power, fixed permanently the latent hostility that French diplomats thereafter encountered in the administration. Americans who understood the revolution and condoned its imperatives soon got over their anguish, but the post-execution attitudes of most government fig-

---

[57]Pautizel, "Mémoire sur l'Etat Publique," f. 49vo.

[58]Rumor of Washington's supposed royalist sympathies reached Paris in the summer of 1794 from Prieur de la Marne, one of the government's representatives at Brest. Prieur's dispatch of 8 July is in *Actes du CSP*, 15: 15–16. Files of U.S. newspaper clippings, collected by government agencies, testify in a more general way to official discomfiture. See AD XX[B], doss. 83, ANF. The difficulty of combatting anti-revolutionary sentiment was perhaps best summed up by Antoine Duplaine in his "Observations sur les circonstances actuelles, relativement aux intérêts de la République Française, et celles des Etats-unis de l'Amérique," Philadelphia, [February 1794], DXXV, carton 59, doss. 582, ANF, written when he was president of the French Society of the Friends of Liberty and Equality in Philadelphia. For official efforts to re-educate American public opinion, see Didot, *Précis*.

ures, he wrote, became "marked by the most striking character of cold-
ness and reserve."[59]

Fauchet's own mission to Philadelphia, 1794–95, played out the last
act in the French effort to obtain "reciprocity" before Jay's treaty dropped
the final curtain. Ill-served and neglected by those who sent it, this Jacobin
embassy stumbled across a darkening scene, rent by internal dissension,
believing itself deceived, and groping vainly for what the French call a
point d'appui on the increasingly slippery terrain of American politics.
With him Fauchet brought three fellow "commissioners," all equally
charged with the mission, but two of them, Antoine Delaforest and Jean-
Baptiste Petry, he soon suspected of having treasonous *émigré* associations
and from whom he quickly dissociated himself by opening a separate,
private correspondence with the Foreign Office. By putting these two
well-seasoned American "hands" at a distance, Fauchet managed to isolate
himself from persons best able to advise him on strategy and fell instead
among American advisers whose political motives were more anti-admin-
istration than they were pro-French.[60]

At the outset, however, the Fauchet mission seemed to succeed ad-
mirably in some of its major objectives. On orders from Paris, the Commissioners promptly disavowed Genet, decommissioned his privateers,
disbanded his "invasion" forces, and managed to reassure the administration of France's wish not to disrupt further its chosen course of neutrality. The emissaries also completed the herculean task of sending off massive
shipments of American grain, indeed in such quantities as to make a critical difference in France's food supply in the year 1794. Even the tides of
congressional politics seemed to be running in France's favor. Fauchet
and his colleagues came on the political scene just as Thomas Jefferson in
a valedictory report to Congress had furnished that body with both the
motive and the statistical ammunition to launch a legislative assault on
British mercantilism which, by its nature, could not help but benefit
France. Jefferson's famous report on commerce applauded France for past
concessions, damned Britain for not having followed suit, and signaled
Congress what it should do to reward the former and punish the latter.
Picking up the cue, James Madison had introduced in the House resolutions that proposed to levy "countervailing" (that is, higher) tariffs and
tonnage duties against the cargoes and ships of nations with which the

---

[59]"Mémoire" (1796), 97.

[60]This last was Otto's judgment (*Considérations*, 16–17). Fauchet's suspicions of Delaforest
and Petry first surfaced in his Nos. 3 and 4 (politique), to MAE, Philadelphia, 4 and 5 June 1794,
CFM, 372–77, and 378–81, respectively.

United States had no commercial treaty. Had the resolutions passed, even though their foremost object was to force concessions from London, until such concessions were forthcoming, French commerce would have been the principal beneficiary. Fauchet and the Commissioners arrived in the midst of this momentous debate on the Madison Resolutions.[61]

Looking back, Fauchet expressed deep regret at not having lobbied more actively for their passage. Two years later he recalled the resolutions as having presented "one of the most beautiful opportunities" of his mission. His slackness can, however, be explained. Getting off the grain convoy had seemed more important. Moreover, the rising crisis in Anglo-American relations seemed likely to push the resolutions through Congress without need for lobbying. On an exonerating note, Fauchet also recalled that he, for one, had wanted to organize "a plan of procedure" for seconding Madison's efforts. His legation colleagues, however, had thought so little of Madison's proposals that he had yielded to their counsel and done little to show open support.[62]

Not for a moment, however, did Fauchet doubt that the Madison Resolutions, though aimed at coercing Britain, also expressed the good-will of pro-French forces in the House. His contemporary dispatches, moreover, showed he hoped to capitalize on that goodwill by pushing for a new commercial treaty. The idea of linking congressional action with a new treaty occurred to him when a further worsening of relations between Philadelphia and London that spring led Congress to shelve the resolutions in favor of stronger anti-British measures. Madison's countervailing duties, he reported, were now deemed "insufficient" to meet the torrent of British abuse. By mid-March, news was pouring in of widespread British seizures of American vessels in the Caribbean. This, combined with word of British troop maneuvers in the Northwest, moved Congress with unaccustomed swiftness to impose an embargo and to begin to talk of military preparations. In the end, Washington was persuaded by his advisers that only a direct approach to London could prevent war, and nominated John Jay to undertake the mission.[63]

Against the outcome of that mission Fauchet made desperate calcula-

---

[61]See Jefferson, "Report of the Secretary of State on the Privileges and Restrictions on the Commerce of the United States in Foreign Countries," Philadelphia, 16 December 1793, *ASP,FR*, 1: 300–304.

[62]Cf., Fauchet's "Mémoire" (1796), 105–107; and his No. 16 (politique) to CRE, Philadelphia, 16 pluviôse, an 3 (4 February 1795), *CFM*, 560–61.

[63]See Fauchet to MAE, No. 2 (politique), Philadelphia, 28 floréal, an 2 (17 May 1794), ibid., 340–44; and Ritcheson, *Aftermath of Revolution*, chap. 14, for details of the Anglo-American crisis of early 1794.

tions. Jay's success, he foresaw, would put an end to the Madison Resolutions. On the other hand, his Republican friends told him that if Jay failed, Congress might revive those punitive measures at its next session. Fauchet was impressed. A blow at British commerce, if ultimately enacted, would produce "a commercial revolution" potentially favorable to France. "The renewal of the Treaty with France," he wrote, "ought to be the forerunner of it." In any event, his course seemed clear. Even if Jay returned with a British treaty in hand, what better way to forestall its ratification than for him already to have offered Congress a French alternative?[64]

The French minister's conjectures by no means reflected optimism. It was already mid-May and John Jay had sailed when Fauchet began to explore in depth the possibilities for treaty-making. Thus far his overtures to Jefferson's successor, Edmund Randolph, had borne no fruit. Moreover, the whole idea of treaty renewal was undergoing a change in scale and purpose his instructions had not envisioned. What those instructions had billed as a fairly routine demand for "reciprocity"—i.e., a tonnage exemption—loomed small alongside the now pressing need for action to prevent what Fauchet sensed might become a complete turnabout in America's relationship with the great powers. Jay's mission, he knew, was pregnant with untoward possibilities. If France did not act firmly, Americans might slip the leash of French fraternity and bed down in the camp of the enemy.

As time passed, his treaty efforts still stalled, Fauchet pinpointed the circumstances he felt most inhibited his taking a diplomatic offensive. The Foreign Office, for its part, had not instructed him fully enough as to what specific articles it wanted. Worse, it persisted in leaving him uninstructed as to how he should respond to the new threat posed by the Jay mission. In Philadelphia, meanwhile, the Washington administration had apparently fallen under the influence of a pro-British faction whose straining for a reconciliation with London precluded any dealings with France that might even appear to jeopardize that objective. In token thereof, Fauchet had found Edmund Randolph evasive to the point of being downright deceitful.[65]

In the latter phases of the French quest for reciprocity, this element of deceit, figuring so prominently in Fauchet's dispatches, seemed to con-

---

[64]See Fauchet's No. 2, cited above, *CFM*, 340, 344.

[65]Fauchet's complaint of Randolph was both contemporary and retrospective. Cf., his No. 16 (politique) to MAE, Philadelphia, 16 pluviôse, an 3 (4 February 1794), *CFM*, 561; and his "Mémoire" (1796), 106, 110. See also his *Coup d'Oeil sur la Situation des Affaires entre la France et les Etats-Unis* (Paris 1798) 30–33.

firm the French perception of American perfidy. Two years later when
the government's official press organ, *Le Moniteur*, reviewed the iniquities
of Jay's treaty, it stressed with particular vehemence the lack of candor
the administration had shown during the course of its British negotiation.
Randolph was especially singled out for having hidden the true purpose
of that negotiation.[66]

Fauchet himself found Randolph doubly evasive. Not only was the
secretary suspiciously reticent about the Jay mission; he also seemed ambiva-
lent toward Fauchet's overtures for a new commercial treaty. On the matter
of opening treaty talks, Fauchet ultimately felt more embarrassed than
deceived. Still, though he knew himself to be woefully under-instructed
to enter formal negotiations, the French minister found it difficult to
shake the suspicion that Randolph was playing a double game. Randolph
repeatedly said he would welcome any treaty proposals Fauchet might
offer, but it soon became clear that he would not entertain any explora-
tory or informal discussions. What Fauchet came to realize was that the
secretary would settle for nothing less than a detailed draft of treaty articles. "One can approach the Americans only with '*un plan fait*,' " he
wrote. In sum, Randolph, with or without good reason, refused to discuss generalities. This, Fauchet explained to Paris, was why he so desperately needed fresh instructions. He underscored the point by remarking
how ridiculous he would appear if he asked Randolph to treat simply on
"the principles proposed [to Ternant] by Mr. Jefferson." Until Paris sent
him the specifics, he could make no headway.[67]

For a time, Fauchet hoped that James Monroe, recently posted to
Paris, had been given the power to treat on commercial matters which he
himself lacked. In fact, Randolph was telling Monroe, and truthfully,
that Fauchet had not come forward with proposals for a new treaty of
commerce; and if the French still wanted such a treaty, they should negotiate it in Philadelphia. Fauchet's suspicions deepened when he realized
that Monroe, as well as he, had no instructions to negotiate. Between
Randolph's refusal to discuss anything but specifics and Monroe's lack of
power to negotiate, he wondered whether the administration had not
deliberately created a hiatus so that Jay would have time to complete his
negotiation in London. Ironically, should Jay succeed, the friends of France

---

[66]*Le Moniteur* of 9 germinal, an 4 (29 March 1796) carried a detailed critique of Jay's treaty.

[67]Cf., Fauchet, Nos. 2 and 3 (politique) to MAE, Philadelphia, 17 May and 4 June 1794,
CFM, 344, and 374–76, respectively; same to CSP, No. 4 (particulière), Philadelphia, 24 germinal,
an 3 (13 April 1795), ibid., 635–39; same to CRE, No. 44 (politique), Philadelphia, 14 pluviôse,
an 3 (2 February 1795), ibid., 556; and his "Mémoire" (1796), 107.

would marvel at the negligence that had allowed British diplomacy to outflank them.[68]

Because Fauchet himself was unprepared to open treaty negotiations, Randolph's equivocations on this score were at least susceptible to blameless explanation. His briefing of Fauchet on the Jay mission, however, suggested outright deception. The secretary solemnly assured him —and this much in good faith—that nothing agreed to in London that violated existing treaty engagements to France would be approved. Less ingenuous, however, were his assurances that Jay's *only* purpose was to secure indemnification for maritime spoliations, and *not* to make a commercial treaty. Fauchet heard this last point clearly; Randolph had even shown him that part of Jay's instructions which ostensibly restricted the mission to obtaining indemnity. Having gone thus far, however, Randolph did not disclose subsequent passages which empowered Jay, if he succeeded in winning indemnity plus other concessions, to negotiate a commercial treaty along the lines of some nineteen points spelled out for his guidance.[69] Jay did, of course, produce a commercial treaty. Fauchet complained that he had been lied to. And Randolph felt compelled to defend himself publicly. He denied telling Fauchet that "nothing of a commercial nature was intended." Fauchet had misunderstood him. Why, he asked, would he have hidden from Fauchet the possibility of Jay's negotiating a commercial treaty when such a treaty was of no concern to France as long as no French treaty rights were abridged? Paris clearly was not persuaded of Randolph's candor, nor did it accept the administration's view that Jay's treaty had left French interests unscathed. At the very least a surreptitious negotiation, artfully concealed, had placed American shipping under its enemy's ultimate control. Only Monroe's restraining influence, and the possibility that neither Senate nor House would implement the treaty, prevented France from taking immediate reprisals.[70]

Earlier, when no news came from London, Fauchet's worst fears had fed on rumor and conjecture. Word that Jay had negotiated a full-scale commercial treaty began to circulate in the fall of 1794. The administration's silence, he thought, "leads to believing that M. Jay does more

---

[68]Randolph to Monroe, Philadelphia, 10 June 1794, *ASP,FR* 1: 668. See particularly *CFM*, 344, 562, and 630, for Fauchet's dispatches previously cited wherein his suspicions can be seen to escalate between May 1794, and April 1795.

[69]Fauchet to MAE, No. 3 (politique), Philadelphia, 16 prairial, an 2 (4 June 1794), ibid., 375. See Randolph's instructions to Jay, Philadelphia, 6 May 1794, *ASP,FR*, 1: 472–74.

[70]"Declaration of Edmund Randolph," 8 July 1795, ibid., 593. The best recent treatment of the Monroe mission is by Edward Angel, "James Monroe's Mission to France, 1794–1796," (unpublished Ph.D. dissertation, The George Washington University, 1979).

things in London than is admitted." By spring, the fact of Jay's treaty was no longer denied. Randolph, however, would say only that whatever its details, the treaty would do no harm to French interests. If that were true, Fauchet reflected, why was Randolph so secretive? When at last the treaty arrived, Fauchet asked to see it and, of course, was refused. He could only conclude that for want of any other source of national strength, the administration had forged the weapon of secrecy.[71]

As his mission drew to a close, Fauchet penned a dispatch dated 13 April 1795, which for clarity of thought and hard-hitting language has few equals among the written explanations of why France so persistently missed opportunities to secure a new commercial treaty. None of his later writings on this subject—and they were copious—made so forceful a case. The major defect in the French quest for "reciprocity," he wrote, was this: no French government had ever developed a fully thought-out commercial strategy based on a realistic assessment of means and ends. Beginning with the "indifference" of the royalist past, Fauchet traced the obstacles familiarly believed to have prevented the making of a new commercial treaty. Americans had been put off, in turn, by what he called "our revolutionary phases," the execution of the king, France's early military setbacks on the continent, and, most recently, by the "astonishing" conduct of Citizen Genet. Throughout, French ministers had lacked adequate directives. Neither Genet nor he could have carried out a treaty negotiation from the vagueness contained in their instructions. This was not surprising, he thought, when one considered how eagerly French regimes had seized on Jefferson's four treaty proposals without really examining their import. Fauchet then put some questions that had not been asked before. If at any time a negotiation had been launched, would the acceptance of Jefferson's proposals have truly benefited France? "Would they have changed anything in the British monopoly?" he asked. "Would they have augmented importations from France? Has anyone compared them with the existing state of things, or studied their future results?"[72]

Unerringly Fauchet put his finger on the most intractable problems France had long confronted in her American commerce. Americans bought too little from France, too much from Britain (which they paid for with French gold), and carried more of France's colonial trade than was healthy

---

[71]To CRE, No. 37, Philadelphia, 7 nivôse, an 3 (27 December 1794), *CFM*, 522; same to CSP, No. 7 (politique), Philadelphia, 26 ventôse, an 3 (16 March 1795), ibid., 605, 607. See also his earlier No. 7 (particulière) to CRE, Philadelphia, 30 fructidor, an 2 (16 September 1794), and No. 14 (politique) to CDRE, Philadelphia, 29 brumaire, an 3 (19 November 1794), ibid., 422, and 482, respectively.

[72]To CSP, No. 4 (particulière), Philadelphia, 24 germinal, an 3 (13 April 1795), ibid., 634–41.

for her external economy. Nothing proposed thus far would alter these realities. On close scrutiny, Jefferson's proposals, if accepted, would work more to the profit of American merchants than French, and the long-sought tonnage exemption would neither create a consumer demand for French exports, nor make them more competitive with those of the British. "For the most part," he concluded, "we lack the necessary materials for establishing our commercial ties solidly with America."[73]

The French Foreign Office obviously did not concur in Fauchet's despairing conclusion. Nor did it heed his plea that thought be given to detailing more explicitly the instructions to emissaries charged with treaty-making. As though nothing had intervened since Fauchet had been instructed, Paris gave his successor the same, slightly warmed-over enjoinders to demand a tonnage exemption and to blow the dust off Jefferson's treaty proposals of 1792.[74] What Pierre Adet soon discovered was that Jay's treaty, if implemented, would destroy the French government's prospects of renewing with advantage its earlier treaty engagements with the United States in several important respects. Ostensibly, the "saving clause" in Jay's Article 25 preserved intact the exclusive port and privateering rights France had won from the United States in 1778. In the same Jay article, however, the *exclusive* claim to those rights could not be renewed to France in any future Franco-American treaty; Britain could claim them as well.[75]

Not surprisingly, in their anger at Jay's treaty, French policymakers by 1796 began to think more in terms of reprisal than of accommodation, more in terms of political action than of trying to patch up a commerce which British cruisers had in any case nearly destroyed. As French leaders considered how rapidly their influence in American affairs was shrinking, plans for political action often tinged with retributive violence seemed to multiply. Most spectacular was the threat of French vengeance Pierre Adet carried openly into the presidential election of 1796. If Americans did not elect Jefferson whom, he made clear, he expected to undo the effects of Jay's treaty, they could expect reprisals on the high seas. In fact, French corsairs were already preying on American shipping, their predatory operations destined to increase as time went on. Equally menacing in its

[73]Ibid., 640. Fauchet's sense of frustration was echoed in his "Mémoire" (1796) 114–15, and only slightly less so in his memorandum dated April 1796, entitled "Considérations sur un traité de Commerce avec les Etats-unis," AF III, carton 64, doss. 260, ANF.

[74]"Instructions pour le Ministre plénipotentiaire, de la République, près les Etats Unis d'Amérique," Paris, 2 brumaire, an 3 (23 October 1794), CFM, 725–26.

[75]For Article 25, see Miller, *Treaties*, 2: 262; and for Adet's awareness of its implication, see Adet to Randolph, Philadelphia, 30 June 1795, *ASP,FR*, 1: 594–95.

way was the renewed appeal of what might be called the "Louisiana solution." Fauchet, now back in Paris, picked up on this project, first suggested by Moustier, touting it as a sure means to compel Americans to show a proper regard for French interests. If returned to France, Louisiana would not only become an alternative source of food supply for the islands, but it would also give France a command of the Mississippi Valley certain to elicit from Philadelphia a greater respect for French *politik*.[76]

By mid-1795, when Adet replaced Fauchet, the time was already long past when French statesmen could reasonably expect to negotiate a new commercial treaty. Although such a treaty was still talked of in official circles, the worsening of Franco-American relations made clear that France's hopes for reordering her American commerce must await a less impassioned era. Looking back from the flash-point of Jay's treaty, French observers could not stare down the fact that they themselves had missed opportunities for securing "reciprocity." They were equally certain, however, that Americans had been woefully remiss in not according, freely and out of gratitude, some small advantage to French shipping that might have allowed France to compete with Britain in the sea lanes of the Atlantic, or by their restraint permitted France to retain her vested interest in the Indies trade. The French perception of ungenerous Americans, underscored by this stubborn refusal to grant "reciprocity," gave added sting to the outrage they felt when Jay's treaty swept aside their last hope of commercial survival in the New World.

---

[76]"Mémoire" (1796) 119. While still in Philadelphia, Fauchet recurred to the Louisiana "solution" in no fewer than three dispatches written in February 1795. See his Nos. 16 and 17 to CRE and his No. 1 to CSP, dated 4, 8, and 16 February, *CFM*, 567, 574, and 580, respectively.

VI
THE CLASH OF VALUES

French ill-will toward the young republic sprang from more than disappointed hopes for trade and commerce. Clashes of values, especially in the realm of individual freedom, also begot resentment. To a society still relatively authoritarian America incessantly challenged and laid open to question the traditional restraints French governments were accustomed to imposing. Whether royalist or republican, French regimes expected their nationals overseas to continue to obey French law and submit to official direction quite as if they were still on home soil. How little control they in fact retained once their countrymen had tasted the opportunities of the New World came as an unpleasant surprise. It galled them to know that Frenchmen, for whatever reason, though usually discreditable, could find escape and refuge in a land that welcomed newcomers, eagerly offered them citizenship, and put its laws and protections at their disposal. Thousands of Frenchmen—seamen, businessmen, refugees, and *émigrés*—would pass through the port cities of the United States in the 1780s and early 1790s. From their passage French officialdom soon learned to its discomfiture that America was a place where French seamen could make good their desertions, French businessmen their conspiracies to circumvent their country's trade regulations, and from which political dissidents could snipe at Paris with impunity.

French consuls who sought to curb such activities often found that their best efforts were defeated by a permissive environment. Schooled to believe that one's countrymen should submit to the nation's authority no matter where, they came ultimately to deplore that aspect of America some of their countrymen most admired: the freedom it offered for individual action unfettered by almost any authority.

The remedy for this state of indiscipline, as French officials regarded it, lay tantalizingly within reach. Congress needed only to ratify the Franco-American consular convention Franklin and Vergennes had signed in 1784. This document had spelled out the kinds of powers French consuls traditionally used to maintain law and order among overseas communities. Unfortunately, although Franklin was later shown to have stayed within his instruction, Congress in 1785, and for several years thereafter, was persuaded that he had not. The master persuader in this sequel was John Jay who, as secretary for foreign affairs, professed to see in Franklin's draft French consular powers dangerous to American sovereignty. In some respects this fear was warranted, but the arguments he gave Congress for not ratifying blinked the fact that an earlier Congress had approved these powers. The judgment seems well founded that John Jay's personal animus toward France, more than anything else, explains the influence he brought to bear on Congress to delay action on the consular convention. From the French standpoint this delay, so obviously a retreat from the earlier commitment, constituted a breach of faith the more serious for the perceived and pressing need of French consuls to have the powers they lacked. Not until November 1788 did Jefferson win Montmorin's consent to a slightly modified version, and not until April 1790 did Washington's proclamation bring the convention into effect.[1]

Although Jay worked to delay the convention out of a personal distrust of France, the specific alarms he raised nonetheless echoed serious and widespread popular misgivings about the kinds of activities consuls might engage in. Members of Congress who feared their government might be forced to repatriate persons fleeing injustice and persecution were already half persuaded to delay action. Conjectures as to whether the convention might lead to unacceptable demands for extradition or somehow abridge the right of states to naturalize French-born immigrants were not lightly dismissed. Recent memory of the Longchamps Affair wherein Paris had sternly demanded custody of a French officer guilty of assaulting the French chargé d'affaires put an edge on the first; and France's well-known aversion to losing population through emigration gave reason to be careful of the second.[2]

Jefferson in Paris, meanwhile, managed to win textual changes that went far to alleviate congressional fears. In final form, the convention made no direct reference to American naturalization procedures or to extradition. It assured that consuls could not arbitrarily deport French

---

[1]For details of Jay's delay tactics, see Julian P. Boyd, "Two Diplomats Between Revolutions," *Virginia Magazine of History and Biography* (April 1958) 131–46; for the text of the consular convention, see Miller, *Treaties*, 2: 228–41.

[2]Though Congress debated in secrecy, Marbois learned of its concerns from Jay, and Otto from confidential conversations with individual members. Marbois to MAE, No. 430, New York, 17 July 1785, AECPE-U, 30: 143–46; Otto to same, No. 5, New York, 6 September 1785, ibid., ff. 270–71.

nationals, while stipulating that American courts would facilitate the recovery and return of deserters and other ships' personnel, but, significantly, not "passengers." As Jefferson told Montmorin, such a bar to free immigration would "violate our bill of rights." With certain other modifications which Montmorin agreed to regard as formal rather than substantive, the convention won the Senate's consent on 29 July 1789.[3]

Ironically, having their powers formally defined by treaty gave French consuls little cause for rejoicing. Indeed, some believed the convention saddled them with more problems than when their powers had been left to chance and discretion.[4] So it seemed, at least, when a document ostensibly intended to clarify their legal powers became instead a playground for American lawyers whereon French consuls found themselves playing games of litigation they suspected were more often intended to defeat those powers than to uphold them. To examine the consular condition both before and after the convention is to reveal how painful the sense of grievance Paris experienced in the realm of consular difficulties over the years.

In the spring of 1788 Antoine Delaforest painted a panoramic scene of French consular activity in late eighteenth-century America. Reporting on the establishment over which he presided, Delaforest omitted no important detail of his consuls' wide-ranging responsibilities. Although the latter were well defined by French law and tradition, his was a description of what his consuls actually did. As information-gatherers, they regularly informed the minister plenipotentiary of local political happenings. They reported four times a year the arrivals and departures of all shipping, wrote annual summaries of business conditions, and translated all newspaper articles relating to commerce. In what he called their "administrative objectives," they watched to make sure the commercial treaty was observed, sought additional port and tax privileges for French vessels, encouraged Americans to send cargoes to French ports, arranged contacts among French and American businessmen, and saw to it that incoming French cargoes paid no higher duties than were required. Their official status, he wrote, required them to live as well as their salaries permitted, mix with local political leaders, keep tabs on other foreign consuls, transact no personal business, and treat all French subjects fairly and without partiality. When he came to describe their exercise of "powers," however, he noted that until the convention took effect his consuls would have to continue to tread softly. They met no obstacle in such routine duties as provision-

---

[3]Cf., Jefferson to Montmorin, Paris, 20 June 1788, ibid., 33: 197vo; "Observations sur la lettre de M. Jefferson du juin 1788," undated but in Montmorin's hand, ibid., ff. 204–206.
[4]Otto to MAE, No. 57, Philadelphia, 12 March 1791, ibid., 35: 307–308.

ing warships or maintaining naval hospitals, but they did encounter difficulties in their dealings with American courts. Delaforest obviously felt no need to elaborate because these difficulties had already figured so vividly in earlier dispatches.[5]

By 1788 the record showed that French consuls were most often frustrated whenever they tried to assert what they regarded as their traditional authority in legal matters. Local magistrates, they discovered, either refused to back up their authority or openly contested it. Typically, French jurisdictional claims fell short whenever a consul tried either to recover seamen-deserters, settle civil disputes among French nationals, or extricate Frenchmen from the American judicial process. Whether their authority was challenged or merely not upheld, consuls felt sure the outcomes would have been different had they been vested with the powers promised by the unratified convention. They also expected the convention to help them deal with French smugglers, although here the problem was less one of jurisdictional dispute than of American court and customs officials not caring one way or the other whether French maritime regulations were complied with. Nor, as it turned out, did the ratified convention enlist American authority in support of the French navigation system. Jefferson quashed this project of extraterritoriality when he told Montmorin that he could not agree to a clause "proposing that the Navigation code of each nation be established in the territories of the other."[6]

Jurisdictional difficulties tended to vary from one consular district to another. New England and Virginia, for example, produced problems principally related to the high incidence of desertion. The annual visits of the French fleet to Boston, sometimes to Newport, kept Philippe Létombe seasonally occupied tracking down French seamen who had taken "English leave." Similarly, Martin Oster spent much of his time recovering seamen who jumped French tobacco carriers that regularly put in to Norfolk, Portsmouth, and Williamsburg. Whether crewmen deserted from naval or merchant vessels, consuls bore responsibility for apprehending them. Success depended on local attitudes. The amiable and well-respected Létombe generally found authorities in Boston cooperative, whereas Oster, perhaps because he was more abrasive, often collided head-on with Virginia magistrates.[7] As a rule, however, Southerners were seen to be

---

[5]"Raport demandé par M. le Cte. de Moustier sur l'établissement consulaire de France en Amérique," enclosed in Delaforest's No. 255, New York, March 1788, CC (New York), 910: 21–31.

[6]In a cover letter to Montmorin, Paris, 16 September 1788, AECPE-U, 33: ff. 266–66vo, enclosing Jefferson's alterations to the draft convention.

[7]Cf., Létombe to MMC, No. 13, 11 July 1787, CC (Boston), 210: 188vo; Oster, "Articles à soumettre à l'Examen de Monsieur le Comte de Moustier," enclosed in No. 60 to MMC, 18 October 1788, CC (Norfolk), 927: 173–84vo.

more indulgent toward the exercise of consular authority. Louis Otto ascribed this to an aristocracy's greater tolerance for the uses of power. Consul D'Annemours in Baltimore, for example, seemed to exercise full judicial authority without the sort of struggle that beset consuls farther north. This was Otto's view, although D'Annemours's own appraisal differed somewhat. French deserters, he noted, regularly signed on American merchantmen out of Baltimore, and could not be recovered on their return because "they disperse the moment they arrive." Be that as it may, Baltimore itself differed from other consular seats. It saw fewer French vessels than most and had only a small French business community. What, for Otto, passed as a quiet exercise of consular powers more likely spoke to a consul little troubled by what few problems arose.[8]

In cities like New York and Philadelphia where desertion was only one of many legal problems, Otto was right. Consuls here met more formidable opposition to their jurisdictional claims. It stood to reason that in the larger cities more Frenchmen would either be "going to the law" or running afoul of it. Here, too, lawyers seemed to be more numerous and more avid, and judges more conscious of being watched for their decisions. In New York, however, when it was the seat of government— and the same was true later in Philadelphia—consuls had the advantage of being able to call on the French minister or chargé d'affaires to back them up. Charleston, too, was an active center of litigation, complicated by its being a major port of entry for French smugglers. It was here that consuls felt most painfully their lack of authority as French vessels, routinely breaking out American "papers," sailed in to drop off "illegal" cargoes of sugar and coffee.

In disputes among Frenchmen a consul's traditional jurisdiction disappeared abruptly whenever litigants chose to take their cases into American courts. If pressed too far, they could always take the extra step, acquire American citizenship, and escape French jurisdiction altogether. Shortly before he left, La Luzerne noted the increasing frequency with which "bad intentioned" Frenchmen were dragging their countrymen into American courts whenever they foresaw that a consul would rule against them. Four years later, Louis Otto cited as typical the case of a French sea captain, three of whose crewmen were demanding to be discharged with pay, who had been haled before an American judge. They won their case, he wrote, as had many others, because they sought out

---

[8]Cf., Otto to MAE, No. 6, New York, 10 September 1785, AECPE-U, 30: 292–92vo; D'Annemours to MMC, No. 3, 11 May 1782, CC (Baltimore), Tome 1, 14.

judges whose rulings were known to encourage "a dispersion of crews."[9]

By and large, consuls were forced to use "great circumspection" in dealing with all litigants. "The least annoyance," wrote Otto, "enrages them and leads them to throw themselves into the arms of Americans always open to receive them." A consular decision that Frenchmen would accept without question in the Levant or in some African port, he continued, "takes on the appearance of an arbitrary act in America and can be eluded without difficulty by decorating oneself with the title of Citizen of the United States."[10]

Consuls did not always find local authorities resistant to jurisdictional claims. In the case of the three sailors who had won their case for discharge, for example, Otto was able to write a satisfactory denouement. The mayor of New York, he reported, had subsequently ordered them arrested for desertion. Otto made clear, however, that success in this instance was an exception to the rule.[11] Much depended, as well, on the French business community's own attitude toward consular authority. In Charleston, for example, Delaforest proved his mettle early in his career when he secured enough backing from resident Frenchmen to get them to submit to him all cases in dispute. These included the policing of vessels in port as well as the disciplining of seamen ashore. Local authorities apparently took the cue. Magistrates in Charleston, he reported, agreed to hold deserters at his request and until he asked for their release. It spoke well for Delaforest's tact and force of personality that only six months earlier legal problems arising "daily" had often provoked bitter disputes with those same authorities.[12]

His successor enjoyed less cooperation. Avistay de Chateaufort ran into a typical problem: that of Americans suing French sailors for debt and persuading a judge to send a constable on board a French vessel to make an arrest. The first time this happened, Chateaufort invoked a clause of the convention, still unratified, requiring that he be notified before an arresting officer went on board. The governor of South Carolina promised to honor the formality. On a second occasion, however, the consul was told that no law required such prior notification, and was reminded

[9]Cf., La Luzerne to MAE, No. 378, Philadelphia, 17 May 1784, AECPE-U, 27: 367–68; Otto to same, No. 21, New York, 16 August 1788, ibid., 33: 254.

[10]"Mémoire remis par le Sr. Otto," ff. 285vo–86.

[11]To MAE, No. 22, New York, 20 August, 1788, AECPE-U, 33: 255–56.

[12]Cf., Delaforest to MMC, Nos. 8 and 10, 23 April and 25 October 1784, CC (Charleston), 372: 36vo–38vo, and 45–56, respectively.

that the convention had not yet taken effect. Chateaufort pressed his argument no further.[13]

Sending a law officer aboard a French vessel took on graver implications if the latter happened to be a warship of his majesty's navy. Hector Saint-John de Crèvecoeur suffered through such an episode in early 1788 when a city constable in New York tried to arrest a cannoneer serving on the French frigate *Aigrette*. An American named Pessendlow had accused the cannoneer of stealing his silver watch. According to Mayor James Duane, the captain of the frigate had not only refused the constable permission to board, but had also "abused" him. The mayor warned Crèvecoeur that he might secure a special admiralty order to gain custody, but preferred that the consul simply deliver the accused man for trial and let justice take its course. With Moustier advising him, Crèvecoeur replied that the evidence of theft was questionable, and denied as "absolutely false" the allegation that the constable had been ill treated. More to the point, he expressed astonishment that New York authorities could imagine they had a right to board a naval vessel for any reason. Refusal was based on the law of nations which protected all public vessels from such intrusions. There the matter ended, or at least became moot when *Aigrette* set sail from New York harbor the following Tuesday.[14]

Moustier, who followed the "silver watch" affair closely, complained to Paris that Americans seemed to believe their police powers extended to naval as well as merchant vessels in their ports. He also noted that John Jay, for reasons unexplained, had persuaded Congress to defer action on a resolution that would have adopted international practice in this regard. Merchant captains, meanwhile, had become so vulnerable to American legal process as to suffer delays tantamount to an "embargo." Sailings were often held up while officers or crew spent time in court answering charges of one sort or another.[15]

When Americans sued Frenchmen or vice versa consular jurisdiction was not an issue; but when both parties were French, and one of them opted for American justice, the legal procedure was, by French standards, notoriously drawn out. As often as not, however, when scheduled sailings were prevented by legal process, captains themselves were to blame. The latter had an unsavory reputation among the consuls. Whenever they were not being sued by crewmen for back wages or maltreatment, they

---

[13]To same, No. 20, 30 March 1786, ibid., ff. 168–69.
[14]Crèvecoeur's account, enclosing copies of his correspondence with Mayor James Duane, is in his No. 2 to MMC, 25 April 1788, CC (New York), 910: 41–44vo. Moustier, meanwhile, kept Montmorin informed in his No. 7, New York, 5 March 1788, AECPE-U, 33: 124–28vo.
[15]Ibid., f. 128vo.

were seen to be making off with their owners' cargoes or otherwise dis-
porting themselves in ways which brought on legal action. In a moment
of disgust, Martin Oster described them as men "who rejoice only in disorder." They lived by robbery and boasted of their lawlessness.[16] The
consuls, meanwhile, lived for the day when a ratified convention would
enable them to bring these lawbreakers to justice, French justice.

Oster himself figured prominently in one of the most publicized of
these "lost jurisdiction" cases—that of Captain Joseph Ferrier who, having stolen his owners' cargo, made use of the Virginia court system to
escape Oster's custody. Virginia's refusal to surrender Ferrier brought
thunderous sounds of displeasure from Paris, even the threat of retaliation. More than any other event, the Ferrier case warned Congress that it
had dallied too long over ratifying the convention.[17] It is interesting to
note that Oster might not have pursued Ferrier so zealously—nor might
the case itself have assumed such ominous proportions—had he not been
successful in detecting and punishing a similar offender three years before.
Even in this earlier episode, the consul had not prevailed without difficulty, though jurisdictional conflict had been less of a problem than the
refusal of local law enforcement officials to back him up.

Sometime in the spring of 1784, the French merchantman *Aimable
Louise* put into Norfolk from the Cap. The ship's cargo, sugar and coffee,
made its arrival in Norfolk highly suspect. The captain's claim that a bad
leak had prevented his sailing to Nantes, for which he had been cleared,
roused Oster's suspicions further, especially when the crew testified that
the leak was insignificant. Meanwhile, the captain, a man named Hallot,
complicated matters by charging the owners' agent with having misappropriated part of the cargo. Oster's investigation led him to conclude
that captain and agent had both conspired to cheat the owners and had
also cheated each other in the process. Ultimately, the consul managed to
impound the cargo, appoint a new captain, and dispatch the vessel to
Nantes with a load of tobacco. Not, however, before he spent some tense
moments with an outraged captain. Hallot, he wrote, "has not ceased to
disobey me because he knows the justice of [this] country refuses me both
its help and its prisons." On 6 June, Hallot appeared at dockside, loudly

[16]To MMC, No. 1, Richmond, 30 May 1784, CC (Norfolk), 927: 15. Jean Toscan wrote
that legal cases in New England usually took two years to reach judgment. See his "Mémoire du
Consulat de Boston pour 1785," to the Controller General, April 1786, Mem. et doc., 9: 70. For
strictures on the misconduct of French sea captains, see Marbois to MMC, No. 40, 26 July 1783,
CC (Philadelphia), 945: 342–42vo; Delaforest to same, No. 2, 29 March 1784, CC (Charleston),
372: 4; and Moustier to MAE, No. 7, New York, 5 March 1788, AECPE-U, 33: 129.
[17]Boyd, "Two Diplomats," 136–37.

announced that he was owner of the *Louise*, and drove off the crew with his sabre. Again, Oster appealed to local authorities for help and was refused. "I have not been able to get the crew back on board until this morning," he wrote the next day.[18] Several years later when Moustier asked the consuls to make full reports on their activities, Oster seized the occasion to submit a long list of tough amendments he urged be added to the original draft of the consular convention. Had they been adopted, French consuls would have acquired extraterritorial powers the like of which were not to be seen until the West made its unequal treaties with China half a century later.[19]

Oster must have been struck by how similar in circumstance the Ferrier case was to the earlier Hallot episode. Certainly Moustier saw the parallel. Indeed, when the French minister complained to Congress about Virginia's interference in the Ferrier case, he pointed out that state officials under very like circumstances had not prevented Oster from dealing summarily with Captain Hallot three years before. To Moustier, a salutary precedent for a state's not interfering in such matters had been violated.[20]

In the sequel the facts were as follows: Joseph Marie Anne Ferrier, captain of the brigantine *David*, cleared Cap Français for Nantes on 1 July 1787, carrying a cargo of coffee owned by several parties. Three weeks later, Ferrier sailed into Norfolk, claiming that his ship had a severe leak and requesting Oster's permission to sell his cargo before it spoiled. Leaks as a pretext for offloading contraband were familiar enough for Oster to launch an inquiry. From interviews with crew members the consul realized that something more serious was afoot. The crew's testimony strongly suggested that Ferrier had already sold off part of the cargo before he sailed from Saint Domingue, and more of it to an American shipmaster with whom he had made a rendezvous at Caiques. In pocketing the proceeds, Ferrier had committed the crime of barratry, cargo embezzling. By this time, alarmed by the mounting evidence against him, Ferrier took flight. Oster managed to capture him, however, and locked him up aboard his own vessel where on 6 September he signed a confession. To complete the formalities, Oster then called an "assembly" of local French businessmen. The latter agreed that Ferrier be shipped back to Nantes for trial by admiralty officials. Just before the *David* was due to sail, however, a county

---

[18]Oster to MMC, Nos. 2 and 4, 7 June and 18 October 1784, CC (Norfolk), 927: 18–21, and 56–57, respectively.

[19]See Oster, "Articles à soumettre," ff. 173–84vo.

[20]"Notte remise au Congrès le 28 May 1788," copy enclosed in Moustier to MAE, No. 12, New York, same date, AECPE-U, 33: 176.

sheriff appeared with a writ and arrested Ferrier for an unpaid debt of fifty pounds, owed to one Louis Breton, a French resident of Norfolk. When Ferrier was whisked off to answer a debt complaint, Oster had no doubt as to its collusive character. His suspicions were confirmed when the county judge released Ferrier on bond. Thereafter the captain remained at large.[21]

Efforts to regain custody soon took a political turn. Thus far, Oster had kept the governor of Virginia, Edmund Randolph, fully informed of his actions. He now wrote Randolph demanding Ferrier's return. So, too, did the Comte de Moustier who went to the additional length of sending Congress a formal note of protest in May 1788. When congressional entreaties proved fruitless, Moustier met with members of the Virginia congressional delegation and sternly explained to them why Ferrier should be returned. Neither letters, nor notes, nor solemn enjoinders, however, brought the desired result. Randolph equivocated; Congress could only request; and the Virginia congressmen, though appropriately apologetic, were noncommittal.[22]

Earlier, in Paris, Montmorin thought he saw here an opportunity to jolt Congress into approving the consular convention. Pending Moustier's arrival, the Foreign Minister instructed Otto to link the Ferrier case with congressional stalling on the convention. Otto was to remind Congress that Franklin had had full powers when he signed the convention, and that France had fully complied with its terms ever since. Under Article 10, the king expected swift compliance with his request for Ferrier's surrender.[23] As it turned out, it was Moustier who soon after he arrived acted on this instruction. In a note to Congress of 28 May 1788, the French minister skillfully combined reproaches. He was astonished, he told Congress, that a French national jailed by a French consul for a criminal offense should have been removed from his custody for a civil offense involving only fifty pounds, and then allowed to go free on bond. As to

[21]Oster to MMC, Nos. 40 and 46, 7 July and 8 November 1787, CC (Norfolk), 927: 135–36, and 144–44vo, respectively.

[22]Oster's correspondence with Randolph is contained in his No. 48 to MMC, Norfolk, 6 December 1787, ibid., ff. 154–55vo, 158–58vo, and 162. Moustier described his own role in his "Notte remise au Congrès," ff. 174–77vo; and in his Nos. 12 and 19 to MAE, New York, 28 May and 4 August 1788, ibid., ff. 170–72vo, and 242–44vo, respectively.

[23]Montmorin to Otto, Versailles, 19 February 1788, AECPE-U, 33: 108–109; same to same, Versailles, 26 February 1788, ibid., ff. 111–13. In Paris, Montmorin received advice on the Ferrier case from several quarters. See letter of 12 January 1788 from Pouget, member of the "American Committee," to Gérard de Rayneval, chief of the Bureau des Fonds, urging that La Luzerne be consulted; and the latter's subsequent note to Montmorin, Versailles, 26 January 1788, ibid., ff. 10–10vo, 13–13vo.

the convention, he urged Congress "to put an end as promptly as possible to the last formalities" by instructing Jefferson to signify ratification.[24]

Efforts to link the two issues were, in fact, unnecessary as far as expediting the convention was concerned. Jay having already decided to pose no further obstacle, it was only a matter of time before Jefferson would sign an acceptable version. This he did on 14 November, while Moustier still waited to hear whether the state of Virginia intended to comply with Congress's "recommendation" that Ferrier be surrendered. Not until January did the French minister learn that his efforts had been to no avail. Governor Randolph's reply, he wrote, was nothing but "sophisticated lawyers' arguments." Exasperated, Moustier relished the prospect that once the new federal government convened, France might confront it with peremptory demands. If the new Constitution meant what it said, deference to state sovereignty in such matters would no longer excuse inaction. By the end of June, however, he doubted whether federal authority could be invoked to recover Ferrier until the convention had been formally ratified.[25] A month later, the United States Senate did just that. Thereafter, however, the Ferrier affair disappears from view. Doubtless, Moustier's departure and Otto's intense preoccupation with the multitudinous activities of the first federal Congress help to explain why this knot of irritation remained unresolved. More likely, the Senate's ratification of the consular convention satisfied Paris that similar losses of jurisdiction would not recur in the future.

Hopes for a trouble-free exercise of consular powers faded quickly in the spring of 1790. Hardly was the convention proclaimed in April than French officials began to spot its shortcomings. Ironically, the document defined clearly enough the problems known to have beset consular authority in the past, but it fell short of specifying solutions. Language setting forth intent dwindled off without spelling out the means of fulfilling that intent. Wherein the intent was only suggested, the consuls soon realized that American magistrates, well known for their narrow reading of legal phrases, would continue to be of little support.

Of the two articles that proved most troublesome, numbers 9 and 12, the latter illustrated how difficult would remain the problem of enforce-

---

[24]"Notte remise au Congrès," ff. 176–77.
[25]To MAE, Nos. 1 and 19, New York, 19 January and 29 June 1789, AECPE-U, 34: 7–7vo, and 204–204vo, respectively.

ment. Article 12 ostensibly gave consuls the power to settle "all differences and suits between the subjects of the Most Christian King in the United States." Particular reference to legal problems arising between captains and seamen did not limit this article's application to shipboard discipline. Settling disputes among French nationals residing ashore also fell, by implication, within a consul's authority.[26]

Létombe in Boston first noted the defect in Article 12 when he wrote that his new authority to adjudicate disputes meant very little unless he could call on local peace officers to enforce his decisions. Because the convention had omitted this detail, he was petitioning the Massachusetts legislature for authority to summon constables and sheriffs when needed. The power to decide cases at law, he added, surely implied the power to enforce such decisions. Létombe later reported that Bay State legislators, though they looked with favor on his petition, had referred his request to the new federal government. Taking the cue, the consul immediately signaled Delaforest to urge Otto to begin lobbying Congress. Unfortunately, Congress had already adjourned until the following December.[27]

From New York, meanwhile, the consul general explained to the Navy ministry how gravely the omission of coercive means was affecting consular activity. Without power to enforce their decisions, consuls felt constrained not to intervene in shipboard discipline except in cases of desertion. Thanks to Article 9, U.S. authorities were expressly enjoined to render assistance in recovering deserters. For any infraction short of desertion, however, consuls could not secure "arrest orders." As a result, insubordination was becoming seriously disruptive on board French vessels. His consuls, he wrote, could neither compel defendants to appear before them, nor require those found guilty to submit to sentencing. When they asked for assistance, American magistrates replied that the convention forbade them to take cognizance of disputes among French subjects.[28]

When Congress reconvened in late 1790, Otto easily persuaded Jefferson to have a bill introduced that would authorize American admiralty officers to enforce consular decisions on simple request. Although the bill was subsequently enacted, its equivocal wording still left consuls without the essential power of enforcement. Fauchet thought that the law might have helped for a year or so, but by 1793 judges were again construing

---

[26]Miller, *Treaties*, 2: 239.

[27]To MMC, Nos. 6 and 9, 9 June and 17 August 1790, CC (Boston), 210: 415–18, and 425–26vo, respectively.

[28]To same, No. 298, 25 July 1790, CC (New York), 910: 311–12.

the language of the convention so narrowly as to have all but destroyed the effects of this supportive legislation.[29]

What troubled French officials, aside from an angry awareness of their own impotence, was the flagrant denial of justice. French litigants, when judges refused to hear their cases, were sent back to consuls whose decisions could not be upheld. Only if both parties agreed to abide by a consul's ruling was there any prospect of a satisfactory resolution.[30] In cases touching the most sensitive of personal interests, litigants faced a painful dilemma. Fauchet explained why. French law required nationals overseas to submit to consular jurisdiction in matters of divorce, marriage, and child custody. They risked a fine of 1500 livres if they resorted to a foreign court. Rather than suffer a consul's uncertain jurisdiction, however, many such litigants opted for American courts. Here the party less likely to prevail could halt the proceedings by invoking the convention, leaving the party who had the stronger case without legal recourse. In sum, American magistrates, by refusing to hear cases that touched on consular jurisdiction while also refusing to honor that jurisdiction, read Article 12 so as to deprive French plaintiffs of the fundamental right of all legal systems, the right to have one's case decided. Small wonder French consuls bristled, not only at the indignity of being deprived of the power to uphold decisions which were properly theirs, but also at the spectacle of French nationals being deprived of a sure remedy at law.[31]

The indignation French officials felt at the shortcomings of Article 12 took on a sharper edge when they realized that Article 9, having to do with the recovery of deserters, was no less susceptible to obfuscation. Article 9 prescribed what appeared to be an iron-clad formula for availing French sea captains of all the legal apparatus needed to keep their crews intact. On its face, the procedure spelled out in this article seemed proof against judicial quibble. To cause a deserter to be arrested and held, a consul needed only to exhibit to an American magistrate explicit proof that the escapee was part of a ship's crew. Proof was to be adduced by show-

[29]Fauchet and the Commissioners to CDRE, No. 25 (politique), 22 brumaire, an 3 (12 November 1794), CC (Philadelphia), Tome 3, 152; and Létombe's similar complaint to MMC, No. 144, 6 March 1793, CC (Boston), Tome 3, 28vo–29. For the act of 14 April 1792, see U.S., *Statutes at Large*, 1: 254–57.

[30]See, for example, Létombe to MMC, No. 2, 20 January 1791, CC (Boston), 210: 438–40; Otto to MAE, No. 57, Philadelphia, 12 March 1791, AECPE-U, 35: 307–08; Oster to same, No. 3, (July 1791?), CC (Norfolk), 927: 321vo; and Hauterive, "Mémoire," 25 December 1793, enclosed in No. 8 to same, 30 December 1793, CC (New York), Tome 3, 38vo–39.

[31]Cf., Fauchet and the Commissioners to CDRE, No. 30 (politique), 28 brumaire, an 3 (18 November 1794), CC (Philadelphia), Tome 3, 168–69; and Hauterive, "Mémoire" of 25 December 1793, cited above.

ing the deserter's name on "the registers of the vessel or the ship's roll." (The latter was known to the French as a *"rôle d'équipage,"* a standard document carried by all French vessels.) Upon such presentment, American authorities were obliged to assist in searching for, seizing, and imprisoning deserters until they could be sent back to France. Detention, significantly, was limited to a period of three months dating from the day of arrest. If not repatriated within that time, deserters were to be "set at liberty and shall no more be arrested for the same cause."[32]

Létombe instantly discerned a practical defect in the three-month holding limitation. Seamen who jumped ship late in the fall might often make good their escape, even if jailed, because three months would have elapsed before vessels returning from France could provide means of repatriation. From November to March few French ships either came or went in New England waters. Most likely to be hard hit were the ships of his majesty's navy. The fleet visits to Boston in August and September might have to be discontinued if too many would-be deserters reckoned a few months in a Boston jail against the probability they would go free before the spring sailings arrived from France. In a petition to the Massachusetts legislature, Létombe argued cunningly that unless that state empowered him to return deserters not within three months but, as he suggested, "by the first opportunity," they risked cancellation of fleet visits that would cost local merchants a good deal of business. Meanwhile, he chafed at the thought of losing even one deserter to the statute of limitations. By January 1791, however, he reported that Pierre Jiran, alias John Walker, having served his three months, was now married and living in Boston, his detention and court costs having set the consulate back 181 livres. Next time the fleet put in, he wrote, it should choose Newport instead, where deserters could be more easily apprehended.[33]

Desertions from naval vessels increased after 1793 when France, once more at war with Britain, found herself engaged in widespread naval operations. While French naval seamen generally supported the Revolution they were no less highly politicized than the rest of their countrymen. Politics inevitably bred unrest, and on shipboard where revolutionary ideas loosened traditional disciplines, crews became mutinous, and individual crewmen fearing punishment often defected. Deser-

---

[32]Miller, *Treaties*, 2: 237–38.

[33]See Létombe to MMC, Nos. 6, 9, and 2, 9 June, 17 August 1790, and 20 January 1791, CC (Boston), 210: 415–18, 425–26vo, and 438–40, respectively. For Paris's awareness of the problem, see anon., "Mémoire sur la Convention Consulaire avec les Etats-unis d'Amérique pour servir au Citoyen _____, Envoyé de la République près du Congrès," an 4 (23 September 1795–21 September 1796), Mem. et doc., 10: 123vo–24.

tions were especially high among seamen stationed in the Antilles who, with soldiers and thousands of civilian refugees, were forced to flee Cap Français in July after a pitched battle in which black and mulatto insurrectionaries had purportedly set fire to the city. Like the refugee *"colons,"* members of French forces blamed their humiliating exodus on the misguided policies of the Girondin regime. The latter, they believed, had touched off a powder keg of racial conflict by foolishly promising to enfranchise the mulatto population. The opening afforded by this folly inevitably led to a slave uprising. Soon, with blacks fighting for emancipation, mulattoes for political status, and whites resisting both, a bloody turmoil ensued to which no white Frenchman, witness to it, could remain indifferent. Discipline on board warships arriving from the French islands suffered accordingly. Indeed, it was in quelling a major mutiny among the demoralized crews arriving in New York harbor that Edmond Genet, the Girondin minister, was at his most effective.[34]

Desertion, meanwhile, depleted the crews of French merchant ships. The temptingly higher wages paid by American owners were a function of rising profits. The traditional bonanza afforded to neutral carriers in wartime meant that owners looking for deck hands gladly signed on any seaman, regardless of the man's previous commitments. Also, with naval complements shorthanded and press gangs active, French seamen not surprisingly looked for safer berths aboard American vessels outbound.[35]

As sailors found more reasons to desert, American judges seemed to find more reasons not to assist in their recovery. By 1796, the Foreign Office had in hand an unsigned memorial (possibly written by Fauchet) which described American magistrates as showing "unimaginable skill in evading the demands of our agents in this regard." The writer of this *"mémoire"* voiced particular anger at judges who chose to read too rigorously the letter of the convention respecting proof. Because the convention specified that consuls present in evidence a ship's *"rôle d'équipage"* showing thereon the name of the alleged deserter, judges were disinclined to accept any other kind of evidence. *"Rôles d'équipage,"* as part of every French vessel's official papers, were required to be kept on board or at least within reach lest its departure be delayed. Moreover, deserters tended to move about from one jurisdictional area to another. The writer summed up the problem when he wrote, "These roles or registers absolutely can-

[34]Harry Ammon, *The Genet Mission* (New York 1973) chap. 9; also T. Lothrop Stoddard, *The French Revolution in San Domingo* (Boston and New York 1914).

[35]See, for example, Hauterive, "Compte Provisoire, rendu pendant la relâche de l'Escadre à New York," to Genet, 15 September 1793, in carton labeled "Marines Archives, BB 7/9," Archives de la Marine Française (Château de Vincennes).

not be taken out of vessels and chancelleries in order to be produced at tribunals which are situated far from the roads and seaports." Nor, it turned out, were judges always willing to accept certified copies of these crew rosters.[36]

Article 9 received a major testing in the summer and fall of 1794 when a spectacular instance of a consul's being unable to collar a deserter reached the highest levels of government attention. The fugitive was no mere seaman but the captain of a French corvette, one Henri Barré who, rather than face his fleet commander's wrath, gave himself permanent shore leave. Purportedly, during a skirmish with British cruisers off Sandy Hook in mid-July, Barré failed to respond quickly enough in support of the line ship, *Concorde*. His superior, Admiral Mahé, denounced him as a "fop," and vowed to have him guillotined when they all got back to France, reason enough for Barré to jump ship at Cape Henlopen.[37]

Before the consul in Philadelphia could arrest him, Barré escaped to New York where Vice Consul Louis Arcambal took up the chase. Pursuit reached a familiar impasse when Federal District Judge John Lawrence refused to issue a warrant. Fauchet, who followed the case closely, demanded of Randolph, now secretary of state, that the executive branch intervene to force Lawrence to comply with Article 9. The judge, however, remained unmoved, ruling that he would not order Barré's arrest because Arcambal had not produced the corvette's *rôle d'équipage*. He said he found the convention very explicit in its requirement that a consul seeking to recover a deserter present a personnel roster bearing the alleged deserter's name. To Fauchet's consternation, Lawrence refused to accept in evidence a multitude of other ship's papers on which Barré's name appeared as commanding officer. To meet the judge's ruling, Fauchet instructed the French consul in Boston (where the corvette was now on post) to copy off a list of crew and officers, attest to its accuracy, and forward it to New York. Again, Lawrence balked, this time because the document was copied. By the language of the convention, he said, he could take judicial cognizance only of the original. Fauchet now began to question Lawrence's good faith. He pointed out to Randolph that in a similar recovery action, another federal judge, Richard Peters, had ordered the arrest of deserters in Baltimore on evidence other than a crew roster. Moreover, Fauchet had received the opinion of Attorney General William Bradford that in instances where vessels left port taking their rosters with

[36]Anonymous, "Mémoire sur la Convention Consulaire," Mem. et doc., 10: ff. 122vo–24.

[37]Fauchet and the Commissioners to CDMC, No. 11, Philadelphia, 15 fructidor, an 2 (1 September 1794), *CFM*, 398–401.

them, a consul could still obtain arrest warrants on presentment of other kinds of identifying documents.[38]

Randolph's response was firm but conciliatory. He explained to Fauchet how improper it would be for the executive to intrude on the judicial branch, then pointed out that Lawrence's decision might be appealed. He even arranged to have the attorney general expedite the appeal.[39] Half a year later when the Supreme Court did rule on the issue, Fauchet thought its decision most unsatisfactory. Far from overturning Lawrence, the Court left federal judges to exercise their individual judgment as to whether to accept in evidence only the original *rôles d'équipage* or consul-attested copies. To Fauchet this raised the absurd prospect that French consuls in pursuit of deserters would henceforth have to carry the original copies of crew rosters "from one end of the continent to the other." The rate of desertion, already high, would, he predicted, climb still higher.[40]

In criminal cases generally, French officials usually had no quarrel with the standards of protection afforded by state laws. Marbois and Otto early decided that American justice was "gentle" enough that only a blatant miscarriage of it would cause them to intervene. In March 1785, for example, Marbois noted that a relatively large number of Frenchmen were being jailed for crimes ranging from murder and theft to counterfeiting. Pennsylvania authorities had asked whether he wanted to be consulted in their cases. He made it a rule, he reported, not to intercede. Too many such cases cropped up for him to keep track of, but more to the point, sentences were absurdly light. Three Frenchmen convicted of murder had recently been pardoned on condition they leave the state. Two had subsequently committed other crimes and been re-imprisoned. A few months after Marbois left, Otto took a similar line in explaining to Vergennes that he and Delaforest had agreed to assist only those Frenchmen accused of crimes who "deserved help." Otherwise, it was best to let American criminal justice run its usually mild course.[41]

Conversely, the law's solicitude for criminal offenders appeared

---

[38]Fauchet's copies of correspondence on the Barré affair include: Bradford to Randolph, Philadelphia, 15 March 1794; Fauchet to same, Philadelphia, 11 August 1794; Lawrence to same, New York, 15 August 1794; and Fauchet to same, Philadelphia, two letters of 5 September 1794, all in CC (Philadelphia), Tome 3, 75, 77–78vo, 80–82, 83, and 84–87vo, respectively.

[39]Cf., Randolph to Fauchet, 8 September 1794; and copy of same to Bradford, Philadelphia, 7 October 1794, ibid., ff. 88–88vo, and 90–90vo, respectively.

[40]Cf., *United States vs. Judge Lawrence*, 3 Dallas (U.S.), 42–54 (1795); and Fauchet and the Commissioners to CDRE, No. 1 (politique), 17 floréal, an 3 (6 May 1795), *CFM*, 681–83.

[41]Cf., Marbois to MAE, No. 417, Philadelphia, 20 March 1785, AECPE-U, 29: 116–17vo; Otto to same, No. 23, New York, 28 November 1785, ibid., 30: 425.

much too lax when the victims were Frenchmen. An incident in New York harbor that same spring brought reproving observations from Marbois. Purportedly, a party of French sailors coming ashore from a warship had had their long-boat beaten back by a dockside mob throwing rocks. Getting satisfaction in such cases was difficult. Governors might issue condemnatory proclamations, legislatures pass resolutions, but magistrates did nothing. No branch of a state government, he concluded, wanted to make enemies among its constituents.[42]

Marbois's interest in criminal offenders had a distinctly personal side. Himself the victim of physical assault in May 1784, he was thrust into the center of an international incident seriously disturbing to Franco-American relations. His government's demand for custody of the man who attacked him, an adventurer named Longchamps, made Marbois advocate as well as victim in the republic's first extradition controversy. Repercussions from the so-called Marbois–Longchamps affair touched not only questions of foreign jurisdiction and diplomatic status, but also freedom of the press, the validity of American naturalization procedures, and the concept of the United States as a haven for refugees. Marbois's reading of American reactions, as they unfolded, became a text for Paris in its understanding of American sensitivity in matters of sovereignty and self-perception.

The incident began when a French cavalry lieutenant, Charles Julien de Longchamps, a sometime resident of Philadelphia, eloped with a very young girl whose family disapproved both of the marriage and of Longchamps. To vent their dislike, the family purportedly slurred Longchamps in the press, planting stories of his "low and ridiculous origins."[43] To vindicate his good name, Longchamps on 16 May 1784 presented himself at the French consulate, armed with brevets, commissions, and other personal documents which he asked to have authenticated. Specifically, he hoped to prove both his claim to a title and his previous military distinction. When Marbois refused his request (for reasons never disclosed), Longchamps shouted angrily that he would "dishonor" the consul general, and called him a "rogue" and a "saucy devil." For this, the Supreme Court of Pennsylvania later found him guilty of "violent and opprobrious language." La Luzerne and Otto both witnessed the encounter. The incident did not end there, however. Next day, Longchamps swore allegiance to the state of Pennsylvania and thereby became an American citizen. The following day, accosting Marbois in Front Street, Longchamps abused

---

[42]To same, No. 423, New York, 7 May 1785, ibid., 29: 234vo–36.

[43]*Courier de l'Amérique*, 27 July 1784.

him verbally, began to cane him, and called for a pistol. Marbois managed
to defend himself until bystanders pulled them apart. After his arrest,
Longchamps escaped, was recaptured, tried, found guilty, and sentenced
to twenty-one months in prison. Enough persons witnessed the assault
that Longchamps's guilt was never in doubt. Other questions, however,
plagued the Franco-American diplomatic scene for more than a year.[44]

By early August, with Marbois reporting to Navy Minister de
Castries and La Luzerne to Vergennes, the royal government had a clear
idea of how matters stood. The king's ministers knew that despite La
Luzerne's request for custody, a Pennsylvania court had tried Longchamps
and found him guilty, but had not yet sentenced him. No matter what
the punishment, de Castries thought representations should be made to
Franklin to have Longchamps extradited. The issue admitted of no alternative: a French army officer had assaulted a French diplomat; neither the
pretext of American citizenship nor the jurisdictional claims of Pennsylvania must be allowed to stand in the way of French justice.[45]

In Philadelphia the affair became a *cause célèbre* when the *Courier de
l'Amérique* published interviews with Longchamps's attorney. In the face
of adverse publicity, Marbois kept a discreet silence. For trial purposes,
he made a deposition to Pennsylvania authorities but refused to go into
the newspapers in any sort of *"guerre de plume."* For his silence the consul
general was made to suffer. The *Courier* "abused" him, he thought, and
when that newspaper lost its low postal rates and went out of business,
another, the *Independent Gazetteer*, took up where the *Courier* had left off,
berating him for his efforts to make an international incident of a simple
assault case. As for public opinion generally, Marbois reported that everyone agreed that Longchamps was guilty of assault. Opinion was divided,
however, as to whether the crime was deserving of more severe punishment because the law of nations had been breached with respect to the in-
violability of a foreign diplomat. The prevailing view, he wrote, held
that nothing in the law of nations required that Longchamps be extradited as long as Pennsylvania justice exacted an appropriate punishment.
The sentencing judge also held this view.[46]

---

[44]For a short account, see Alfred Rosenthal, "The Marbois–Longchamps Affair," *Pennsylvania Magazine of History and Biography* 63 (July 1939) 294–301.

[45]At Versailles ministerial exchanges on the affair included: de Castries to Vergennes, 8
August; Vergennes to de Castries, 9 August; de Castries to Vergennes, 15 August, and finally,
Vergennes to Marbois, No. 4, 12 October 1784, AECPE-U, 28: 90–91vo, 92, 144–44vo, and
319–20, respectively.

[46]Cf., Marbois to MAE, No. 416, Philadelphia, 14 March 1785, ibid., 29: 104–105vo; and
earlier, to same, Nos. 383 and 389, Philadelphia, 1 July and 14 August 1784, ibid., 28: 7–8, and
136–38, respectively. For Judge Thomas McKean's opinion, see *Respublica vs. De Longchamps*, 1
Dallas (Pa.), 111–13 (1784).

Although a jury found Longchamps guilty on 12 July, sentencing was delayed until 8 October. The interval allowed both sides to make conciliatory gestures. On 28 September, the Pennsylvania legislature enacted a law placing stiffer penalties on crimes against the "public ministers of foreign princes." Vergennes, meanwhile, told Marbois that failing extradition—for which he was to make formal request to Congress—he must at least assure that Longchamps be punished "in a way that can satisfy his Majesty." Louis, however, was not altogether pleased when he learned of Longchamps's sentence. A fine of 100 crowns, imprisonment until July 1786, and seven years' bonding for good behavior was not the king's idea of a sentence "proportionate to the offense," although Vergennes reported that his majesty thought it useless to make further representations.[47] How well Paris foresaw frustration became clear when, as Jay predicted to Marbois, Congress rejected the latter's request for extradition, and instead urged the states to adopt a model law affording greater protection to the persons of foreign diplomats. Only Virginia followed Pennsylvania's example in this regard. Irritably, Marbois summed up the intransigence he had met throughout. Americans believed their own laws to be sufficiently protective. The United States, he concluded, "will not suffer any crime committed within its bounds to be submitted to a foreign jurisdiction."[48]

That matters of high policy could be influenced by newspapers or popular opinion troubled French officials unaccustomed to heeding such political forces. To Marbois, during the Longchamps affair, these elements of a free society intruded annoyingly. Smarting under the *Courier's* criticism in the summer of 1784, he said he dared not challenge the newspaper's right to attack him. Freedom of the press, he noted drily, is "one of the dearest rights of the people." The following spring, however, when the *Gazetteer* picked up the attack and continued to harass him, he told of his effort to persuade Congress to pass a law that would punish those who published libels against foreign emissaries. Not to protect himself, he explained to Paris, so much as to defend the honor and dignity of the king's government. He found members of Congress predictably wary. "That assembly," he wrote, "shows the greatest repugnance to touch a chord as delicate as that of liberty of the press." Privately, Congressmen told him they would like to protect ministers from abuse, but

---

[47]Cf., Vergennes to de Castries, Versailles, 1 October 1784; and to Marbois, No. 4, Versailles, 12 October 1784, AECPE-U, 28: 287–87vo, and 319–20, respectively; and same to Marbois, Versailles, 8 February 1785, ibid., 29: 43–43vo.

[48]To MAE, No. 423, New York, 7 May 1785, AECPE-U, 29: 233. See also congressional resolution of 27 April 1785, *Journals of the Continental Congress, 1774–1789* (Washington 1933) 28: 214–15.

feared to take measures that would "lose them the affection of the People."[49]

His demand for extradition, Marbois felt, had awakened a variety of popular conceits. At one level, those who objected to Longchamps's being sent back to France for trial seemed pridefully defensive about the propriety of trying him here. That the offender had lodged a claim of American citizenship was, perhaps, not as important as the fact that he had breached the peace of Pennsylvania whose authorities were felt competent to try and punish him. Beyond this sort of jurisdictional jealousy, however, Marbois detected a deeper, more heart-felt concern. Some believed that relinquishing Longchamps would set a precedent unworthy of a nation that beheld itself as a haven for refugees. Though he termed it "ridiculous," Marbois heard the fear expressed and repeated that if France succeeded in recalling a subject for punishment, other monarchs, especially the German princes, might clamor for the return of fugitives far less blameworthy. In a country which welcomed immigrants and whose government was susceptible to popular pressures, Marbois told Paris, extradition was likely to remain a sensitive issue.[50]

Ten years later, Fauchet and the Commissioners learned anew the American distaste for extradition when they were refused permission to arrest Edmond Genet. The Washington administration made clear to Fauchet that it was sufficiently satisfied that his predecessor had been "recalled"; it would not permit that he be forced to return to France. Genet's decision to seek asylum here probably saved his life. Some months later, commenting on Captain Barré's success in eluding capture, Fauchet singled out extradition—the American aversion to it—to explain why, in his view, American authorities so persistently contested the efforts of French consuls to recover deserters. Like Marbois, he connected the dislike of extradition with Americans' perception of their country as a protected place for persons who, for whatever reason, chose to join them. Americans, he wrote, seemed to be preparing themselves to welcome "an epoch of general emigration from Europe."[51]

The procedures in Article 9 for recovering deserters were the closest France ever came to a formal extradition arrangement. Nor was it particularly surprising that American authorities should contest its operation. Efforts to restrict the free movement of individuals inevitably put French

[49]To MAE, Nos. 387 and 416, Philadelphia, 24 August 1784, and 14 March 1785, AECPE-U, 28: 138; and 29: 104–105, respectively.

[50]To same, No. 401, Philadelphia, 10 November 1784, ibid., 28: 366.

[51]Fauchet and the Commissioners to MAE, No. 1 (politique), Philadelphia, 1 germinal, an 2 (21 March 1794), CFM, 308–309; and same to CDRE, No. 25 (politique), Philadelphia, 22 brumaire, an 3 (12 November 1794), CC (Philadelphia), Tome 3, 151vo.

and American authorities at odds, especially when the latter tended to regard all newcomers as possible refugees from Old World tyranny. On the French side, attempts to retain jurisdiction over those who, like deserters, tried to escape it sprang from the conviction that Frenchmen should not be allowed to leave France in the first place unless they intended to return. To the extent that emigration meant a loss of population and Article 9 contained a mechanism for recovering at least the seafaring part of that population, the two phenomena—emigration and extradition— were closely related aspects of the mercantilist view that people were a valuable national resource. Article 9 was apiece with French laws dating from the era of Colbert which explicitly forbade laborers and artisans from leaving the country. That French officials should frown on their departure, and Americans rejoice in their arrival, spoke to feelings deeply rooted in opposing attitudes toward freedom of movement.[52]

From first to last, official concern over emigration seemed curiously exaggerated. Of the thousands of French nationals who spent time in the United States in the 1780s and early 1790s, few remained permanently. Few, indeed, intended to remain. Whenever the circumstance that brought them changed, they seemed glad to leave. This was as true of Rochambeau's soldiers after Yorktown as it was a decade later when island planters fleeing war and insurrection stayed in American port cities only long enough to find passage to France, or back to the Antilles. Political émigrés were equally transient, returning as soon as proscriptions were lifted. Though noting how few came to settle permanently, French officials nonetheless worried that they might be witnessing the vanguard of a mass movement. Those whose job it was to keep track of such arrivals felt uneasy at having to explain to Paris how dangerously attractive the United States might become, perhaps to a whole generation of Frenchmen. Even when the fears proved groundless, consuls kept up what might be called an emigrant watch, pleased whenever they could report large boatloads of Irish and English arriving but few French.

Various preventive measures were developed during the 1780s. Officials tacitly agreed, first of all, that it would take more than legislation to stop individuals who were determined to cross the Atlantic. Any large-scale exodus, however, could probably be prevented if would-be emigrants were properly cautioned that life in America was not as idyllic as some had painted it. Thus, warnings that most Frenchmen would find themselves ill-suited to the rigors of the frontier played an important part

---

[52]See Charles W. Cole, *Colbert and a Century of French Mercantilism* (New York 1939) 2: 463.

in the anti-emigration propaganda fostered by French regimes. Coupled with caveats to settlers were warnings to investors. Those who hoped to profit from land speculation should know the perils of securing clear title and the dangers of fraud in dealing with undercapitalized American land companies. Such was the familiar grist of consular warnings passed back to Paris.[53]

As early as 1781, Marbois reported the presence of Frenchmen among the investors in all four of the huge land companies spawned during the war, Illinois, Vandalia, Wabash, and Indiana. The consul general had mixed feelings. On the positive side, a wartime trade balance favorable to France meant that French businessmen in America had surplus funds to invest. The profits from such investment, he supposed, would ultimately find their way back to France. There was political advantage, too. By investing in American lands, these businessmen "will bind the two Nations and multiply the ties which they have in common." Less salubrious was the likelihood he foresaw that French investment would attract other Frenchmen as settlers. Already, French soldiers marching through the countryside "see how easy it is in this country to become farmers." Nor could they fail to notice that "the condition of the peasant in America is infinitely superior to that of a man of the same class in Europe." With nuclei of Frenchmen already settled at New Rochelle, N.Y., and New Bordeaux, S.C., the tide of emigration once started would be difficult to stem.[54]

Psychologically, the ground seemed well prepared for a mass movement of Frenchmen to the New World. France already boasted a voluminous literature that proclaimed Americans to be among the world's freest and most prosperous peoples. Liberated from Europe's corrupting influence and passionately devoted to political and social equality, they were virtuous exemplars of humankind's potential for all things good. Notwithstanding the explanation, convincingly offered by the historian Durand Echeverria, that these projections of an American idyll spoke more to their authors' calculated effort to discredit the political and social climate of France than to any accurate knowledge of the New World, the myth exerted a powerful hold on the French imagination.[55]

To French officials who feared its stimulating effect on emigration, Edenic portrayals of life in America provided a framework for their con-

---

[53]On the futility of legislation, see, for example, Marbois to MAE, No. 434, New York, 22 August 1785, AECPE-U, 30: 234–34vo; and Otto to same, No. 15, New York, 21 January 1790, ibid., 35: 37–38vo.

[54]To MMC, No. 2, Philadelphia, 10 November 1781, CC (Philadelphia), 945: 150–59.

[55]*Mirage in the West*, 79–80, 174.

cerns. It worried the Comte de Moustier, for example, that Saint-John de Crèvecoeur, the French consul in New York, found an eager readership for his *Letters from an American Farmer*. Crèvecoeur's depiction of pastoral serenity, he wrote, "does more credit to his sensitivity and his imagination than to his judgment, and it is desired that he not continue this work which has induced many French emigrants who have come here to find misery in a country where they counted on making a brilliant fortune." And yet, success stories abounded. Marbois awesomely described how new settlers often cleared lands without taking title, sold out, and moved farther west. Some individuals had repeated this process five or six times. Even those who came penniless, he concluded, could prosper if they were "thrifty and industrious."[56]

Such mixed assessments of what awaited French emigrants were neither uncommon nor mistaken. America offered opportunities for failure as well as success. Still, few Frenchmen could remain oblivious to the high drama they perceived in a people who boldly tested political and social ideas and whose incessant activity added new dimensions to the notions of personal and national wealth. Here in its totality a grand experiment was afoot which, to Frenchmen of adventurous spirit, beckoned irresistibly. How France might share in this enterprise—but without losing population—doubtless helps to explain why, apart from strategic considerations, French regimes showed increasing interest in Louisiana. Here where a French population already existed a union with liberty-loving Americans beyond the Appalachians might make France an active participant. Writing to Létombe in late 1794, the Committee of Public Safety caught the sense of challenge when, after requesting him to size up the hoped-for affinities between American Westerners and "our former brothers, the inhabitants of Louisiana," it gave rein to its visionary enthusiasm. The Great Committee called on Létombe to predict the impact of "the revolutions which this vast country will surely experience as agriculture, industry, and above all, the powerful genius of Liberty will make the forests which cover it disappear, replacing them with fertile fields and commercial cities." In this wise, ironically, did a government that had no thought of encouraging emigration glowingly describe what would be its ultimate accomplishment.[57]

Nor were Americans themselves reticent in proclaiming the virtues of immigration. Thanks to their chronic and well-publicized shortage of

---

[56]Cf., Moustier, "Distribution des Consulats," f. 191vo; and Marbois to MMC, No. 43, 16 August 1783, CC (Philadelphia), 945: 362–63vo.

[57]Paris, 12 brumaire, an 3 (3 November 1794), ibid., Tome 3, 116–16vo.

labor, skilled and unskilled, and their not insubstantial offering of religious and political liberties, no one expected them to remain silent. As Louis Otto wrote in 1785, "they are too carried away [by the idea] that they can make the entire universe enjoy what they call the rights of humanity." And while Franklin in Paris was contemporaneously warning would-be emigrants not to act precipitately, there were always sea captains ready to sign articles of indenture with persons willing to take temporary servitude as a gateway to a freer existence.[58]

Once the revolution began to deposit its flotsam, even *émigrés* were found who joined in the approving chorus. The fallen Girondin leader, Brissot de Warville, wrote ecstatically of American egalitarianism. Moreau de St. Méry, whose Philadelphia bookstore became a regular meeting place for *émigrés*, called it "this land of freedom," and hoped that the United States would someday "impose upon the universe the law of being happy like itself." Even Talleyrand in exile, for all his disdain of Americans, thought well enough of U.S. government securities and public lands to become an ardent investment counsellor to European colleagues. Though their opinions of Americans differed widely, these observers seldom failed to agree on one point: anyone who came to the United States willing to work would probably get ahead.[59]

By mid-1785, the spell seemed broken. Marbois and Otto quietly exulted that despite a postwar inpouring of Scots, Irish, English, and Palatinate Germans, perhaps as many as 50,000 in all, few Frenchmen were among them. Even those few seemed, to Otto, to have come "by chance and not by any design to establish here." He and Marbois vied in offering smug explanations. The "gentleness" of the French government, Marbois suggested, gave their countrymen less reason to emigrate; and Otto thought he saw an explanation in their Gallic sense of self-respect. French peasants, he ventured, unlike the German and Irish, were too proud to suffer five or six years of "slavery," i.e., indentured service, for their passage. A Frenchman, he wrote, "would rather beg his bread than sell his liberty and his labor to a foreigner."[60]

---

[58]Cf., "Mémoire remise par le Sr. Otto," f. 285vo; and Edward Hale and Edward Hale, Jr., *Franklin in France* (Boston 1888) 2: 256.

[59]See Kenneth Roberts and Anna M. Roberts, *Moreau de St. Méry's American Voyage, 1793– 1798* (Garden City, N.Y. 1947) 34; and Hans Huth and Wilma J. Pugh, eds., "Talleyrand in America as a Financial Promoter, 1794–96," vol. 2 of the *Annual Report of the American Historical Association for the Year 1941* (Washington, D.C. 1942); as well as La Rochefoucauld-Liancourt, *Voyage*, 1: 45, 66; and Marquis de Chastellux, *Voyages dans l'Amérique septentrionale dans les années 1780, 1781 & 1782* (Paris 1788) 2: 534–35.

[60]Cf., Marbois to MAE, No. 429, New York, 15 July 1785; and Otto to same, No. 16, New York, 19 October 1785, AECPE-U, 30: 139vo–40, and 356, respectively.

One minor leak—from Alsace—illustrates how closely French officials monitored incoming passenger groups. In August, Marbois reported the arrival of a dozen Alsatian families who had made their way down the Rhine and shipped out from Holland. Word getting back that they had been well received would swell the tide, he wrote, unless Paris moved quickly to choke off the emigration at its source. Otto, himself an Alsatian, made a point of following up on this immigrant group after Marbois left for Saint Domingue. From interviewing them, he learned why they had left and why they had chosen the United States. As to the first, he urged Vergennes to investigate their complaint that they had been driven out by excessively high taxes and unjust administrators. He thought there might be some truth in it. As to why the United States had been their refuge of choice, he noted helplessly that Rochambeau's veterans had spread among them "the most alluring tableaux of wellbeing which the American people enjoyed."[61]

Occasionally, a plan surfaced for using French nationals as temporary labor for exploiting American resources for which France had particular need. Martin Oster, for example, aware of the Navy's constant need of ship timbers, suggested putting French lumbermen to work in the hardwood forests of southside Virginia. The production of charcoal, tar, turpentine, etc., would constitute equally useful side ventures. In detailing his plan, the Norfolk consul showed how well he understood the need to reassure those above him. The notion of bringing French laborers to the United States without losing them required a formidable mustering of argument. Using French rather than American timber cutters, he began, would assure that the money paid in wages would return to France when the individual himself returned at the end of his term of employment. The point was well taken: keeping cash from leaving one's country was soundly mercantilist and reassuringly familiar. The duration of the worker's employment, he continued, must be precisely stipulated to leave no doubt as to the eventuality of repatriation. Few would defect, he argued, if they were well paid, well treated, came with the expectation of returning, and were kept in isolated company with other Frenchmen while they were here. Then, with a bow to the normal Frenchman's "strong and natural loyalty," Oster admitted that some few might opt to stay. Like Marbois, Oster made the best of an unwelcome possibility: those who remained would serve a good purpose in tightening the bonds between "the two friendly and allied people." And finally, however

---

[61]Marbois to same, No. 434, New York, 22 August 1785; and Otto's No. 16, cited above, ibid., ff. 234–34vo, and 357–58, respectively.

many the defections, they must be weighed against the Navy's need for timber.[62]

Proposals like Oster's cropped up from time to time. Paris took no interest in them. Even had the safeguards against losing members of the French work force been credible, no French government of the period had either the energy or the capital to pursue them. Official interest in deploying population generally required the driving force of some greater strategic or political purpose. Settling Frenchmen in Louisiana, for example, if France could recover that territory, was about the only project likely to win official sanction for emigration unless, of course, the United States came to be viewed as a suitable dumping ground for persons disaffected by the Revolution. Delaforest picked up a rumor to that effect when the first Scioto settlers began to arrive in early 1790. Though he doubted its truth, Delaforest reported hearing that the government was encouraging the Scioto emigration because it wanted to be rid of "malcontents." If this were true, he wrote, surely France did not intend to settle large numbers of Frenchmen in the Ohio Valley unless she also intended to acquire Louisiana, since their presence there would only rouse Spain's suspicions. Delaforest was right to doubt any change in anti-emigration attitudes. The Scioto experiment, so widely publicized for its failures, had no official backing. More importantly, that venture marked the high point, as well as the end, of fears that America might drain France of valuable human resources.[63]

Born in secrecy, the Scioto land company flourished on duplicity and ended in bankruptcy, but not before it deposited perhaps as many as a thousand ill-assorted Frenchmen in the marshy wilds between the Scioto and Ohio rivers in the year 1790. Bitter memories of this venture, especially the dubious role of its American promoters, added another unsavory component to the French perception of being made the victims of American enterprise.

Scioto took shape in 1787 when two speculators, Manasseh Cutler and Winthrop Sargent, contracted to pay Congress a million dollars worth of veterans' bounties for one and a half million acres of public lands to be conveyed to their Ohio Company. Simultaneously, by a second contract, Cutler and Sargent acquired a pre-emption, that is, the right to buy but not title to another four million acres lying west and north of the Ohio tract and known as the Scioto lands. The Cutler group promptly made over its pre-emption to this larger tract to William Duer as payoff for the

---

[62]To Moustier, "Questions Répondues," ff. 225–26.
[63]To MMC, No. 289, New York, 23 May 1790, CC (New York), 910: 295–95vo.

latter's having ably used his official position as Secretary of the Treasury
Board to grease both deals. Because both contracts had been made with
the Ohio Company, Duer and his associates kept their acquisition of the
pre-emption a closely guarded secret. From this point nearly everything
went awry. Unlike the Ohio Company which set about to finance its
purchase with veterans' bonuses, Duer's Scioto group planned to operate
in Europe, offering pre-emptions in return for depreciated U.S. government securities. Unfortunately, by the time the Scioto group got under
way, the rapidly rising value of those securities made their holders, principally Dutch investors, prefer not to sell. This necessitated a more direct
sales approach to the European public at large. Hence the dispatch to Paris
of Duer's agent, Joel Barlow, erstwhile poet and now purveyor of Scioto
lands to Frenchmen presumably eager to find a safe hedge for their savings
or even to leave revolutionary France for a less troubled environment.

For want of business acumen, Barlow might have failed had he not
teamed up with an aggressive and well-connected English promoter named
William Playfair. The latter proceeded to enlist a group of French businessmen and, with Barlow in tow, touched off a "land office" sales campaign that swept Paris in the fall of 1789. Boosting sales, however, required
that buyers be kept from knowing that they were merely buying pre-
emptions and not title, a deception not necessarily fraudulent inasmuch as
the Scioto associates could expect to gain clear title when they had amassed
enough money to meet the Ohio Company's original contract with Congress. This, unfortunately, was not to be. Playfair shattered the company's financial expectations when he absconded with the Paris receipts.
Barlow was audited; Playfair disappeared altogether; and although efforts
were made to reorganize the Paris operation, the Scioto company ultimately collapsed.[64]

For the Scioto emigrants uncertain land title was only one of their
problems. Settlers arriving in Alexandria, Virginia, in early 1790, at first
found no one on hand to greet them. A company agent turned up belatedly
and managed to organize what, by then, had become an angry and disillusioned group of Frenchmen. From then on, the company did its best
to give satisfaction. Despite an acute shortage of funds, Duer and his
associates furnished the means of transportation west and sent along

---

[64]For documentary sources on the Scioto venture, see Theodore T. Belote, ed., *The Scioto
Speculation and the French Settlement at Gallipolis* (Cincinnati University Studies, ser. 2, III, 1907);
and for summary accounts, E.C. Dawes, "The Scioto Purchase in 1787," *Magazine of American
History* 22 (December 1889) 470–82; Echeverria, *Mirage in the West*, 134–35; Francis S. Childs,
French Refugee Life in the United States (Baltimore 1940) 37–49, passim; and Shaw Livermore, *Early
American Land Companies: Their Influence on Corporate Development* (New York 1968) 139–41.

several score of professional hunters to provide fresh game. Earlier, the company had sent out an advance party of experienced woodsmen. Near the mouth of the Great Kanawha river they built four stockades and two parallel rows of log cabins on a site to be known as Gallipolis. Not only did the settlers arrive to find rough housing, but the company also arranged to feed them, albeit meagerly, through their first winter. Neighboring Indians, though eager to steal their horses, were not unfriendly, at least not until General Harmar's "pacification" campaign the following year stirred them up. Fever and disappointment were the principal enemies. The site itself, low and swampy, proved to be notably unhealthful. After a year or two, settlers began to drift away, down river to New Orleans or back east. By 1795, the few who remained finally secured land title by buying the lands they had already paid for at $1.25 an acre.[65]

The historian Theodore Belote in his insightful study of the Scioto phenomenon concludes not unreasonably that the Gallipolis settlers, for all their well-publicized trials, suffered no more than the usual discomforts of Europeans transplanted to the American frontier. Their anguish was the worse, perhaps, for having believed Barlow's picturing of how blissfully uncomplicated their lives would be on the banks of the Great Kanawha and then coming face to face with rigors for which their largely urban backgrounds had not prepared them. Wigmakers, confectioners, lackeys, and musicians were among them, Otto noted, and as they began to filter back east, he hoped they would find employment in the towns more suitable to their talents.[66]

Scioto's major significance, however, lay in the propaganda windfall it handed to a government eager to discredit the putative attractions of the New World. Reports of what happened to these settlers, embellished by repetition, continued to decorate official dispatches and unofficial travellers' accounts long after the event. Gratefully to Paris regimes, Scioto became the widely accepted symbol of misadventure, the sort of predictable emigrant disaster which, for Frenchmen, ought to dispel forever the image of America as a land of opportunity. Efforts began almost at once to discredit the company and to portray the settlers as victims cruelly deceived.

At its outset, however, the Scioto venture put French officials in a state of suspense which only its failure could entirely allay. From the mo-

---

[65]Belote, *Scioto Speculation*, 45–49, passim; Dawes, "Scioto Purchase," 482; Howard Mumford Jones, *America and French Culture, 1750–1848* (Chapel Hill 1927) 148–49.
[66]Cf., Belote, *Scioto Speculation*, 59; Otto to MAE, No. 43, New York, 12 November 1790, AECPE-U, 35: 196vo.

ment the earliest arrivals set foot in New York in February 1790, they
fretted over the emigrants' every move. Delaforest, struck by the aura of
secrecy surrounding this first group, reported that they had been hustled
to a place some twenty-seven miles outside the city where they remained
virtually incommunicado. From this staging area they were to rendezvous
with others arriving at Alexandria. Only with difficulty had he managed
to secure from them copies of the company's handbills and to have a look
at the contracts they had signed. Tensions increased when more settlers
arrived in May. Otto, also in New York, reported the landing of about a
hundred after a stormy passage aboard a British vessel, and the presence
of another three hundred already in Virginia. Worse, rumors circulated
that some 12,000 were expected to follow.[67]

Amid these developments, both men sought to be reassuring. This
"passion for emigrating," Otto thought, would soon run its course. But
until it did, he and Delaforest urged their respective ministries to give
serious consideration to financing the repatriation of those who were
having second thoughts. The best way to discourage other emigrants
would be to expedite the return of the disillusioned. Knowing how effectively word-of-mouth publicity had worked to excite the emigration
"fever," they argued that tales brought home of suffering and disappointment would do much to cool it. In June, Otto repeated Delaforest's report
that a delegation of Scioto settlers had already asked to be taken back to
France at government expense. The request posed an interesting question. French seamen stranded overseas were routinely sent home at the
Navy's expense. Would Paris in the case of these settlers do the same?
Delaforest had no authorization, but Otto ventured to estimate that for
an outlay of 8000 livres, France could get back at least 250 "honest citizens"
whose return would help dampen any further enthusiasm for emigration.
Reading Otto's recommendations, Montmorin agreed that many settlers
would doubtless want return passage, but felt that requests for government-
funded repatriation should be relayed to the Navy ministry. Whether the
latter undertook this project in any systematic way is not recorded.[68]

Accounts of the colony's ultimate dispersal generally told of persons
moving on to Marietta, New Orleans, or back east to the coastal towns.
In any event, by the time Montmorin responded, the Scioto bubble had

---

[67]Cf., Delaforest to MMC, No. 289, 23 May 1790, CC (New York), 910: 294vo; and Otto
to MAE, No. 27, New York, 11 May 1790, AECPE-U, 35: 92–92vo.

[68]See same to same, No. 31, New York, 10 June 1790, ibid., ff. 111–13; Delaforest's No.
289, cited above, f. 295vo; and Montmorin to Otto, Nos. 2 and 3, Versailles and Paris, 11
September and 13 November 1790, AECPE-U, 35: 168vo, and 199vo, respectively.

burst at its source. By early spring 1790, Paris land-buyers began to suspect they had been bilked. Rumors of the company's uncertain land title combined with unhappy reports filtering back from the settlers brought a sharp drop in land sales. Dissatisfied investors went so far as to threaten the company's Paris offices with arson and its principal promoters with bodily harm.[69] Given the company's disrepute in Paris, it must have seemed superfluous to bring home these "unhappy victims of their credulity," as Montmorin called them, to bear further witness to the follies of emigration.

It struck Otto, meanwhile, that the colony might not fail, after all. In mid-August, he remarked approvingly on the settlers' "surprising perseverance" and on how much "zeal" the financially straitened company had shown in providing for their needs. He later confirmed its hiring of woodcutters, carpenters, and hunters. Nor, as widely predicted, had the settlers been troubled by Indians. For the moment all seemed well. Winter would tell whether the venture had truly succeeded. To be sure, persons unsuited to frontier life were beginning to return east. But these, the most dissatisfied, would presumably return to France where they could be counted on to discourage others from following. By spring of 1791, Otto seemed almost relieved to report news that the colony was breaking up. Unwilling to write it off entirely, however, he supposed that those who remained might survive if they showed "prudence, industry and perseverance."[70]

Even as the Scioto colony dwindled, what might have been its success left a lasting impression. In May 1791, Otto alerted Paris to rumors of a land company backed by the financier Robert Morris reportedly recruiting settlers in France for a colony in upstate New York. In Baltimore a year later, Consul D'Annemours got wind of a scheme to sell shares in Virginia lands to French investors "in the same manner as the Scioto company was launched." The agent for this Virginia group, he wrote, was "a supple and insinuating genius" named Fitzmealy who had changed his name to O'Mealy and would probably arrive in France under still another alias. So that French authorities could identify him, D'Annemours sent an unmistakable description of a thin, red-headed, very bowlegged Irishman, having blue eyes, blanched eyebrows, and a markedly pimpled complexion.[71]

---

[69]Belote, *Scioto Speculation*, 34–35.

[70]To MAE, Nos. 37, 43, and 60, 12 August, 12 November 1790, and 7 May 1791, AECPE-U, 35: 158–58vo, 194–97, and 343–43vo, respectively.

[71]Cf., Otto to MAE, ibid., f. 434vo; and D'Annemours to MMC, No. 2, 16 March 1792, CC (Baltimore), Tome 1, 67–68.

How firmly fixed "Scioto" had become in the French lore of the era was illustrated by an irritated allusion made offhandedly by Michel Mangourit in late 1793. One of Genet's most activist consuls, Mangourit took vehement exception to Jefferson's written warning to consuls not to judge and condemn prize vessels. Outraged, he wrote: "I think they have a Russia here where they threaten representatives of the Republic with the knout or with Siberia. The circular letter addressed to all consuls by Thomas Jefferson . . . doubtless threatens us . . . with exile on the Scioto."[72]

Later French visitors to Gallipolis, describing what they saw, helped to strengthen the conviction that nothing but misery awaited Frenchmen who were so foolhardy as to emigrate. The Comte de Volney in 1795 described the survivors as pale, thin, and unhappy, the community itself forlorn and miasmic. The settlers had been lured by deception, but they had also let themselves be victimized by "their own infatuation and temerity." A year later, General Victor Collot, on a supposedly secret mission designed to sample Western attitudes toward a possible French takeover of Louisiana, met some of the Scioto survivors when he visited Marietta. Collot could express only distaste for countrymen so naive as to be taken in by land agents' promises of prosperity.[73]

Reinforced by travellers' accounts, the saga of Scioto came to symbolize all that French regimes most hoped for: a perception of America not as a land of beckoning opportunity, but as an alien world where French emigrants were sure to be worse off than if they had stayed at home. The revolution in France strengthened this perception. It was one thing for unwanted *émigrés* and Antillean refugees to use the United States as a temporary haven, but quite another to imagine that any liberated Frenchman would turn his back on the blessings of the new Republic. Otto sensed the anomaly when, on greeting the Scioto arrivals, he chided them for having come so far and so perilously to find a liberty they could enjoy at home. Others, like Joseph Fauchet, suspected emigrants of being anti-revolutionary at heart, persons of means who were using Scioto-like projects as a cover for transferring their wealth, and themselves as well, beyond the Revolution's reach.[74]

To revolutionaries of all stripes, then, America appeared increasingly

---

[72]To same, No. 37, 15 October 1793, CC (Charleston), Tome 2, 133.

[73]Cf., Volney, *View of the Soil and Climate*, 1: 322–27; Collot, *A Journey in North America* (Florence, Italy: Reprints of Rare Americana, No. 4, 1924) 71–72.

[74]Cf., Otto to MAE, No. 27, New York, 11 May 1790, AECPE-U, 35: 93–93vo; Fauchet and the Commissioners to the Commission du Commerce et des Approvisionnements, Philadelphia, 15 fructidor, an 2 (1 September 1794); and Fauchet to CDRE, No. 12 (politique), Philadelphia, 19 brumaire, an 3 (9 November 1794), *CFM*, 396, and 465–67, respectively.

to be an asylum for those who had something to hide, their money, their past, or their dangerous politics. Its freedoms were a bit too free for an all-controlling Republic whose zest for managing the lives of individuals far exceeded that of the decrepit monarchy it replaced. As to which nation stood more truly for the ideals of liberal philosophy, Frenchmen and Americans would remain divided, differing reproachfully over the fundamental question of what role government and the claims of nationality should play in the comings and goings of their respective peoples.

CONCLUSIONS

Although French officials of the 1780s never lacked for evidence of Americans' high regard for France, they gradually despaired of France's being able to derive any substantial advantage from that goodwill. Whether it was France's inability to compete with Britain for American markets, the loss of her Antilles trade to American interlopers, the absence of "reciprocity" in commercial relations, or ideological differences respecting the rights of individuals, they soon realized how unavailing were the claims of goodwill when ranged against the imperatives of American self-interest.

Disappointment registered more keenly because the American partiality for France seemed secure. Americans still appeared to appreciate the wartime assistance afforded by the French alliance, and gave no serious thought to rejoining the British Empire. Their wartime memories continued to cast Britons in the role of recent enemy; and London's postwar decision to keep its Indies ports closed to American vessels made the outlook for an Anglo-American rapprochement seem remote. As between the two great European powers, French officials could report, usually with confidence, that France stood more favorably in the estimation of most Americans.

Against this semblance of a French "ascendancy," however, these same observers often noted how fragile the affection in which France was held, and how limited her means to exploit it, or even to preserve it. A closer reading of the American scene reminded them—and they in turn reminded Paris—that a rival British presence persisted, manifesting itself in the unbroken ties of commerce and more subtly in the commonalities of language, culture, and tradition. Happily for those who feared that Britain might by some gesture of reconciliation seek to regain influence in American councils, British ministries of the era remained indifferent to the low state of Anglo-American relations. In the end, it took a renewal of Anglo-French warfare in 1793 to shatter the facade of American francophilia. Only then, when the Washington administration embarked on neutral policies that proved to be pro-British in their operation, was the frailty of the French "ascendancy" revealed.

How long France might enjoy her standing as friend and ally caused less immediate concern at the outset of the postwar decade than did the precipitate decline in Franco-American trade. A relatively flourishing wartime trade did not produce reliable postwar markets. Instead, French exporters steadily lost ground to their British competitors. Frenchmen who studied the phenomenon usually explained it unflatteringly. They pointed to the shoddiness of French export commodities, the government's toleration of monopolistic controls, and the unwillingness of French manufacturers to adapt their products to American consumer tastes. These and other deficiencies they usually held up as being in marked contrast to the boldness, freedom, flexibility — and resultant success — of British marketing operations.

Whenever they proposed remedies, the more reflective French consuls stationed here focused on France's central need to broaden its American market for French exports. Paris, some concluded, should at least underwrite the sort of market research that would make French products more suitable to American tastes. Or, they proposed, the government should establish warehouses here the better to regulate both the quality and flow of French goods. Periodically, they also called on the home government to relax its import restrictions, arguing that if France were to export in greater volume, she must make it easier for incoming shipmasters to sell off their American cargoes. These and other proposals, perhaps understandably, evoked little response from a government beset by awesome financial difficulties and soon to be caught up in political crises. Although Paris during the 1780s did make a few minor concessions to American imports, it lacked both the will and the means to implement its consuls' urgings to expand the French export market. Likewise in the private sector, the French export community, cautious by nature and hampered by restrictions, took few initiatives.

France's inability to induce Americans to become regular customers was matched by her failed efforts to keep Americans out of her West Indies islands. Here where possession should have guaranteed the fruitful operation of a closed trading system, American interlopers and renegade Frenchmen made short work of France's presumed monopoly. Here need and greed combined to favor the smuggler's pursuit. The islands, for their part, were not economically self-sustaining. To survive they needed foodstuffs, principally grain which they could legally import only from France. Only from the United States, however, could they obtain it in sufficient quantities. Whether they took grain legally from France or illegally from the United States depended throughout the 1780s on the uncertain bounty of French harvests. The trend, however, was toward increasing dependence on American sources and, finally, almost total dependence. First rent by revolution and then cut off from France by war, the islands ultimately yielded to the reality that mainland America, not France, could feed them more reliably and, as always, more cheaply.

Just as the island peoples increasingly fed on American grain, so Americans eagerly consumed or re-exported much of the islands' output of sugar and coffee. Incoming American grain-ships, rather than return in ballast, made off with these illicit cargoes (otherwise reserved for French carriers) whenever wile and inventiveness permitted. The patterns of traffic in contraband sugar and coffee soon became as varied as they were profitable. Vessels bearing two sets of "papers," two flags, two names and, when necessary, two captains—one French, the other American—plied back and forth between islands and mainland, their masters seizing whatever new ruse was necessary to evade official scrutiny. While French officials, the consuls in particular, offered unceasing advice on how to quash this brisk trade in contraband, no sure remedy ever surfaced. Well before the onset of the French Revolution, the bulk of the Antilles trade had fallen into the hands of Americans.

French officials whether they deplored the persistent Anglo-American customer relationship or lamented American depredations on their island trade at least understood why. They knew that consumer preferences and the profit motive, not malevolence, were working to France's disadvantage. Less easily explained, however, was the indifference they found among American political leaders. These presumed custodians of American gratitude, they felt, showed far too little interest in sponsoring legislative measures aimed either at favoring French imports or curbing American smugglers. Some were willing to ascribe such legislative inaction to the Articles of Confederation, that organic law which denied Congress the power to regulate commerce. Others came to expect few favors from the state legislatures as they discovered how subservient these bodies were to their merchant constituents. Still, there was no mistaking the singular breach of goodwill French officials thought they discerned at the highest levels of government. Frenchmen reading the clauses of the Franco-American commercial treaty of 1778 clearly expected French ships and cargoes to receive preferential treatment in American ports. Congress, however, insisted on reading the same clauses to mean that all trade partners be treated equally. To be placed on the same commercial footing as the British seemed to signal a shameless indifference to the claims of gratitude.

Despite hopes repeatedly dashed, French officials never entirely despaired of obtaining what they came to call "reciprocity." Americans, they believed, once properly aware that France expected their gratitude, would gladly extend favor to French goods and vessels. Paris needed only to find and seize an opportune moment. The adoption of the Constitution, for example, led the French minister, Comte de Moustier, to venture that members of the first federal Congress, if pressed, might flex their new-found regulatory powers explicitly to benefit French commerce. Whatever opportunity inhered in this new beginning, however, passed unexploited in part because neither Paris nor its minister to Philadelphia knew precisely what favor to ask for. When, instead, the first Congress promptly enacted a tax law that placed equal tonnage duties on all incoming foreign-flag vessels irrespective of nationality, it became clear that France could expect more harm than good from a new government left to its own devisings. Indeed, "reciprocity" now ceased to be a word that expressed a vague hope for some unspecified favor, and came to be equated with a French demand that French vessels be exempted from such duties.

The refusal of Congress, then and later, to accord a tonnage exemption to French carriers became variously a symbol of American ingratitude, a target of periodic retaliation and, most importantly, the source of a decade-long effort by French regimes to negotiate a new commercial treaty. Curiously, this effort, while retaining its initial goal—to gain exemption from U.S. tonnage duties—never produced a full set of treaty proposals. French governments appeared not to feel the need to specify what other concessions they might wish to see written into a new treaty. The waning monarchy left its minister, Jean de Ternant, woefully under-instructed in this respect, and then toyed with a treaty proposal from Thomas Jefferson which, inexplicably, it left unanswered, indeed unexamined. Only much later did one of Ternant's successors, Joseph Fauchet, point out how little Jefferson's "treaty" in fact offered France, had anyone in Paris seen fit to analyze it.

Edmond Genet, best remembered for his spectacular breaches of American neutrality, was also the bearer of treaty proposals. His Girondin masters, however, put political objectives ahead of commercial. Sent to negotiate a formidable military alliance, Genet wrecked whatever chances he had for any negotiation when he behaved as if such an alliance were already in effect. On commercial matters, however, he was remarkably short of instruction except, of course, that he was to renew the demand for a tonnage exemption. Worse, the Girondin regime snatched away his bargaining chips when, in early 1793, it opened all Indies ports to American vessels and agreed, without *quid pro quo*, to impose no tax on them that was not also levied on French carriers.

Hope for commercial favor revived briefly during the Fauchet mission. Genet's successor arrived in early 1794 to find Anglo-American relations so strained that Congress seemed ready to place retaliatory duties on British ships and cargoes. Realizing that such duties would simultaneously improve the competitive position of French ships and cargoes, Fauchet saw no need to press for a new commercial treaty. He was to change his mind, however, when the Anglo-American crisis began to cool. Washington's announced intention to send John Jay on a "peace" mission to London not only led Congress to put its retaliatory tax measures on hold, but also awakened Fauchet to the possibility that Jay might negotiate a full-fledged rapprochement. Should Jay return from London with a commercial treaty—and Fauchet increasingly suspected he would—French interests would suffer accordingly. Summer and fall of 1794, then, found Fauchet earnestly importuning the administration to make a new commercial treaty with France, if only to give the Senate when it reconvened a diplomatic alternative to whatever Jay might have arranged. Ultimately, Fauchet's treaty offensive came to nought. Whether he failed because the administration deliberately put him off or because he had no detailed draft to present, Fauchet in retrospect emphasized the latter. In a bristling dispatch he told the foreign office that it should blame itself for its persistent failure to obtain commercial reciprocity. French policymakers, he charged, had never given thought to exactly what they wanted by way of commercial concessions (except for the tonnage exemption). As a result, their emissaries had never been specifically enough instructed to enter a serious negotiation. The record bears out the accuracy of this judgment.

Recriminations in the realm of Franco-American commerce had their counterpart in strongly voiced differences over the rights of the individual vs. the state. French governments of the era, whether royalist or republican, shared an authoritarian tradition dismayingly at odds with American views in such matters. How far the state might regulate the activities and movements of its citizenry often divided French and American officials, sometimes bitterly. Put simply, France expected to wield an authority over French nationals, whether at home or abroad, that Americans found distasteful, even oppressive. The controversy centered, in part, on the powers accorded to French consuls by the Franco-American consular convention, signed in 1784 but stalled in Congress and left unratified throughout most of the decade. Jefferson, while still minister to France, negotiated enough new wording to assure Congress that French consular powers would not be excessive, but when the new Senate ratified the convention, French officialdom saw little improvement. As before, the consuls complained of American magistrates who either refused them the coercive means to enforce their judgments, or who blocked the exercise of their powers by construing the convention too narrowly. As a result, Frenchmen presumably subject to consular jurisdiction took their disputes instead to American courts, and sometimes clothed themselves in U.S. citizenship to avoid consular justice. When the legal proceedings involved French sea-captains and their crews, sailings were delayed and expenses mounted.

One such case of "lost jurisdiction" Paris found extremely rankling. In this instance, French jurisdiction seemed unassailable. A French consul arrested and detained a French shipmaster named Joseph Ferrier who had confessed to having misappropriated his owners' cargo. French officials fully expected to meet no obstacle to their plan to repatriate him for trial. Despite protests from the French minister himself, however, Ferrier made good his escape when he had his friends arrange for a Virginia magistrate to find him guilty of a lesser charge and released on bail. Efforts to regain custody were in vain.

Even in such routine matters as recovering French deserters, the convention proved to be defective. American judges often refused to hear desertion cases on grounds that the convention gave such jurisdiction to the consuls, and then defeated the effectiveness of that jurisdiction by refusing to issue warrants for arrest. Jurisdictional assertiveness reached a climax in the widely publicized case of Henri Barré. Here, a French Navy captain who, according to his fleet admiral, had deserted under fire, sought asylum, fleeing from one American port city to another. Efforts to recover Barré failed because a literal reading of the convention required his accusers to present an original copy of his ship's crew-roster showing his name. French authorities brought to court other evidence of Barré's desertion, including a reproduced sworn copy of the roster on which Barré's name appeared. A sworn copy was not sufficient. Two U.S. judges refused to issue an arrest order, and their refusal was later upheld by the Supreme Court.

French requests for extradition touched an even more sensitive nerve. Thus the refusal of U.S. authorities to surrender one Charles de Longchamps evoked repeated protests and gave the decade one of its major *causes célèbres*. Longchamps was a former French army officer residing in Philadelphia who felt himself slighted by bureaucratic indifference. In May, 1784 he accosted and physically assaulted the French chargé d'affaires, François de Barbé-Marbois. Because Paris felt Marbois to be entitled to the special protections traditionally afforded to diplomatic persons, it demanded that Longchamps be extradited. The incident became further complicated when Longchamps, claiming American citizenship, was arraigned before a Pennsylvania judge. Before it ended, the Longchamps affair raised a public furor over such delicate issues as freedom of the press, the rights of naturalized citizens, the right to asylum and, above all, the sufficiency of American justice. It made little difference to Paris that Longchamps was found guilty and sent to prison. The refusal of extradition, later repeated when Washington declined to repatriate Citizen Genet, bitterly impressed on French officials that Americans, given a pretext, would shelter aliens from what they perceived as the more severe justice of their homelands.

Finally, while such denials of jurisdiction caused irritation, some French officials foresaw even greater loss—that of population—should the attractions of life in America take hold of the French popular imagination. That Frenchmen might be gullible enough to yield to the blandishments of American real estate promoters was at least a daunting possibility. A mass migration depleting France of her human resources, indeed a source of her national vitality, appeared the more threatening because Americans so often made clear they would welcome these additions to their workforce. Knowing the temptations, French officials resented the tempters and strove incessantly to discredit them, taking every opportunity to expose as schemers, laying traps for the unwary, those Americans who glowingly touted this country as a place of refuge and opportunity. For reasons not altogether clear, the much-feared migration, when it came, took the distinctive French form of *aller et retour*. Many came, to be sure, but most left, apparently satisfied to have found temporary respite from violence at home or in the islands. Among French officialdom, however, the suspicion died hard that the lure of life in the New World might prove irresistible; they kept a baleful eye on their countrymen's comings and goings. Not until the failure of the French colony at Scioto were their fears laid to rest; their resentments lingered.

The foregoing essays have depicted on the French side a Franco-American relationship increasingly fraught with disappointment and chagrin. Whatever moral ascendancy Frenchmen hoped to enjoy in this country, whatever their expectations of gratitude, whatever their plans to expand their American commerce or to keep Americans out of their West Indies—had by 1793 eroded to near extinction. Instead, self-serving Americans, preoccupied with commercial expansion and caught up in the heady freedoms of new nationhood, made short work of French expectations. Eaten away by repeated disappointments, Franco-American goodwill rested on a much narrower base in 1793 than it had in the first year of peace.

By 1793 Europe was again at war, with Americans opting for a neutrality that could satisfy either their British trade partner or their French ally, but not both. With the new era came new and different problems, none with easy solutions, few even predictable. None could foresee, for example, that within the following decade the United States would have accomplished a full rapprochement with Britain and, as a result, found itself in open warfare with France. By the same token, because the wars of the French Revolution so drastically altered the context of Franco-American relations, one cannot draw a straight line of causality from the frustrations of the 1780s to the much worse relations of the 1790s. And yet, unmistakably, the ill-will generated in one decade set the tone for worse to come.

BIBLIOGRAPHY

SELECT ARCHIVAL SOURCES

Archives des Affaires Etrangères

Principally used in this study were:

(1) the bound volumes of ministerial dispatches, numbered 26 through 36 (1783–1792), identified as: Archives Etrangères, Correspondance Politique, Etats-Unis, and cited herein as AECPE-U by volume number;

(2) supplementary volumes to the Correspondance Politique, listed by volume number below;

(3) the bound series known as Mémoires et documents, cited throughout as Mem. et doc., by volume number; and,

(4) that part of the B^1 *série* from the Archives de la Marine which is held by the Archives des Affaires Etrangères. This partial holding contains the bound volumes of French consular dispatches from the United States after 1792. They are cited herein as CC (Correspondance Consulaire), followed by the name of the American city from which the dispatch was sent, and by volume number. (Dispatches dated prior to 1792 and bearing the same B^1 designation are housed in the Archives Nationales.)

Correspondance Politique, Etats-Unis. Correspondence of French Ministers to the United States (vols. 26 through 36 for the period 1783–1792).

Supplementary volumes (Correspondance Politique, Etats-Unis):

5 Citoyen Mangourit, Correspondance aux enterprises contre la Louisiane et les Florides, 1793

5 (1re série). Dépêches des consules aux Ministre de la Marine, puis des Relations Extérieures, 1790–1813

19 (2e série). Liquidation de la dette américaine, 1783–1797

20 Correspondance entre la légation et le Ministre, les autorités américaines, Finance, 1789–1794

24 Subsistances: correspondance, comptes et documents divers, 1794–1796

25 Subsistances: correspondance, comptes et documents divers, 1794–1796

30 (2e série). Correspondance et documents relatifs aux affaires de la marine et des colonies d'Amérique, 1778–1794

31 (2e série). Correspondance et documents relatifs aux affaires de la marine et des colonies, 1795–1797

179

Mémoires et documents, Etats-Unis.

Memoranda relating to American politics and commerce in the 1780s and 1790s may be found in volumes:
  9 (1784–1815)
  10 (1793–1812)
  14 (1778–1786)

Correspondance Consulaire, Etats-Unis.

  Baltimore, Tome 1 (1781–1817)
  Boston, Tome 3 (1793–1795); Tome 4 (1796–1824)
  Charleston, Tome 2 (1793–1799)
  New York, Tome 3 (1793–1805)
  Norfolk, Tome 2 (1793–1814)
  Philadelphia, Tome 3 (1793–1796); Tome 4 (1796–1798)
  Wilmington, one volume, unnumbered (1783–1810)

Archives de la Marine (Château de Vincennes, Paris)

One carton labeled "Marine Archives, BB 7/9" contains papers relating to the United States: mémoires, observations, statistical abstracts, and a collection of Rochambeau-Fauchet correspondence.

Archives Nationales de France

Among vast and well-catalogued holdings the following *séries* contain manuscript and printed materials that contributed directly and indirectly to this study:

AD XV (Affaires Etrangères: Espagne, Etats-unis, 1790–1839)
  See carton 48 for printed brochures, pamphlets and mémoires of the 1790s, including a 1797 edition of Fauchet's *Coup d'Oeil.*

AD XX[B] Clippings from U.S. newspapers of the mid-1790s forwarded by consuls to various departments of the French government. See Dossier 83.

AF II (Conseil exécutif et Convention, Rapports des Ministres au Conseil exécutif, Marine et Colonies, 1793–94). Dossiers 59 and 60 in Carton 9 contain correspondence relating to U.S. shipping. See also Dossier 468 in Carton 63 for official correspondence on American affairs.

AF III Carton 64 holds the ANF's largest random collection of documents relating to Franco-American political and commercial matters in the 1790s. Its six dossiers, numbered 259 to 264, are labeled "Relations Extérieures, Etats-Unis d'Amérique, Fonds de la Secrétairérie d'Etat, Directoire exécutif."

B[1]   (Correspondance Consulaire). This ANF collection contains bound volumes of French consular dispatches from the United States, 1778–1792, cited herein as CC, followed by the name of the American city from which the dispatch was sent, and by volume number:
  209–210 Boston
  372   Charleston
  909–910 New York
  927   Norfolk
  945–946 Philadelphia
  1183   Williamsburg

B[7]   (Service général, pays étrangères, et consulats: Amérique: Etats-Unis, 1778–
       1789). Dossiers 459–461 include items of interministerial correspondence.

BB[1] Dossiers touch peripherally on matters of Navy concern with the United
       States. For shipboard discipline and refugee arrivals, see Dossier 8 (Rapports
       de la Commission de la Marine et des Colonies au Comité de Salut public,
       1794); for disposition of vessels at sea, Dossier 9 (Décisions du Ministre, 1794);
       and for Navy reports to the Committee of Public Safety as early as 1793, Dos-
       sier 11 (Rapports au Directoire, 1795).

BB[2] This collection contains reports and requests to, and orders from, the Com-
       mission de la Marine et des Colonies in the early 1790s, with only occasional
       references to naval matters as they related to the United States. For fragmen-
       tary references, see Dossiers 17, 23, 24, 25, 58, and 59. Dossier 87 (Service
       général, Correspondance, Consuls de France, 1795) contains copies of much of
       Fauchet's correspondence with the Navy Commission.

D XXV Carton 59 with dossiers numbered 576 to 586 contains items of corre-
       spondence between officials in the Antilles and French ministers to the United
       States, 1791–95.

F[11] Carton 223, labeled "Mémoires sur les grains, les approvisionnements, le com-
       merce, an II," contains a copy of James Swan's "Plan de Commerce, No. 1,"
       dated 22 frimaire, an II (12 December 1793).

SELECT MANUSCRIPT SOURCES

Alexander, William. 7 September 1784. "Memorial on the Trade with Virginia and the
    other United States" (Richmond). AECPE-U, 28: 188–90vo.

_____, 26 November 1788. "Quel est le système que l'on pourrait substituer au Contract
    de Mr Morris" (Norfolk). CC (Norfolk), 927: 241–44.

Anon. 25 frimaire, an V (26 December 1796). "Extrait d'un Mémoire Sur la Situation
    Commerciale de la France avec les Etats-unis d'Amérique." AF III, carton 64, doss.
    261, 12 pp.

_____, An IV (23 September 1795–21 September 1796). "Mémoire sur la Convention
    Consulaire avec les Etats-unis d'Amérique pour servir au Citoyen _____, Envoyé de
    la République près du Congrès" (Paris). Mem. et doc., 10: 119–25.

_____, October 1788. "Mémoire sur la Dette du Congrès envers le Roi et sur les moyens
    d'en faciliter le remboursement" (Paris). AECPE-U, Liquidation de la dette améri-
    caine, 1783–1797, 2e série (supplément), 19: 84–108vo.

_____, 1 May 1786. "Observations sur le Mémoire concernant le commerce de France
    avec les Etats-Unis" (Paris). AECPE-U, 31: 268–79.

_____, 23 May 1786. "Propositions pour le Commerce des Etats Unis" (Paris). Ibid.,
    ff. 368–77.

_____, 15 October 1787. "Rapport sur le Commerce des Etats-unis de l'Amérique avec
    la France, fait à Monsieur le Contrôleur Général." Mem. et doc., 9: 102–89.

_____, 29 March 1784. "Réflexions problématique proposées à Philippe Mazzei par un
    Seigneur Français." AECPE-U, 27: 224–34vo.

_____, 24 May 1786. "Résultat du Comité tenu à Berni chez M. le Contrôleur général, en presence de M. le Comte de Vergennes, et auquel assisté MM. de St. Amand, Paulze et La Perrière, représentant la ferme générale." AECPE-U, 31: 378–79.

Barbé-Marbois, François, Vicomte de. [1783]. "Supplément au précis remis à Fontaine-bleau de toutes les dépêches d'Amérique concernant le commerce des Etats Unis avec nos colonies et avec le Royaume" (Philadelphia). B⁷, doss. 460, doc. 1.

Bérard, Jean Jacques. 10 January 1786. "Mémoire sur le commerce de la France avec les Etats Unis" (Paris). AECPE-U, 31: 31–41.

Crèvecoeur, Hector Saint-John de. 29 December 1788. "Tableau de la Navigation active et passive de New York dans les Années 1784, 1785, 1786, 1787, 1788" (New York). CC (New York), 910: 85–94.

Delaforest, Antoine-René-Charles-Mathurin. 18 February 1789. "Mémoire sur la situation actuelle des Etats unis relativement à L'industrie intérieure et au Commerce Etranger" (New York). B⁷, doss. 461.

_____, 2 October 1790. "Observations" [on the Nootka Sound Crisis] (New York). AECPE-U, Dépêches des consuls aux Ministres de la Marine, puis des Relations Extérieures, 5 (1ʳᵉ série): 12–21.

_____, March 1788. "Raport Demandé par M. le Cte. de Moustier sur l'établissement consulaire de France en Amérique" (New York). CC (New York), 910: 21–31.

Ducher, G.J.A. 1787. "Notes remises par Ducher" (Wilmington). CC (Wilmington), 1: 65–66.

Duplaine, Antoine Charbonnet. August 1794. "Notes sur le Commerce de la France avec les Etats Unis d'Amérique" [Philadelphia]. Mem. et doc., 9: 200–10.

_____, [February 1794]. "Observations sur les circonstances actuelles, relativement aux intérêts de la République Française, et celles des Etats-unis de l'Amérique" (Philadelphia). D XXV, carton 59, doss. 582.

Fauchet, Jean-Antoine-Joseph. 17 April 1796. "Considérations sur un traité de Commerce avec les Etats-unis" (Paris, 28 germinal, an IV). AF III, carton 64, doss. 260.

Hauterive, Alexandre Lanouette, Comte d'. 15 September 1793. "Compte Provisoire, rendu pendant la relâche de l'Escadre à New York" (New York). BB 7/9, Archives de la Marine Française, Château de Vincennes.

_____, 18 October–8 December 1793. "Journal" (New York). New York Historical Society.

_____, 25 December 1793. "Mémoire" (New York). CC (New York), 3: 38–39.

Hauteval, Lucien. 24 July 1798. "Mémoire" (Paris). Mem. et doc., 10: 146–51.

_____, 13 February 1796. "Notes sur les raports des Etats-unis de l'Amérique avec la République française" (Paris). Ibid., 10: 134–41vo.

Lafayette, Marie-Joseph-Paul-Yves-Roch Gilbert du Motier, Marquis de. n.d. "Observations sur le Commerce entre la France et les Etats Unis" [Paris]. B⁷, doss. 460, doc. 54.

Létombe, Philippe-André-Joseph. 15 December 1795. "Extrait d'un Mémoire sur la situation commerciale de la France avec les Etats unis de l'Amérique" (Philadelphia). Mem. et doc., 9: 244–49.

_____, February 1784. "Mémoire des Affaires du Consulat Général de France à Boston pour L'Année 1783" (Boston). CC (Boston), 209: 277–94.

_____, 1785. "Mémoire des Affaires du Consulat de France à Boston pendant l'Année 1784" (Boston). Ibid., ff. 367–85.

_____, April 1788. "Mémoire des Affaires du Consulat de France à Boston pendant l'Année 1787 (Boston). Ibid., 210: 258–70.

_____, 1789. "Mémoire des Affaires du Consulat de France à Boston pendant l'année 1788" (Boston). Ibid. ff. 330–35.

_____, 6 thermidor, an 2 (24 July 1794). "Mémoire de l'Alliance entre la République française et des Etats-unis de l'Amérique aux Representans du Peuple composant le Comité de Salut Public." Mem. et doc., 10: 62–69.

_____, 1794. "Réponse de Létombe à une libelle, trouvée dans les cartons du depôt des Relations Extérieures" (Philadelphia). CC (Philadelphia), 3: 105–07.

Luzerne, Anne César, Chevalier de la. April 1784. "Résumé des affaires de l'Amérique" (Annapolis). AECPE-U, 27: 313–19vo.

Mangourit, Michel Ange. An III (22 September 1794–22 September 1795). "Mémoire sur la Situation Politique de la France avec les Etats-unis." Mem. et doc., 10: 70–73vo.

Montmorin de Saint-Hérem, Armand-Marc, Comte de. (1788). "Observations sur la lettre de M. Jefferson du Juin 1788" (Paris). AECPE-U, 33: 204–206.

Moustier, Eléonore-François-Elie, Comte de. June 1789. "Analyse de mes recherches sur le Service des Consuls" (New York). AECPE-U, 34: 147–51vo.

_____, 1788. "Distribution des Consulats et Vice Consulats de France dans les Etats Unis" (New York). Mem. et doc., 9: 186–99.

_____, July 1789. "Extrait d'un Mémoire du Cte de Moustier sur le Commerce des Etats unis" (New York). AECPE-U, 34: 221–24.

_____, May 1788. "Notte remise au Congrès le 28 May 1788" (New York). Ibid., 33: 174–77vo.

Oster, Martin. 18 October 1788. "Articles à soumettre à l'Examen de Monsieur le Comte de Moustier, Ministre Plénipotentiaire de France, comme étant relatifs à la Convention qui doit fixer les fonctions et prérogatives des Consuls, Vice-Consuls, Agents et Commissaires dans les Etats Unis, de la part du Roy: et en France, de la part du Congrès" (Norfolk). CC (Norfolk), 927: 173–84vo.

_____, 26 October 1785. "Etablissement du Vice-Consulat de Virginie par M. Oster, Vice-Consul du Roi, 1784" (Williamsburg). Ibid., ff. 85–103.

_____, 27 December 1785. "Mémoire sur le Commerce de Virginie, presenté au Ministre, par M. Oster, Vice Consul de France" (Norfolk). B[7], doss. 460, doc. 64.

_____, 26 November 1788. "Questions Répondues sur la Population, L'Agriculture, Le Commerce et Les Finances de Virginie" (Norfolk). CC (Norfolk), 927: 194–244.

Otto, Louis Guillaume. 17 May 1785. "Mémoire remis par le Sr. Otto pour demander des instructions avant son départ" (Paris). AECPE-U, 29: 271–94vo.

Pautizel, [   ]. 19 February 1794. "Mémoire sur l'Etat Politique des affaires de la République française dans les Etats-unis de l'Amérique." Mem. et doc., 10: 45–55.

Petry, Jean-Baptiste. 30 January 1788. "Etat des Importations de France dans le Port de Charleston & ses Exportations de ce port en France Pendant L'année 1787" (Charleston). B[7], doss. 461, doc. 9.

Rochambeau, Donatien Marie Joseph de Vimeur, Vicomte de. 5 December 1794. "Mémoire sur la situation de l'agriculture et du Commerce des Etats-unis" (Philadelphia). Mem. et doc., 9: 223–41vo.

———, 25 November 1794. "Sur les rapports avenirs des Etats unis de l'Amérique septentrionale avec la France." Ibid., ff. 211–22vo.

Swan, James. 12 December 1793. "Plan de Commerce, No. 1, aux comités de Salut Public & de Finances Le unis" (Paris). F[11], carton 223.

Toscan, Jean. April 1786. "Mémoire du Consulat de Boston pour 1785" (Boston). Mem. et doc., 9: 46–80vo.

Valcoulon, Savary de. 15 May 1785. "Extrait d'une lettre de M. Savary de Valcoulon, George Creek sur les bords de la Monongahela." AECPE-U, 29: 248–60.

SELECT PUBLISHED SOURCES

Almanac National de France, L'An Troisième de la République (Paris n.d.).

American State Papers, Foreign Relations. 1832–59. (6 v., Washington 1832–59), 1.

Analyse des loix commerciales, avec les tarifs, des Etats des deux Carolines et de la Géorgie (Fayette-Ville, Etat de la Caroline du Nord n.d.).

Archives parlementaires de 1787 à 1860. 1862–1937. (188 v., Paris).

Arnould, Ambroise Marie. 1791. *De la Balance du commerce et des relations commerciales extérieures de la France* (3 v., Paris).

Aulard, A., ed. 1889. *Recueil des Actes du Comité de Salut Public* (27 v., Paris).

Bonnet de Fréjus, J. Esprit. 1795. *Réponses aux principales questions qui peuvent être faites sur les Etats-Unis de l'Amérique* (2 v., Paris).

Boyd, Julian P., ed. 1950– . *The Papers of Thomas Jefferson* (Princeton).

Brissot de Warville, Jacques Pierre. 1964. *New Travels in the United States of America*, ed. Durand Echeverria (Cambridge).

———, 1791. *Nouveau Voyage dans les Etats-Unis de l'Amérique septentrionale* (3 v., Paris).

Bulletin des lois de la République française [1794–1799] (9 v., Paris).

Chastellux, François-Jean, Marquis de. 1963. *Travels in North America in the Years 1780, 1781, and 1782*, tr. Howard C. Rice, Jr. (2 v., Chapel Hill).

———, 1788; 1791. *Voyages dans l'Amérique septentrionale dans les années 1780, 1781 & 1782* (2 v., Paris).

Chateaubriand, François René, Vicomte de. 1838. *Voyage en Amérique* [1791] (Paris).

Clavière, Etienne, et Jacques Pierre Brissot de Warville. 1787. *De la France et des Etats-Unis, ou de l'importance de la révolution de l'Amérique pour le bonheur de la France, des rapports de ce royaume et des Etats-Unis, des avantages réciproques qu'ils peuvent retirer de leurs liaisons de commerce, et enfin la situation actuelle des Etats-Unis* (London).

Collot, Victor. 1924. *A Journey in North America* (2 v., Florence; Reprints of Rare Americana, No. 4).

Crèvecoeur, Hector Saint-John de. 1787. *Lettres d'un cultivateur américain* (2 v., Paris).

Courier de l'Amérique

Courier de Boston

Courier Français (Philadelphia)

Debates and Proceedings in the Congress of the United States. 1834–1856. (42 v., Washington).

Debidour, Antonin, ed. 1910. *Recueil des actes du Directoire Exécutif (Procès-verbaux, arrêtés, instructions, lettres et actes divers)* (4 v., Paris).

Didot, Aristarque. 1793. *Précis sur la Révolution et le caractère français, adressé aux citoyens des Etats-Unis d'Amérique* (Paris).

Ducher, G. J. A. 1792. *Nouvelle Alliance à proposer entre les Républiques Française & Américaine* (Paris).

Extraits des Registres du Conseil d'Etat

Fauchet, Jean-Antoine-Joseph. Fructidor, an V (18 August–16 September 1797). *Coup d'Oeil sur l'état actuel de nos rapports politiques avec les Etats-unis de l'Amérique septentrionale* (Paris).

———, 1798. *Coup d'Oeil sur la Situation des Affaires entre la France et les Etats-Unis* (Paris).

———, 20 March 1796. "Mémoire sur les Etats Unis d'Amérique," in *Annual Report of the American Historical Association for the Year 1936* (Washington, 1938) 85–119.

Fitzpatrick, John Clement, ed. 1931–40. *The Writings of George Washington* (37 v., Washington).

Gazette Nationale ou Le Moniteur Universel. 1789–1810.

Genet, Edmond Charles. 1793. *The Correspondence between Citizen Genet, Minister of the French Republic, to the United States of North America, and the Officers of the Federal Government*, ed. Benjamin Franklin Bache (Philadephia).

Holroyd, John Baker (Lord Sheffield). 1789. *Observations sur le commerce des Etats américains, par le Lord Sheffield* (Rouen).

Journals of the Continental Congress, 1774–1789. 1904–1937. (34 v., Washington).

La Rochefoucauld-Liancourt, François-Alexandre-Frédéric, Duc de. An VII (22 September 1798–16 September 1799). *Voyage dans les états-unis d'Amérique fait en 1795, 1796, et 1797* (8 v., Paris).

Létombe, Philippe-André-Joseph. 1793. *Recueil de diverses pièces en faveur du Citoyen Létombe* (Paris).

Lois et Actes du Gouvernement [1789–1794]. 1806. (8 v., Paris).

Mangourit, Michel Ange. 1794. *Mémoire de Mangourit* (Paris). Copy in AD XV, carton 48, ANF.

Mayo, Bernard, ed. 1941. *Instructions to the British Ministers to the United States, 1791–1812* (Washington).

Michaud, Louis G., ed. 1968. *Biographie universelle ancienne et moderne* (45 v., reprinted in Gratz, Austria).

Miller, David Hunter, ed. 1931–48. *Treaties and Other International Acts of the United States of America, 1776–1863* (8 v., Washington).

Les Ministères français (1789–1911). 1911. (Paris).

Moustier, Eléonore-François-Elie, Comte de. 1903. "Correspondence of the Comte de Moustier with the Comte de Montmorin, 1787–1789." *American Historical Review* 8: 709–33; 9: 86–96.

———, 1935. "Moustier's Mémoire on Louisiana," ed. E. Wilson Lyon. *Mississippi Valley Historical Review* 22: 251–66.

———, 1790. *Observations sur les différents rapports de la liberté ou de la prohibition de la culture du tabac, suivis d'une lettre à M. Necker* (Paris).

Otto, Louis Guillaume. 1945. *Considérations sur la conduite du gouvernement Américain envers la France, depuis le commencement de la Révolution jusqu'en 1797* (Princeton).

Randolph, Edmund. 8 July 1795. "Declaration of Edmund Randolph" (Philadelphia). *ASP,FR* 1: 472–74.

Recueil des lois relatives à la marine et aux colonies. 1797 (Paris).

Richardson, James D., ed. 1896. *Messages and Papers of the Presidents, 1789–1897* (10 v., Washington).

Roberts, Kenneth, and Anna M. 1947. *Moreau de St. Méry's American Journey, 1793–1798* (Garden City, N.Y.).

Swan, James. 1790. *Causes qui se sont opposées aux progrès du Commerce entre la France et les Etats-Unis de l'Amérique, avec les moyens de l'accélérer* (Paris).

Talleyrand, Charles Maurice de. 1799. *Mémoire sur les Relations commerciales des Etats-Unis avec l'Angleterre* (Paris).

Tanguy de la Boissière. [1796]. *Mémoire sur la situation commerciale de la France avec les Etats-Unis de l'Amérique depuis l'année 1775, jusque & y compris 1795* [Paris].

Turner, Frederick Jackson, ed. 1904. "Correspondence of the French Ministers to the United States, 1791–1797." *The Annual Report of the American Historical Association for the Year 1903* (Washington).

Volney, Constantin François Chasseboeuf, Comte de. 1804. *A View of the Soil and Climate of the United States of America: with Supplementary Remarks upon Florida; on the French colonies on the Mississippi and Ohio, and in Canada; and on the Aboriginal Tribes of America*, trans. C.B. Brown (Philadelphia).

Select Secondary Works

Ammon, Harry. 1973. *The Genet Mission* (New York).

Angel, Edward. 1979. "James Monroe's Mission to France, 1794–1796" (unpublished Ph.D. dissertation, The George Washington University).

Appleby, Joyce. 1971. "America as a Model for Radical French Reformers of 1789." *William and Mary Quarterly* 28: 267–86.

Baldensperger, Fernand. 1924. "Le Séjour de Talleyrand aux Etats-Unis." *Revue de Paris* 6: 364–87.

Baldrige, Edwin R., Jr. 1963. "Prince Talleyrand in the United States, 1794–1796" (unpublished Ph.D. dissertation, Lehigh University).

Barthold, Allen J. 1936–37. "French Journalists in the United States, 1780–1800." *The Franco-American Review* 1: 215–30.

Belote, Theodore T. 1907. *The Scioto Speculation and the French Settlement at Gallipolis* (Cincinnati).

Bowman, Albert Hall. 1974. *The Struggle for Neutrality: Franco-American Diplomacy During the Federalist Era* (Knoxville).

Boyd, Julian P. 1964. *Number 7: Alexander Hamilton's Secret Attempts to Control American Foreign Policy* (Princeton).

____, April 1958. "Two Diplomats Between Revolutions." *Virginia Magazine of History and Biography:* 131–46.

Buron, Edmond. November 1931. "Notes and Documents: Statistics on Franco-American Trade, 1778–1806." *Journal of Economic and Business History* 4 (No. 1): 571–80.

Childs, Francis S. 1940. *French Refugee Life in the United States, 1790–1800* (Baltimore).

____, 1949. "The Hauterive Journal." *New York Historical Society Quarterly* 33: 69–86.

Cole, Charles W. 1939. *Colbert and a Century of French Mercantilism* (2 v., New York).

Darling, Arthur, B. 1940. *Our Rising Empire, 1763–1803* (New Haven).

Dawes, E.C. December 1889. "The Scioto Purchase in 1787." *Magazine of American History* 22: 470–82.

De Conde, Alexander. 1958. *Entangling Alliance: Politics & Diplomacy under George Washington* (Durham).

Duncan, Brigham. 1957. "Franco-American Tobacco Diplomacy, 1784–1860." *Maryland Historical Magazine* 51: 273–301.

Duniway, Clyde A. 1904. "French Influence on the Adoption of the Federal Constitution." *American Historical Review* 9: 304–09.

Earl, John L. July 1967. "Talleyrand in Philadelphia, 1794–1796." *Pennsylvania Magazine of History and Biography* 91: 282–98.

Echeverria, Durand. 1966. *Mirage in the West: a History of the French Image of American Society to 1815* (New York).

Faÿ, Bernard. 1927. *The Revolutionary Spirit of France and America: a Study of Moral and Intellectual Relations between France and the United States at the End of the Eighteenth Century,* trans. Ramon Guthrie (New York).

Godechot, Jacques Léon. 1965. *France and the Atlantic Revolution of the Eighteenth Century, 1770–1799* (New York).

____, 1958. "Les relations économiques entre la France et les Etats-Unis de 1778 à 1789." *French Historical Studies* 1: 26–39.

Hale, Edward E., and Edward E. Hale, Jr. 1887–88. *Franklin in France* (2 v., Boston).

Hazen, Charles Downer. 1897. *Contemporary American Opinion of the French Revolution* (Baltimore).

____, 1896. "The French Revolution as seen by Americans of the Eighteenth Century." *Annual Report of the American Historical Association for 1895,* 455–66.

Huth, Hans, and Wilma J. Pugh, eds. 1942. "Talleyrand in America as a Financial Promoter." *Annual Report of the American Historical Association for the Year 1941,* 2.

Hutson, James H. 1980. *John Adams and the Diplomacy of the American Revolution* (Lexington, Ky.).

Hyslop, Beatrice. 1958. "American Press Reports of the French Revolution, 1789–94." *New York Historical Society Quarterly* (October): 329–48.

Ingham, Joseph W. 1916. *A Short History of Asylum, Pennsylvania* (Towanda, Pa.).

James, James Alton. June 1914. "Louisiana as a Factor in American Diplomacy, 1795–1800." *Mississippi Valley Historical Review* 1: 44–56.

Jensen, Merrill. 1950. *The New Nation: a History of the United States During the Confederation, 1781–1789* (New York).

Jones, Howard Mumford. 1927. *American and French Culture, 1750–1848* (Chapel Hill).

Kaplan, Lawrence S. 1972. *Colonies Into Nation, 1763–1801* (New York).

Ketcham, Ralph L. June 1963. "French and American Politics, 1763–1793." *Political Science Quarterly* 78.2: 198–223.

Livermore, Shaw. 1939. *Early American Land Companies* (New York).

Lyon, Elijah Wilson. 1934. *Louisiana in French Diplomacy, 1759–1804* (Norman, Okla.).

Marks, Frederick W., III. 1973. *Independence on Trial: Foreign Affairs and the Making of the Constitution* (Baton Rouge).

Masson, Frédéric. 1877. *Le département des affaires étrangères pendant la révolution, 1787–1804* (Paris).

Morris, Richard B. 1965. *The Peacemakers: The Great Powers and American Independence* (New York).

Murray, Elsie. 1935. *French Exiles of 1793 in Northern Pennsylvania* (New York).

Murray, Louise W. 1917. *The Story of Some French Refugees and Their "Azilum"* (Athens, Pa.).

Nevins, Allen. 1924. *The American States during and after the Revolution, 1775–1789* (New York).

Nussbaum, Frederick. December 1925. "American Tobacco and French Politics, 1783–1789." *Political Science Quarterly* 40: 497–516.

——, 1923. *Commercial Policy in the French Revolution; a Study of the Career of G. J. A. Ducher* (Washington).

——, 1928. "The French Colonial Arrêt of 1784." *South Atlantic Quarterly* 27: 62–78.

O'Dwyer, Margaret M. 1964. "A French Diplomat's View of Congress, 1790." *William and Mary Quarterly* 22: 408–12.

——, 1954. "Louis Guillaume Otto in America (1779–91)." (unpublished Ph.D. dissertation, Northwestern University).

Palmer, Robert R. 1959. *The Age of Democratic Revolution: A Political History of Europe and America, 1760–1800: The Challenge* (Princeton).

——, 1971. *The World of the French Revolution* (New York).

Peterson, Merrill D. 1965. "Thomas Jefferson and Commercial Policy, 1783–1793." *William and Mary Quarterly* 3rd ser. 22.4: 584–610.

Price, Jacob M. 1973. *France and the Chesapeake: a History of the French Tobacco Monopoly, 1674–1791, and Its Relationship to the British and American Tobacco Trades* (2 v., Ann Arbor).

Rice, Howard C. September 1937. "James Swan: Agent of the French Republic, 1794–1796." *New England Quarterly* 10.3: 464–86.

Ritcheson, Charles R. 1969. *Aftermath of Revolution: British Policy Toward the United States, 1783–1795* (New York).

Rosenthal, Alfred. 1939. "The Marbois–Longchamps Affair." *Pennsylvania Magazine of History and Biography* 63: 294–301.

Ryan, Lee W. 1939. *French Travelers in the Southeastern United States, 1775–1800* (Bloomington).

Sears, Louis M. 1960. *George Washington and the French Revolution* (Detroit).

Sée, Henri. 1926. "Commerce between France and the United States, 1783–1784." *American Historical Review* 31.4: 732–52.

Setser, Vernon G. 1937. "Did Americans Originate the Most-Favored-Nation Clause?" *Journal of American History* 5: 319–23.

____, 1937. *The Commercial Reciprocity Policy of the United States, 1774–1829* (Philadelphia).

Sherrill, Charles H. 1915. *French Memories of Eighteenth Century America* (New York).

Sifton, Paul G. October 1965. "Otto's *Mémoire* to Vergennes, 1785." *William and Mary Quarterly* 22: 626–45.

Stewart, Donald H. 1969. *The Opposition Press of the Federalist Period* (Albany).

Stoddard, T. Lothrop. 1914. *The French Revolution in San Domingo* (Boston and New York).

Stover, John F. 1958. "French-American Trade during the Confederation, 1781–1789." *North Carolina Historical Review* 35.4: 399–414.

INDEX

Adams, John: as minister to Great Britain, 23; seen as hostile to France, 24, 30, 31

Adet, Pierre: as French minister to U.S., 20, 114, 136

Alexander, William (Scots tobacco magnate): on warehouses as a factor in Franco-American commerce, 70, 70n

"American Committee": attacks Farmers General, 57–58; inspires whale oil decrees, 76; mentioned, 60, 74, 108

Anglo-American relations: cultural factors in, 2, 38, 39, 42–44; Delaforest on, 34; Ducher on, 17, 29; Létombe on, 23; Marbois on, 23, 39; Moustier on, 25, 26, 27, 28, 32; private indebtedness as a factor in, 50; Talleyrand on, 48–49. *See also* British influence in U.S.; commerce, U.S., with Britain; commercial retaliation, U.S. threat of, against Britain; Jay treaty; Madison Resolutions; Nootka Sound crisis

Arcambal, Louis (French consul at New York), 153

Arnould, Ambroise Marie (French economist), 47, 74

Barbé-Marbois, François, vicomte de: as author of "Marbois Letter," 15–16; as chargé d'affaires, 5, 15–16, 19; on U.S. commerce with Britain, 53; on U.S. commerce with France, 17, 48, 49, 51, 60, 64, 65, 67, 68, 69, 74, 100–101; on commercial reciprocity, 54, 108; on commission agents, 69; on congressional impotence, 111; on economic conditions (post-war depression), 50, 64–65, 67; on emigration to U.S., 161, 162; on French West Indies contraband trade, 54, 80, 84, 89, 93, 94, 100; on justice in U.S., 154, 157; and Longchamps affair, 15, 16, 155–58, 176, 177; as observer, 6, 17; and Otto, 6, 134, 162; on politics (U.S.), 28; on press freedom, 157–58

Barlow, Joel: role of, in Scioto company, 165–66

Barré, Henri (French naval officer charged with desertion), 153–54

Beckwith, George (British agent): Hamilton's dealings with, 35–36

Bradford, William (U.S. attorney general), 153

Brissot de Warville, Jacques Pierre, 39, 162

British influence in U.S.: Delaforest on, 40, 113; Fauchet on, 132; Genet on, 38, 40, 126; Luzerne on, 22, 23; Mangourit on, 40, 41; Montmorin on, 25, Moustier on, 25–31, *passim*, 113; Oster on, 109; Otto on, 23, 24, 26, 35–36, 40; Rochambeau on, 109

Calonne, Charles Alexandre de (French controller general), 57

Castries, marquis de (French Navy minister), 97, 156

Chateaufort, Avistay de: as consul in Charleston, 6, 143–44; on Franco-American commerce, 58–59, 65, 71; on French West Indies contraband trade, 91, 92, 93, 97, 98

Collot, General Victor, 169

commerce, U.S., with France: *ancien régime*'s neglect of, 48–49, 109, 110, 111, 119, 120, 125, 135, 172; Arnould on, 47, 74; balance of, unfavorable to France, 46–48, 54, 57, 65–66, 70, 77, 78, 108, 135; Chateaufort on, 58–59, 65, 71; commission agents as a factor in, 69; compared with Anglo-U.S. commerce, 33, 46–78, *passim*, 106, 107, 136, 171; consumer preference as a factor in, 49, 59–60, 66, 68, 73–75, 172; credit as a factor in, 50, 51, 66–68, 70; Crèvecoeur on, 58, 69–70; D'Annemours on, 49; decline of, 1, 2, 26, 42, 45–48, 63–68, 172; Delaforest on, 56, 73, 74, 77; delay as a factor in, 62; Ducher on, 17–18; Duplaine on, 47–48, 73, 74, 75, 108; economic depression as a factor in, 51–52, 63–66; Fauchet on, 48, 111, 123, 130, 131, 133–37; French concessions to, 54, 75, 76–77, 103, 110, 111, 122, 127; French efforts to improve, 54, 55, 68–78; French restrictions on, 33, 60, 61, 62, 76–77; Jefferson on, 76, 118, 119, 122–27, *passim*, 130, 135; Lafayette on, 60, 62, 74; Létombe on, 58, 59, 66, 73, 74, 106; Luzerne on, 48, 49, 69, 74; Marbois on, 17, 48, 49, 51, 60, 64, 65, 67, 68, 69, 74, 100–101; Montmorin on, 102; Moustier on, 28, 29, 30, 31, 47, 66, 68, 71–73, 120; Oster on, 59, 61, 65, 74–75, 109; Otto on, 51, 52, 60, 65, 67, 68, 78, 119; Petry on, 62, 66; price as a factor in, 49, 60–61, 74–75, 77; quality as a factor in, 49,